Digital Literary Studies

Digital Literary Studies presents a broad and varied picture of the promise and potential of methods and approaches that are crucially dependent upon the digital nature of the literary texts it studies and the texts and collections of texts with which they are compared. It focuses on style, diction, characterization, and interpretation of single works and across larger groups of texts, using both huge natural language corpora and smaller, more specialized collections of texts created for specific tasks, and applies statistical techniques used in the narrower confines of authorship attribution to broader stylistic questions. It addresses important issues in each of the three major literary genres, and intentionally applies different techniques and concepts to poetry, prose, and drama. It aims to present a provocative and suggestive sample intended to encourage the application of these and other methods to literary studies.

Hoover, Culpeper, and O'Halloran push the methods, techniques, and concepts in new directions, apply them to new groups of texts or to new questions, modify their nature or method of application, and combine them in innovative ways.

David L. Hoover is Professor of English at New York University, USA. His publications in stylistics and digital humanities include three books— *A New Theory of Old English Meter*, *Stylistics: Prospect and Retrospect*, and *Language and Style in "The Inheritors"*—and numerous articles on authorship attribution and corpus and computational stylistics.

Jonathan Culpeper is Professor of English Language and Linguistics in the Department of Linguistics and English Language at Lancaster University, UK. His major publications include *Language and Characterisation in Plays and Other Texts* (2001) and *Early Modern English Dialogues: Spoken Interaction as Writing* (2010; coauthored with Merja Kytö).

Kieran O'Halloran is a Reader in Applied Linguistics at King's College, University of London, UK. Publications include *Critical Discourse Analysis and Language Cognition* (2003), *The Art of English: Literary Creativity* (2006 with Goodman), and *Applied Linguistics Methods* (Routledge, 2010 with Coffin and Lillis).

Routledge Advances in Corpus Linguistics

Edited by Tony McEnery, *Lancaster University, UK*

Michael Hoey, *Liverpool University, UK*

.

Digital Literary Studies

Corpus Approaches to Poetry, Prose, and Drama

David L. Hoover, Jonathan Culpeper, and Kieran O'Halloran

LONDON AND NEW YORK

First published 2014
by Routledge

2 Park Square, Milton Park, Abingdon, Oxon OX14 4RN
711 Third Avenue, New York, NY 10017, USA

Routledge is an imprint of the Taylor & Francis Group, an informa business

First issued in paperback 2016

Library of Congress Cataloging-in-Publication Data

A catalog record has been requested for this book.

ISBN: 978-0-415-35230-7 (hbk)
ISBN: 978-1-138-21054-7 (pbk)

Typeset in Sabon
by Apex CoVantage, LLC

Contents

viii   *Contents*

Figures

Tables

Acknowledgments

The authors are grateful to the publishers below for permission to reproduce copyright material.

Bloodaxe Books kindly gave permission to use Fleur Adcock's "Street Song," from Fleur Adcock, 2000. *Poems 1960–2000*. Tarset, Northumberland: Bloodaxe Books.

Chapter 2 is based on Culpeper (2002), and chapter 3 is based on Jonathan Culpeper, 2009, "Keyness: Words, Parts-of-Speech and Semantic Categories in the Character Talk of Shakespeare's *Romeo and Juliet*," *International Journal of Corpus Linguistics* 14 (1): 29–56, by kind permission of John Benjamins Publishing Company, Amsterdam/Philadelphia. www. benjamins.com

Chapter 6 is a revised version of Kieran O'Halloran, "Corpus-Assisted Literary Evaluation," *Corpora* 2 (1) (2007): 33–63, by kind permission of Edinburgh University Press, www.euppublishing.com.

Chapter 7 is a revised version of Kieran O'Halloran, 2012, "Performance Stylistics: Deleuze and Guattari, Poetry, and (Corpus) Linguistics," *International Journal of English Studies* 12(2) (2012): 171–199. It is provided by kind permission of the *International Journal of English Studies*.

The authors would also like to thank the series editors, especially Michael Hoey, for reading and commenting on chapters at various points.

1 Introduction

David L. Hoover, Jonathan Culpeper,
and Kieran O'Halloran

1.1 AIMS

The phrase "digital literary studies," a recent coinage that owes much to the only slightly less recent "digital humanities," has caught fire in academic circles in the last few years. Both phrases usefully focus our attention on the ways that the methods and approaches we present here, among others, are crucially dependent upon the digital nature of our objects of study. In this book, our primary objects of study are literary texts, but not one of them was born digital. In most of our analyses below, these objects themselves are studied in their digitized forms, and in all of them digital texts and collections of texts are crucial to the analysis. Culpeper and Hoover exploit digital forms of (groups of) novels and plays directly by analyzing them computationally. O'Halloran, who focuses on lyric poems that are too short for nearly all methods of computational analysis, instead brings to bear information collected from huge digital collections of natural language or "corpora" ("corpus" being the singular form).

The book presents a broad and varied picture of the possibilities of digital literary studies. We study style, diction, and characterization, both within a single work and across the work of an author, a group of authors, or across an author's career. We use both huge natural language corpora and smaller, more specialized collections of texts created for specific tasks. We apply statistical techniques normally used in the narrower confines of authorship attribution to broader stylistic questions, such as style variation. Finally, we examine important issues in each of the three major literary genres. We have intentionally applied a different selection of techniques and concepts to poetry, prose, and drama, in ways that reflect some of our own current major concerns. Yet, in spite of this variety, we make no attempt to cover all of the possible approaches that are currently being used in this fast-growing field. Rather, we have aimed at a provocative and suggestive sample that will encourage other researchers to apply these and other methods across all genres, periods, and styles of literature. Some of the specific approaches represented here, such as multivariate analysis and text-markup/annotation, have long traditions, others, such as the use of huge corpora, are of more recent origin. We have tried, throughout, however, to push the methods, techniques, and concepts in new directions, to apply them to new groups of texts or to new questions, to modify their nature or method of application, and to combine them in innovative ways.

1.2   DIGITAL LITERARY STUDIES AND CORPUS LINGUISTICS

Most of what we present in this book belongs squarely within the tradition of what might be called rather broadly, "textual analysis." This tradition exploits the digital nature of the texts by analyzing them computationally. At the other end of the spectrum lie studies that focus on the nature of the medium itself and how new media impact literary studies more generally; such studies tend to be more theoretical than practical, and need not make significant use of computation. And there is plenty of room left in the spectrum for many other kinds of digital literary studies. The fact that we have nothing to say about the Text Encoding Initiative (TEI), electronic literature, scholarly digital editions, digital archives and portals, blogging and social media, new media theory, or other areas of digital literary study is a result of our own central interests and not a comment on the significance or value of other approaches.

As reflected in the title of the book, a crucial purpose of ours is to flag the value of corpus linguistics (and corpora in general) for digital literary studies. This is a method that engages in the building and exploitation of corpora, the latter involving software programs that extract particular kinds of linguistic features from the corpus and undertake statistical analyses. It is not as though corpus linguistics is unheard of in the digital humanities. But, it is often seen as one branch of digital humanities that you can take or leave rather than something that has implications for language study generally in the humanities, not to mention the social sciences. This is perhaps, in part, because of "linguistics" in "corpus linguistics"—it looks specialized and forbidding. There are plenty of analytical frameworks in linguistics that are technically sophisticated, demanding to learn, and challenging to apply successfully. But, this is not the case for corpus linguistics. Compared to many other approaches in linguistics, it is accessible, and light on terminology. This is because it is much more of a set of methods and principles for the analysis of electronic language data than a complex theoretical perspective on language. Terminology used in corpus linguistics, such as "collocation," "keywords," "phraseology," "semantic preference," and "semantic prosody," crops up in the book. To promote corpus linguistic methods for use in the digital humanities, we have produced a glossary where these corpus linguistic terms and others are explained.

For our purposes, a corpus can be defined simply as any structured collection of digital texts, and the structuring principles can be quite various. Giant natural language corpora, for example, are typically balanced by genre, containing the same amount of text from genres like spoken language, literature, news reporting, and so forth. Historical corpora are usually balanced by date. Specialized corpora are often specifically designed and created so as to provide a norm against which an author, text, or part of a text can be compared. We use all of these kinds of corpora below. In chapters 2 and 3, for example, Culpeper studies the character parts in *Romeo and Juliet* by comparing the speech of each important character with a specially created corpus consisting of the speech of the remaining characters. In chapters 4 and 5, Hoover uses specially created corpora of novels by contemporaries to investigate the styles of Wilkie Collins, Hannah Webster Foster, and Henry James, and treats early, intermediate, and late James texts as subcorpora to analyze changes in his style over his long career. In chapters 6 and 7, O'Halloran compares the ways words, phrases, and collocations are used in lyric poems and in giant natural language corpora. In all of these uses, the corpora are used in the service of comparison.

1.3   STYLISTICS AND CORPUS STYLISTICS

We cannot neglect mention of a field in which textual analysis engages, typically, literary texts; that is, stylistics—how linguistic analysis can account for readers' interpretations, including their impressions of style and experience of aesthetic effects (for example, Carter and Stockwell 2008; Cook 1994; Jeffries and McIntyre 2010; Leech and Short 2007, Simpson 2004; Verdonk 2002; Wales 2011; Widdowson 1992). Stylistics has been a thriving discipline since the 1960s, but its roots go back further. It can be viewed as the logical outcome of literary criticism in the first half of the twentieth century, which placed emphasis on studying texts rather than authors. Russian formalism (especially the work of Roman Jakobson) and the related Prague school (especially the work of Jan Mukařovský) are key influences on the development of stylistics. Stylistic analysis of literature is a technique we draw on to different degrees in the chapters. The glossary also includes definitions of linguistic concepts we employ.

Another purpose of our book is to broadcast the value of corpus linguistics for stylisticians. The combination of stylistic analysis and corpus linguistic method is relatively recent, but an area of increasing popularity (for example, Semino and Short 2004; Hoover 2010a; Hori 2004; O'Halloran 2007; Stubbs 2005; Mahlberg 2013; Fischer-Starcke 2010). The label "corpus stylistics" perhaps first appears as the main title of Semino and Short (2004), though there are a number of precursors doing corpus stylistic work without using that label (for example, Stubbs 1996, 81–100; Louw 1997; Hoover 1999). Corpus linguistics may seem, at least to some, an alien enterprise in the world of stylistics, but this is an erroneous perception on several counts. Stylisticians, and indeed literary critics, often discuss matters of frequency. Any pattern they point to or tendency they highlight is a matter of frequency, of statistics by the back door. Moreover, key works in stylistics emphasize the need for quantification (for example, Leech and Short 2007, chapter 2), and the empirical study of literature—mostly revolving around informant testing—is an important subfield. Indeed, deviation from statistical norms is one way of characterizing an aspect of foregrounding theory (for example, Mukařovský 1970), a theory that has been a keystone in stylistics for decades. We will touch on some aspects of foregrounding theory in our work, notably in chapter 2.

Corpus linguists do not argue that the corpus-related approach should be all-consuming, but rather that it "should be seen as a complementary approach to more traditional approaches" (Biber, Conrad, and Reppen 1998, 7–8). Moreover, the corpus-related approach itself deploys a mixture of methods; it is not—and this is particularly true of more recent work—a purely quantitative methodology, all computers and numbers, as the following quotations from popular textbooks in corpus linguistics argue:

> both qualitative and quantitative analyses have something to contribute to corpus study. Qualitative analysis can provide greater richness and precision, whereas quantitative analysis can provide statistically reliable and generalisable results. There has recently been a move in social science research towards multi-method approaches which largely reject the narrow analytical paradigms in favour of the breadth of information which the use of more than one method may provide. Corpus linguistics could . . . benefit as much as any field from such multi-method research, combining both qualitative and quantitative perspectives on the same phenomena. (McEnery and Wilson 2001, 76–77)

> it is important to note that corpus-based analyses must go beyond simple counts of linguistic features. That is, it is essential to include qualitative, functional interpretations of quantitative patterns. In each chapter of this book, you will find that a great deal of space is devoted to explanation, exemplification, and interpretation of the patterns found in quantitative analyses. The goal of corpus-based investigations is not simply to report quantitative findings, but to explore the importance of those findings for learning about the patterns of language use. (Biber et al. 1999, 5)

Throughout this book we will be combining qualitative and quantitative analyses.

Still, despite the overlaps between these fields, one might reasonably ask what particular value corpus linguistics brings to stylistics. We would argue that corpus-related techniques allow one's analysis to (1) encompass more than one could possibly encompass with reasonable human labor, and (2) be systematic, and (3) be fine-grained. These are the very features we aim to demonstrate in this book. Through being able to encompass the *whole* of, for example, an author's work, their entire canon, or a large body of language representing a comparative norm, we seek to avoid a major criticism of traditional stylistic analysis, namely, that stylisticians select their examples and textual extracts to fit their interpretations, while paying little attention to the bulk of the works they purportedly analyze (see for example Stubbs 2004, a review of a mainstream stylistics book). Thus, our analyses, as we will show, present a solid basis on which to rest readers' interpretations, and also to make explicit things that readers are only dimly aware of, if at all. All of our chapters could be construed as employing "corpus stylistics" techniques. Perhaps, though with hindsight, the term is not so felicitous. "Corpus stylistics" might seem parochial and highly specialized—as compared with "digital literary studies"—when, in fact, the use of corpus linguistics methods has far-reaching consequences for literary scholarship whether it includes stylistic analysis or not.

1.4 CHAPTER SUMMARIES

Jonathan Culpeper's two chapters on drama begin the book. In chapter 2, "Keywords and Characterization," he argues that the notion of "style markers" (Enkvist 1964, 1973) is synonymous with that of "keywords," but that the term keywords links in with corpus linguistics research in general and the computer program Wordsmith Tools (Scott 1999) in particular. One specific innovation is that dialogue is analyzed for keywords. Dialogue is a "mixed style" text—a collection of different character voices. To enable the analysis of individual voices, a relatively simple tagging system is adopted. Culpeper shows how a keywords analysis offers a way of establishing lexical and grammatical character patterns without a reliance on intuition (something that has characterized much previous research). Specifically, his analysis reveals lexical and grammatical character patterns in Shakespeare's *Romeo and Juliet*. In some cases, it provides solid evidence for what one might have guessed (for example, Romeo's keywords *beauty* and *love*); in others, it reveals what would be very difficult to guess but fits well a possible interpretation (for example, Juliet's keywords *if* and *yet*). Culpeper demonstrates how keywords analysis also offers a way of analyzing function words, such as pronouns, and accounting for their contribution to style and meaning.

Chapter 3, "Developing Keyness and Characterization: Annotation," moves beyond keywords. The point of Culpeper's chapter is to investigate whether the analysis of key parts of speech and key semantic categories simply replicates the keyword findings for the characters of chapter 2 or reveals new things of interest. To enable the computer to identify key grammatical and semantic features, he explains how he first annotates his texts. Consequently, his chapter also engages debates about what is to be gained from analyzing interpretive annotations of the text rather than the text itself. Should we, as Sinclair (2004) puts it, "trust the text"? The answer is, in part. Many of the findings about the characters in *Romeo and Juliet* had already been revealed via keywords. However, the extent to which this is the case depends on the kind of word. Closed class words, words that are more grammatical, match the keywords better, whereas open class words, including parts of speech such as nouns, adjectives, and lexical verbs, fare less well. The grammatical analysis highlights some features overlooked in the keyword analysis, such as Romeo's tendency to use a wide range of adjectives. The semantic analysis, though somewhat error prone, is effective in revealing, for example, metaphorical patterns, including Romeo's penchant for color metaphors.

In the middle two chapters of the book, David L. Hoover turns his attention to fiction. Chapter 4, "*The Moonstone* and *The Coquette*: Narrative and Epistolary Style," focuses on style variations within a single work. In his seminal work on Jane Austen, John F. Burrows was able to demonstrate that Austen's characters can be successfully distinguished from one another on the basis of the frequencies of frequent words within the dialogue of each character—that different characters can, for some purposes, be treated as if they were different authors. Here, Hoover examines two related questions by analyzing two very different novels that contain multiple voices. He uses multivariate authorship attribution techniques to determine how successful each author is in modifying his authorial style to indicate what one might expect to be very marked changes in narrator or letter-writer. In *The Moonstone,* Wilkie Collins divides his narration among several characters, and very successfully creates distinct voices for them. In contrast, although Hannah Webster Foster tells the entire story of her epistolary novel, *The Coquette,* through the letters of the characters, she is not very successful in providing the characters with distinctive voices. In both of these analyses, Hoover also points toward ways in which the presence or absence of character differentiation intersects with more traditional literary questions. In *The Moonstone,* the most problematic distinction is between the narration of Franklin Blake (the rich young man who organizes the narrative) and the mysterious Ezra Jennings (a mysterious, disgraced doctor of mixed ancestry). This fact seems potentially relevant to Collins's interest in social themes, and especially the interaction of the English with colonial peoples. The failure of Foster to create consistent voices supports the general view that the novel is mainly interesting for its social and cultural themes rather than its literary quality.

In chapter 5, "A Conversation Among Himselves: Change and the Styles of Henry James," Hoover shows that authorship attribution techniques that easily distinguish the style of Henry James from that of other authors also confirm the long-standing critical consensus that James's early and late styles are quite distinct. But these quantitative methods can do more than bolster critical commonplaces; they can identify three distinct periods in James's style, periods that correspond exactly with gaps in the publication dates of his novels. Hoover begins by analyzing a specially created corpus of American novels of the late nineteenth century to determine the extent to which traditional multivariate authorship attribution techniques based on frequent words (and some refinements of these techniques) can successfully attribute both James's early and late novels to him and distinguish both from novels by his contemporaries. He then shifts to an examination of the statistical basis for a distinction between James's early and late styles and the extent to which his revisions of novels written in the 1870s and 1880s for the New York Edition of 1907–09 bring them closer in style to his later novels. He shows that, perhaps surprisingly, word frequencies alone are sufficient for this task, in spite of the heavy emphasis in traditional criticism on James's increasingly convoluted syntax (which is much less amenable to computational analysis). Hoover's analysis shows that James's style evolution is extraordinarily uniform and unidirectional, that his unusual style pervades the whole spectrum of word frequencies from the ubiquitous to the unique, and that words that James progressively adopts and abandons over his long career overwhelmingly fall into word-families (almost all forms of the word *sharp* increase progressively, while almost all forms of *keen* decrease progressively over his career).

Kieran O'Halloran's two chapters on poetry complete the book. In chapter 6, "Corpus-Assisted Literary Evaluation," O'Halloran provocatively suggests that it is possible to bring evidence to bear on literary evaluation or judgment, areas that have seemed for a long time to be primarily subjective. He begins with Roger Fowler's evaluation of Fleur Adcock's poem, "Street Song," as "dynamic and disturbing," a literary evaluation with which he agrees. He notes that the poem's unsettling effects take place during the initial response to the poem and help to draw the reader into the work. In other words, they are experienced before any deeper reflection and analysis of the poem or individual interpretation of it. Implicit within Fowler's evaluation is that these effects are likely to be true for readers generally. Traditionally about all critics could do was to describe the effects, point toward parts of the text that they claimed produced them, and hope to persuade readers that they were likely to be general. In contrast, O'Halloran argues that empirical corpus evidence can usefully provide substantiation of such initial evaluations of literary works, drawing on both schema theory and corpus analysis to show whether or not they are likely to be, if not universal, at least widely experienced by a broad spectrum of readers.

Chapter 7, "Performance Stylistics: Deleuze and Guattari, Poetry, and (Corpus) Linguistics," takes as stimulus some key ideas of the philosopher Gilles Deleuze and his collaborator, the psychoanalyst Félix Guattari. O'Halloran begins with Robert Frost's, "Putting in the Seed" as his example, and demonstrates an alternative interpretative engagement with poetry, one he calls "performance stylistics," in which a poem is seen as an invitation to the reader to be creative via a web-based, interpretative journey that is individual, edifying, and refreshing. This approach allows a poem's obliqueness and suggestiveness to trigger, randomly, knowledge and resources on the

World Wide Web that are new for the reader; in turn, these can be used as fresh perspectives on the poem in order to perform it in individual ways, to "fill in" creatively personas and scenarios in the poem. This web-based engagement with a poem, which involves stylistic analysis in order to lead to an interpretative performance of it, is centrifugal, taking the reader outside of the poem, traveling from website to website. This centrifugal movement is balanced, however, by a centripetal one that takes the reader into the patterns of the poem. Stylistic analysis meets this centripetal need effectively. Traditionally, stylistic analysis has been used to provide linguistic evidence for interpretation of a literary work. However, influenced by ideas in the work of Deleuze and Guattari, O'Halloran also uses stylistic analysis in a nontraditional way—to "mobilize" interpretation of a poem—and shows how performance stylistics can also draw on corpus analysis for that same purpose.

With this brief introduction, we leave the book to speak for itself.

2 Keywords and Characterization

An Analysis of Six Characters in *Romeo and Juliet*

Jonathan Culpeper

2.1 INTRODUCTION

One aim of this chapter is to show how the study of an important area within stylistics, namely characterization, can benefit from "keyword" analysis, an empirical and systematic methodology that is becoming popular in corpus-related studies. The other aim is to explore that specific methodology further, to enhance our understanding of what keywords are and what a keyword analysis can do. As far as characterization is concerned, two areas, lexis and grammar, are particularly problematic. There is a large literature on how lexical and grammatical items constitute particular registers and dialects, which may correlate with particular social groups. What we know less about is how such items reflect the speech styles or idiolects of particular personalities. Intuitively, it is reasonable to suggest that lexis plays a significant role. For example, the tendency to use formal lexis may—context permitting—give the impression that someone is rather aloof or pompous; informal lexis that someone is "down to earth." But what the relevant lexical dimensions are and how one goes about revealing them in an analysis have been largely ignored. The situation for grammatical features is similar. For example, Scherer, in his review of personality markers in real-life speech, is surprised that "there is no systematic research on personality differences in cognitive processing and the complexity of syntactic structure" (1979, 170).

One particular problem is that patterns created by grammatical features are often unconsciously observed, with the consequence that an analysis geared towards certain foregrounded features will not be productive. Page, for example, examining speech in the English novel, states: "Grammar and syntax are, apart from the most obvious differences, less readily absorbed by the casual listener, and are used relatively little by writers" (1988, 57). Similarly, Blake (1983), considering Shakespeare, concludes that syntactic differences between characters' speech are less important than other aspects because they are less likely to be noticed: they are "more subtle than marked features of vocabulary or dialect and can readily be overlooked, particularly in the theatre" (1983, 28). The important point is that, although these features are less obvious and therefore less easily observable, this does not mean that we can safely assume that they have a negligible effect on our impressions. It might be the case that the accumulative effect of lexical or grammatical features is decisive. A character's idiolect is the total set of linguistic choices made by the author for that character, and it is thrown into relief by relationships of contrast or similarity with the idiolects of other characters. In other words, an idiolect is a foregrounded style, which may deviate from or be parallel to the idiolectal styles of other characters. Keyword analysis, as demonstrated below, can reveal statistically unusual lexical and grammatical differences from a reference point without reliance on intuitions about what the relevant dimensions or features are.

This chapter starts by arguing that the notion of "keywords" relates to what Enkvist (1964, 1973) calls "style markers," and points out their history in stylometry. Then, it discusses the preparation of the text and the choices that have to be made in conducting a keyword analysis. After the deployment of the KeyWords facility in Mike Scott's WordSmith Tools (1999), a computer program that does the kind of analysis required of Enkvist's definition, it discusses the results of a keyword analysis of character speech in Shakespeare's *Romeo and Juliet*. It examines the function and context of the keywords, in order to validate and account for the results. Finally, it concludes by noting both further possibilities and limitations for keyword analysis.

2.2   STYLE, STYLE MARKERS, AND KEYWORDS

Nils Erik Enkvist's (1964, 1973) definition of style lends itself well to statistical analysis:

> Style is concerned with frequencies of linguistic items in a given context, and thus with *contextual* probabilities. To measure the style of a passage, the frequencies of its linguistic items of different levels must be compared with the corresponding features in another text or corpus which is regarded as a norm and which has a definite relationship with this passage. For the stylistic analysis of one of Pope's poems, for instance, norms with varying contextual relationships include English eighteenth-century poetry, the corpus of Pope's work, all poems written in English in rhymed pentameter couplets, or, for greater contrast as well as comparison, the poetry of Wordsworth. Contextually distant norms would be, e.g., Gray's *Anatomy* or the London Telephone Directory of 1960. (1964, 29)

Style, then, is a matter of "frequencies," "probabilities," and "norms." He goes on to offer the following definition of "style markers":

> We may . . . define style markers as those linguistic items that only appear, or are most or least frequent in, one group of contexts. In other

words, style markers are contextually bound linguistic elements. Elements that are not style markers are stylistically neutral. This may be rephrased: style markers are mutually exclusive with other items which only appear in different contexts, or with zero; or have frequencies markedly different from those of such items.

In the light of this, some otherwise meaningless repetitions of linguistic items acquire meaning as style markers. For instance, the swearing and cursing of a soldier introduces a stream of stylistically significant items—"style reminders"—into statements that would otherwise remain neutral. (1964, 34–35)

Style markers, then, are words whose frequencies differ significantly from their frequencies in a norm. As will be seen in the next section, this is precisely the principle used to identify "keywords." Repetition is the notion underlying style markers and hence keywords, but not all repetition, only repetition that statistically deviates from the pattern formed by that item in another context (that is, it is more or less repetitive than that other pattern).

One other concept worth drawing attention to here, although not one with which we will engage in this book, is that of "style reminders." It is reasonable to suppose that style markers, by virtue of the fact that they are "contextually bound," acquire stylistic meaning (cf. Leech 1981, 14–15) over time and become "style reminders." Thus, a single occurrence of a style reminder may convey certain stylistic associations, regardless of the context in which it appears. For example, informants readily suggest that the word *cast* evokes the biblical register, while *chuck* evokes a colloquial register (with *throw* the rather more neutral term), even when these words are given without context. Clearly, the unusual frequency with which *cast* occurs in the biblical register and *chuck* in the colloquial register (a matter of style markers), has set up the conditions by which they can develop into style reminders.

This chapter will focus on statistically based keywords. The term "keyword" is not to be confused with lexical items that are "key" because they are of particular social, cultural, or political significance (see for example, Williams 1976). It is simply another term for statistically based style markers. In fact, Enkvist (1973, 132–33) acknowledges the connection. Studies in the area of stylometry have long known of statistically based keywords, though perhaps the first to use the term *keyword* (*mots-clés*) was Pierre Guiraud, who contrasts *mots-clés* (based on relative frequency) with *mots-thèmes* (based on absolute frequency) (1954, 64–66):

Toute différente est la notion de *mots-clés*, qui ne sont plus considérés dans leur fréquence absolue, mais dans leur fréquence relative; ce sont les mots dont la fréquence s'écarte de la normale.

[Wholly different is the notion of *mots-clés*, which are not considered in terms of their absolute frequency, but their relative frequency; these are the words whose frequency diverges from the normal.]

In the context of corpus linguistics, the notion of keywords and the practice of keyword analysis has been developed and popularized by Mike Scott, through the KeyWords facility of his program WordSmith Tools (1999), a program designed for the computational analysis of corpora. This program performs the kind of statistical analysis required to identify keywords. It conducts a statistical comparison between the words of a corpus (or word list) and a bigger reference corpus, in order to identify words that are unusually frequent or unusually infrequent. According to Scott (2013, 209; the punctuation is not original):

> To compute the "key-ness" of an item, the program therefore computes: its frequency in the small wordlist, the number of running words in the small wordlist, its frequency in the reference corpus, the number of running words in the reference corpus and cross-tabulates these. Statistical tests include: the classic chi-square test of significance with Yates correction for a 2×2 table; Ted Dunning's Log Likelihood test, which gives a better estimate of keyness, especially when contrasting long texts or a whole genre against your reference corpus. A word will get into the listing here if it is unusually frequent (or unusually infrequent) in comparison with what one would expect on the basis of the larger wordlist.

"Keyness," then, is a matter of being statistically unusual relative to some norm. The statistical operations involved here—a cross tabulation, a chi-square significance test—are among the most basic in statistics, and common in the world of corpus linguistics. However, to apply such operations manually would be extremely time-consuming. In fact, Burrows (1987) did use a computer to examine the vocabulary of characters in Jane Austen's novels using a variety of statistical measures, including cross-tabulation and chi-square (see 1987, chapter 2). However, Burrows's starting point was but three words, *we, our,* and *us,* the incidences of which were then retrieved for every character, and significant differences calculated. This—though in itself a huge task with illuminating results—is much more manageable than calculating the incidences of every single word a character speaks and undertaking statistical comparisons with the incidences of those lexical items for other characters in order to establish significant differences. The chief benefit of the KeyWords facility of WordsSmith Tools is that one can load in the relevant texts, click a few buttons and get all the lexical items of a body of data ranked according to the degree of difference within minutes.

2.3   A NOTE ON PREPARING THE TEXT: GENRE AND HISTORICAL CONSIDERATIONS

The fact that the analysis reported in this chapter concerns a Shakespearean play-text raises a couple of issues that need to be resolved before analysis

can start. The first issue relates to the fact that a Shakespearean play consists of dialogue—it is a play-text. Play-texts are mixed-style texts in that
they contain the speech styles of the different characters. This presents an
obvious problem to the computational analyst wishing to study character
and style: there has to be a way of enabling the computer to distinguish
between the speech of different characters. To that end, we added a simple
tagging system, consisting of a switch-on tag based on the first three letters
of the character's name, and a switch-off tag based on a backslash and
the first three letters of the character's name.[1] A sample of the tagged text
follows:

> Enter SAMPSON and GREGORY, armed with swords and bucklers.
> Gregory, o' our word, we'll not carry coals.
> No, for then we should be colliers.
> I mean, an we be in choler, we'll draw.
> Ay, while you live, draw your neck out o' the collar.
> I strike quickly, being moved.
> But thou art not quickly moved to strike.
> A dog of the house of Montague moves me.

As can be seen from this sample, such a tagging system also enables one
to exclude nonspeech material, such as stage directions. WordSmith Tools
(1999) is well suited to operating with such a tagging system, since it allows
one to examine text between a specific pair of tags or to exclude text between
a specific pair of tags from one's examination.

The second issue relates to the choice of edition. One possibility was
to download an electronic version of *Romeo and Juliet*, the First Folio,
from the Oxford Text Archive. Although this has the merit of being a more
"original" text compared with modernized editions, it also contains much
spelling variation. Spelling variation is perhaps the greatest obstacle to the
computational analysis of historical texts. Computers focus on word forms:
sweete, for example, would not be counted along with *sweet*. For this reason, we downloaded *The Oxford Shakespeare* edition of the play (1914,
edited by W. J. Craig), complete with modern standardized spelling, from
the internet. It might also be noted that each scene of the play constitutes
a separate file. This allows us to track, via WordSmith, changes across the
play (see our dispersion plots in section 2.5).

2.4 SELECTING CHARACTERS, COMPARATORS, AND PARAMETERS

The major criterion determining which and how many characters we investigated was how many words they spoke. Table 2.1 displays in rank order
the total number of words spoken by seven characters in *Romeo and Juliet*.

Table 2.1   The total number of words spoken by seven characters in *Romeo and Juliet*

Character	Total Words Spoken
Romeo	5,031
Juliet	4,564
Friar Laurence	2,901
Nurse	2,369
Capulet	2,292
Mercutio	2,254
Benvolio	1,293

It is clear from this table that a cut-off point presents itself after Mercutio, since the word count for the next character, Benvolio, drops by nearly one thousand words.

In any keyword analysis, the choice of data for comparison (the reference corpus) is an issue. There is no magic formula for making this decision. Scott and Tribble (2006, 58) suggest that the reference corpus "should be an appropriate sample of the language which the text we are studying . . . is written in," and that "appropriate sample" "usually means a large one, preferably many thousands of words long and possibly much more." Precisely what counts as large enough is still a matter of debate. Xiao and McEnery (2005, 70) compared two reference corpora, the hundred-million-word British National Corpus and the one-million-word Freiburg-LOB Corpus, and achieved almost identical keyword lists, thus concluding that "the size of reference corpus is not very important in making a keyword list." However, this does not rule out the possibility of important differences if much smaller reference corpora are used. Apart from the issue of size, we are still left the problem of deciding the language variety or varieties of which the reference corpus should consist. A clue is provided in the quotations from Enkvist in section 2.2 above. A set of data that has no relationship with the data to be examined is unlikely to reveal interesting results (cf. Enkvist's comparison of a Shakespearean sonnet with a telephone directory). What if one simply selects a huge multigenre corpus, such as the British National Corpus, as indeed other studies have done (for example, Tribble 2000; Scott 2000; Johnson, Culpeper, and Suhr 2003)? Let us consider one of those studies: Johnson, Culpeper, and Suhr (2003). Here, the corpus to be examined consisted of newspaper articles that contained political correctness expressions (for example, "political correctness," "politically correct," and "politically incorrect"), the research interest being to discover what characterized the discourse in which those expressions appeared. This corpus was compared with a word list based on the entire BNC set of written texts (90.7 million words). Among the most key keywords were *is*, *has*, *who*, and *says*. These were frequent items in the political correctness corpus and were evenly dispersed, but, upon close analysis, no connection with political correctness matters could be discerned. Two of the items, *who* and *says*, were found by Biber et al. (1999, 375, 610) to be outstandingly frequent in newspaper language generally. Thus the problem with the resulting list of keywords is that some reflected newspaper discourse in general as opposed to political correctness discourse in particular. What this suggests then, is that the choice of the reference corpus will affect whether you acquire keyword results that are all relevant to the particular aspect of the text(s) you are researching. The closer the relationship between the target corpus and the reference corpus the more likely the resultant keywords will reflect something specific to the target corpus. Thus, for the above study, a comparison with a corpus of newspaper texts (excluding political correctness-related texts) should have provided results specific to political correctness discourse, as features of newspaper discourse in general would most likely be common to both target and reference corpus, and therefore not be identified as key. However, this is not to say that the effect of a different reference corpus variety is a radical change in the keyword results. Scott and Tribble (2006) conclude that "while the choice of reference corpus is important, above a certain size, the procedure throws up a robust core of KWs [keywords] whichever the reference corpus used" (2006, 64). This is not surprising when one considers that any one style will stand in contrast to a large number of other styles. The issue is to do with how specific you want *all* your keyword results to be.

Given the research goal here of identifying a character's idiolect, comparing each of the six characters with the rest of the play seems to be the obvious choice.[2] Characters are partly shaped by their context. Thus, it makes little sense to compare, say, the characters of *Romeo and Juliet* with the characters of *Macbeth* or *Anthony and Cleopatra*, since the fictional worlds of Italy, Scotland, and Egypt provide very different contextual influences. Furthermore, characters, like people, are partly perceived in terms of whom they interact with. Indeed, linguists have argued that interaction itself can reveal personality. Brown and Levinson put it thus: "an understanding of the significant dimensions on which interaction varies should provide insights into the dimensions on which personality is built, as well as social relationships" (1987, 232).

The KeyWords program (within WordSmith Tools) allows the user to set various parameters. For the purposes of this study, the minimum frequency for a word to be considered for keyness is five.[3] The point of this parameter is to exclude words that will be identified as unusual simply because they happen not to have occurred in the reference corpus. Proper nouns, for example, are often among these one-off occurrences. This is not to say that such phenomena—which are referred to as "*hapax legomena*"—are uninteresting. We selected the log-likelihood test for significance. (We repeated the analysis with the chi-square test: the same results were revealed with only minor and occasional differences in the ranking that have no effect on our commentary below). The significance test calculates the significance of the difference in frequency between the word in the target data and in the reference corpus. The probability value was set at smaller than or equal to 0.01. Thus, words whose differences were considered to have a one percent chance or less of being a fluke would be included as keywords; words with more than a one percent chance of being a fluke would be excluded. Rayson (2003), evaluating various statistical tests for data involving low frequencies, different corpus sizes, and so on, favors the log-likelihood test "in general" and, moreover, a 0.01 percent significance level "if a statistically significant result is required for a particular item" (2003, 155). However, Scott (2013, 205–6) suggests that "where the notion of risk is less important than that of selectivity, you may often wish to set a comparatively low p value threshold such as 0.000001 (one in one million) . . . so as to obtain fewer keywords" (2013, 195–96). Given varying research questions, it is doubtful whether any general recommendation is possible. In sum, and rather like Baker (2004), the settings used for this chapter were largely derived by testing various possibilities and choosing a combination that resulted in (1) a decent but not overwhelming number of words to analyze, (2) every file (in our case, scene) offering at least some keyword instances, and (3) one-off and extremely rare word types being minimized.

2.5   ANALYSIS AND RESULTS: KEYWORDS IN *ROMEO AND JULIET*

2.5.1   A Note on Raw Word Frequencies

Before examining the keywords results, we shall briefly consider simple raw frequencies for each of the characters. The point of this is to justify why we need to engage in a more sophisticated analysis, such as keyword analysis. Table 2.2 displays the top ten rank-ordered word frequencies for the six characters. For comparative interest, the ten highest word frequencies overall in the play are included, and also the ten highest word frequencies in present-day spoken English and present-day written English. Of course, comparing an early modern English play-text with present-day general spoken language and general written language requires much caution!

What will be clear from this table is that many words are common to many characters (for example, *and* occurs in every list and always in the top three). Thus, they fail to discriminate between characters: they are not style markers that take into account differences of *relative* frequency (that is, whether the density of occurrence for a character is relatively unusual). That said, there are some differences that are noteworthy. For example, a unique feature of the Nurse's list is the presence of the interjection *o*. This would reflect the idea that the Nurse is a rather emotional character, and we will see

Table 2.2 The top ten rank-ordered word frequencies for six characters in *Romeo and Juliet* (present-day data taken from Leech, Rayson, and Wilson 2001)

Romeo	Juliet	Capulet	Nurse	Mercutio	Friar L.	Overall in the play	Pres-day Spoken English	Pres-day written English
and (136)	I (138)	to (61)	I (70)	a (85)	and (93)	and (734)	the	the
I (132)	to (113)	you (49)	a (61)	the (85)	the (83)	the (714)	I	of
the (117)	and (104)	and (48)	and (61)	of (57)	to (67)	I (589)	you	and
to (97)	our (92)	a (45)	the (56)	and (53)	in (51)	to (551)	and	a
our (85)	the (84)	our (45)	you (55)	to (36)	thy (51)	a (473)	it	in
that (84)	that (82)	I (44)	to (45)	that (33)	thou (46)	of (389)	a	to (inf.)
a (78)	thou (71)	is (39)	it (39)	I (31)	of (43)	our (361)	's	is
of (77)	is (68)	the (37)	is (34)	is (31)	is (37)	that (354)	to	to (prep.)
me (73)	a (68)	her (29)	our (33)	in (30)	that (36)	is (342)	of	was
in (72)	be (59)	not (29)	o (26)	thou (27)	a (33)	in (321)	that	it

more evidence of this later. Focusing on rank-order, it is interesting to note that Mercutio's top four words are identical to the words for present-day written English, and Friar Laurence's top four words appear in the top six for present-day written English. In contrast, the other characters all have first or second-person pronouns in the top four (something that is also true of present-day spoken English). It has been suggested that first and second-person pronouns are features of interaction (for example, Biber 1988). Romeo, Juliet, Capulet, and the Nurse are more interactive characters than Mercutio and Friar Laurence, who both tend to extol forth regardless of other characters on stage. Also, the fact that Mercutio's word frequencies have some similarities with "writtenness" is not surprising, since he has an elaborate rhetorical style, something that will be considered further later.

Of course, one can refine such frequency tables. A common strategy, for example, is to remove grammatical or function words from the lists, so that only the frequencies of content words are shown. This path has not been followed here, because it is not the case that grammatical words contain no evidence of style. Indeed, the following keywords analysis will show the contrary.

2.5.2   Keywords

Table 2.3 displays all the keywords revealed for each of the six characters. Positive keywords are keywords that appear because they are unusually frequent; negative keywords are keywords that appear because they are unusually infrequent (all items are rank-ordered according to keyness, that is, how statistically unusual they are compared with the reference corpus).[4] The fact that there are fewer negative keywords compared with positive keywords is not surprising: it is easier to exceed the norm established in a reference corpus than to fall short of that norm, particularly when the reference corpus is small.

Let us begin with some general remarks. Scott comments in a number of publications (for example, 2000, 2013) that keywords tend to be of three types. First, there are proper nouns. Scott's suggestion is that these are of little importance: "a text about racing could wrongly identify as key, names of horses which are quite incidental to the story" (2013, 206). In fictional texts, they may be of some interest, as they relate to key aspects of the fictional world. However, in table 2.3 they are very few—a mere three—and two are highly localized. Friar Laurence uses the place name *Mantua* in act 3, scene 3, for this is where he recommends Romeo to flee after his banishment. Juliet uses the bulk of instances of *Tybalt's* in act 3, scene 2, where she grieves Tybalt's death (he is her relative) and the consequent banishment of Romeo. Interestingly, the other proper noun is *Romeo*, a *negative* keyword for Romeo. This reflects the fact that *Romeo* is a frequent term of address or reference for other characters, but not used frequently in self-reference by Romeo himself (only five instances). This would seem to be some evidence

Table 2.3 Keywords for six characters in *Romeo and Juliet* (in descending order of keyness, with frequency of occurrence given in brackets)[8]

	Romeo	Juliet	Capulet	Nurse	Mercutio	Friar L.
Positive keywords	beauty (10)	if (31)	go (24)	day (22)	a (85)	thy (51)
	love (46)	be (59)	wife (10)	he's (9)	hare (5)	from (23)
	blessed (5)	or (25)	you (49)	you (55)	very (11)	thyself (5)
	eyes (14)	I (138)	ha (5)	quoth (5)	of (57)	her (30)
	more (26)	sweet (16)	thank (5)	God (12)	the (85)	Mantua (6)
	mine (14)	my (92)	her (29)	woeful (6)	he (20)	part (7)
	dear (13)	news (9)	t (5)	warrant (7)	o'er (5)	heaven (10)
	rich (7)	thou (71)	Thursday (7)	madam (10)	an (14)	forth (5)
	me (73)	night (27)	child (7)	lord (11)	eye (5)	alone (6)
	yonder (5)	would (20)	welcome (5)	lady (16)	us (7)	time (10)
	farewell (11)	yet (18)	we (15)	it (39)		married (7)
	sick (6)	that (82)	tis (11)	hie (5)		thou (46)
	lips (9)	Nurse (20)	haste (6)	your (21)		in (51)
	stars (5)	name (11)	gentlemen (5)	faith (7)		then (18)
	fair (15)	words (5)	our (13)	she (21)		letter (5)
	hand (11)	Tybalt's (6)	make (10)	ay (90)		
	thine (7)	send (7)	now (15)	said (6)		
	banished (9)	husband (7)	well (13)	about (5)		
	goose (5)	swear (5)	daughter (5)	sir (13)		
	that (84)	where (16)		ever (5)		
		again (10)		marry (7)		
				a (61)		
				ah (6)		
				o (26)		
				well (13)		
				fall (5)		
				mother (5)		
Negative keywords	he (11)	the (84)	the (37)	thou (11)	what (5)	have (5)
	Romeo (5)	you (27)	that (13)		I (31)	a (33)
	you (14)	her (5)	thou (7)		my (13)	you (16)
						I (32)

that Romeo is a fulcrum for the play. Secondly, there are keywords that relate to the text's "aboutness" or content, a term used by Phillips (1989) among others. Scott (2000, 155) relates aboutness to Halliday's (1994) ideational metafunction, and also suggests that such words "are keywords that human beings would recognize" (2013, 206) or be "likely to predict" (2000, 160). Romeo's most key keywords illustrate this well: surely most people would guess that Romeo's talk was about *beauty* and *love*! Thirdly, there are "indicators more of style than of 'aboutness'" (2013, 206), and Scott cites such examples as *because*, *shall*, and *already*. Juliet's most key keywords illustrate this well: *if*, *be*, *or*, and *I* are all frequently occurring items that most people would be unlikely to predict; they seem to capture her grammatical style. It seems to be the case that aboutness keywords relate to "open class" words, while stylistic keywords relate to "closed class" words.[5] However, caution is needed here. The notion of aboutness is not restricted to words, it is more abstract. Also, the distinction between aboutness and stylistic keywords, while useful, can lead one to assuming a simple "dualist" view of style, whereby choices of content are separable from stylistic choices. A functional, Hallidayan approach would view all choices, including grammatical choices, as meaningful and stylistic.[6] This discussion relates to the debate in stylistics about content and form. We do not have space to review this debate (for details, see Leech and Short 2007, chapter 1). We take the general view that style is any kind of meaningful linguistic choice, but that those choices may vary with respect to how "contentful" or "referential" they are as opposed to how "grammatical" or "textual," or even "interpersonal." Consequently, the analyses below consider all lexical items equally, without excluding, as some researchers have done, more grammatical items.

The following discussion focuses on particularly salient or interesting trends for each character. Comments on pronouns that are keywords, however, will form a separate discussion in the following subsection. Not all keywords, of course, relate to characterization. Only by examining the usage of those keywords (that is, by conducting qualitative analysis), can one determine whether a keyword has anything to do with characterization. An important factor—though not necessarily a decisive one—in determining whether they relate to character or not is whether they are localized or well-dispersed throughout the play.

Romeo's top three keywords, *beauty*, *love*, and *blessed*, as we commented above, seem to match one's intuitions about this character: he is the lover in a romance. Other keywords, such as *dear*, *stars*, and *fair*, fit his "love talk" style, as in, for example (all keywords are underlined in examples cited):

> She hath, and in that sparing makes huge waste;
> For <u>beauty</u>, starv'd with her severity,
> Cuts <u>beauty</u> off from all posterity.
> She is too <u>fair</u>, too wise, wisely too <u>fair</u>,
> To merit bliss by making <u>me</u> despair:
> She hath forsworn to <u>love</u>, and in that vow
> Do I live dead that live to tell it now. (1.1)

Note that it is not until act 1, scene 5 that Romeo notices Juliet; prior to this, Rosaline is the subject of his infatuation. This has some implications for the way the keyword instances are dispersed across the play, as shown in figure 2.1 (in these figures, the keywords in bold at the bottom are negative keywords).

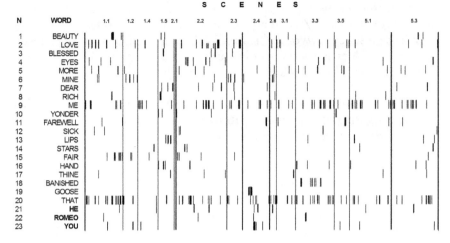

Figure 2.1   The dispersion of Romeo's keywords

Love is dispersed widely, appearing in every scene that Romeo does, except two: clearly this is a consistent feature of his characterization. However, one can see something of a concentration in two scenes: in act 1, scene 1, Romeo extols his love for Rosaline to his cousin Benvolio; in act 2, scene 2, he extols his love for Juliet, who appears on the balcony. *Beauty* is used of both women, but *blessed* only of Juliet, who is metaphorically deified as the object of his love.

Keywords relating to body parts–*eyes*, *lips*, and *hand*–underlie Romeo's concern with the physical:

> If I profane with our unworthiest <u>hand</u>
> This holy shrine, the gentle sin is this;
> Our <u>lips</u>, two blushing pilgrims, ready stand
> To smooth that rough touch with a tender kiss. (1.5)

Interestingly, as is clear from the quotation above, Romeo often reflects on aspects of his own body. This hint at his egocentric nature is also reflected in the pronominal keywords, as we shall see in the following section. The dispersal of these body keywords is not even: *lips* and *hand* concentrate in act 1, scene 5, the scene of the above quotation, and *eyes* in act 2, scene 2. Here, where Romeo first sees her on the balcony and refers to her as "blessed," he deifies her eyes as heavenly stars ("two of the fairest stars in all the heaven, Having some business, do entreat her <u>eyes</u> To twinkle in their spheres till they return").

The dispersion plot of figure 2.1 usefully shows that two keywords are highly localized. Romeo's keyword *banished* only occurs in act 3, scene 3: it is a localized reaction to the circumstances he finds himself in and not a general feature of his character. *Goose* only occurs in act 2, scene 2, where Romeo word-plays with Mercutio about a "wild-goose chase."

Juliet's most key keyword, *if*, is striking, because, unlike many of Romeo's keywords, it does not seem so obviously guessable, partly because it is a more grammatical word. Here are some examples:

> If he be married, / Our grave is like to be our wedding-bed (1.5.) [at her first sighting of him, whether Romeo is married]
> If they do see thee, they will murder thee (2.2.) [whether Romeo will be spotted during a covert visit]
> But if thou meanest not well (2.2.) [whether his intentions are honourable and his love will lead to marriage]

The keyword *if* seems to reflect the fact that Juliet is in a state of anxiety for much of the play. Other keywords support this. Consider these examples of *or*:

> Is thy news good, or bad? answer to that; / Say either, and I'll stay the circumstance: / Let me be satisfied, is 't good or bad? (2.5) [whether the Nurse has good news or bad]

And these of *yet*:

> Tis almost morning; I would have thee gone; / And yet no further than a wanton's bird (2.2.) [whether Romeo should go]
> I fear it is: and yet, methinks, it should not, / For he hath still been tried a holy man (4.3.) [whether the Friar has supplied sleeping potion or poison]

Also, we see examples of the subjunctive *be* (see the first instance in the first example for Juliet above), and the modal *would* (see the penultimate example for Juliet above, where it expresses her mixed wishes). All these keywords are more grammatical items. Together, they create a grammatical style that is meaningful: it articulates Juliet's anxieties. Moreover, figure 2.2 shows that these keywords are fairly evenly dispersed throughout the play: anxiety is a characteristic of Juliet.

Even *yet*, with only eighteen occurrences, occurs in six scenes, with just a slight preponderance in act 2, scene 2. In contrast, keywords like *news*, *name*, *Tybalt's*, *husband*, and *swear* relate much more to the immediate event at hand.

Capulet's most key keyword is *go*. It is widely dispersed, occurring in all but two of the nine scenes in which he appears. It is usually an imperative command directed variously to, for example, Tybalt (1.5.82), Paris (3.4.31), the Nurse (3.5.171), his servants (4.2.2), Juliet (4.2.9), and Lady Capulet (4.2.41). There are no surprises here: as Capulet is the head of a noble household, his function in the play is largely to direct the others. The

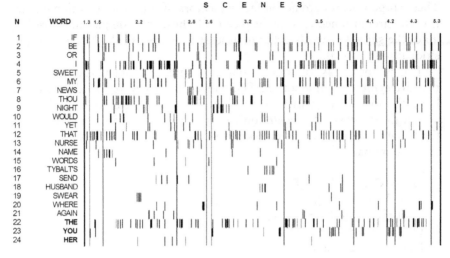

Figure 2.2 The dispersion of Juliet's keywords

keywords *make* and *haste* are also part of this directive pattern, as can be seen from the following quotation:

> Go wake Juliet, go and trim her up;
> I'll go and chat with Paris. Hie, make haste,
> Make haste; the bridegroom is come already:
> Make haste, I say. (4.4)

Of course, it is Capulet's conspicuous failure to direct Juliet that constitutes part of the tragedy of the play.[7]

An interesting pattern in the Nurse's keywords is that many are what have been referred to as "surge features," a term that refers to linguistic items that reflect "outbursts of emotion" (Taavitsainen 1999). The Nurse's keywords that are clearly surge features include: *warrant, faith, marry, ah, well, o,* and *well-a [-day]*, and also various vocatives sometimes used in an exclamatory way: *god, madam, lord, lady, sir*. The following quotation illustrates the usage of some of these:

> Mistress! What, mistress! Juliet! Fast, I warrant her, she.
> Why, lamb! Why, lady! Fie, you slug-a-bed!
> Why, love, I say! madam! sweetheart! Why, bride!
> What, not a word? You take your pennyworths now.
> Sleep for a week; for the next night, I warrant,
> The County Paris hath set up his rest
> That you shall rest but little. God forgive me!
> Marry, and amen! How sound is she asleep! (4.5.)

These surge features are not in fact indicators of transitory emotional reactions to circumstances. As can be seen from the dispersion plot in figure 2.3, all of the surge keywords occur in at least four scenes. The Nurse is dispositionally emotional.

This is not to say, of course, that the context cannot trigger keywords that are symptoms of emotion. The Nurse's most key keyword is *day* and her fifth most key keyword is *woeful*. As can be seen from figure 2.3, these are localized keywords: *woeful* only occurs in act 4, scene 5, and fifteen of the twenty-two instances of *day* occur in that scene. Here, the Nurse discovers Juliet apparently dead:

> O wo, O <u>woeful</u>, <u>woeful</u>, <u>woeful day</u>,
> Most lamentable <u>day</u>, most <u>woeful day</u>,
> That <u>ever</u>, <u>ever</u>, I did yet behold.
> O <u>day</u>, O <u>day</u>, O <u>day</u>, O hateful <u>day</u>,
> Never was seen so black a <u>day</u> as this:
> O <u>woeful day</u>, O <u>woeful day</u>. (4.5.)

The Nurse, already an emotional character, reacts with extreme emotion (compare, for example, Capulet's rather more controlled and sophisticated rhetorical reaction). Finally, it is worth noting that many of the Nurse's keywords reflect her more colloquial register. This includes the surge features listed above (including the vocatives), the item *ay*, and the speech report verbs *quoth* and *said* (which are evidence of the fact that the Nurse delights

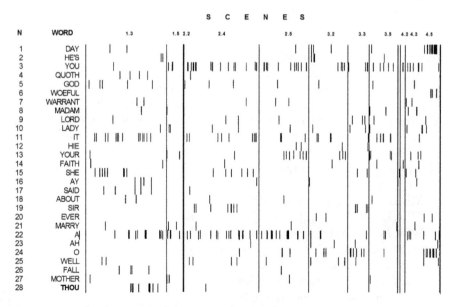

Figure 2.3   The dispersion of the Nurse's keywords

in oral narratives). Shakespeare is well-known for attributing a more colloquial style to characters of the lower social orders (see, for example, Gilbert
1979, chapter 2, for a discussion of "high-style," "middle-style," and "low-
style" in Shakespeare).

Mercutio's most key keyword is *a*, his fourth is *of*, and his fifth is *the*.
On the face of it, this appears to be an unexciting result. Note that such
central grammatical items are often deleted when raw word frequency lists
are considered, as we mentioned above. In fact, they reveal an important
aspect of Mercutio's style. They confirm an observation made earlier that
Mercutio has a more "written" and less interactive style. More specifically,
he has a "nominal" style: he has a tendency to use lists of noun phrases or
prepositional phrases, as can be seen from the quotation below:

> Ben.   Why, what is Tybalt?
> Mer.   More than Prince of Cats. O, He's the courageous captain of
>   compliments. He fights as you sing prick-song: keeps time,
>   distance, and proportion; he rests his minim rests, one, two,
>   and the third in your bosom; the very butcher of a silk button,
>   a duellist, a duellist; a gentleman of the very first house, of
>   the first and the second cause. Ah, the immortal passado! the
>   punto reverso! the hay!—(2.4.)

Mercutio's function in the play is to give dazzling rhetorical displays, as well as
to raise the emotional temperature and further the plot by getting killed. The
dramatic focus is not on his social relations with other characters. All of his
keywords are fairly well dispersed, except his five instances of *hare*, his second
most key keyword, which all occur in a small cluster towards the end of act 2,
scene 4, his five instances of *oer*, which occur in a cluster in act 1, scene 4, and
his eleven instances of *very*, all but one of which occur in act 2, scene 4, from
which the above quotation is drawn (see there, for examples of *very*).

Friar Laurence is a man of the Church, and hence the presence of *heaven*
as the seventh-ranked keyword is not surprising. However, his three most
key keywords, *thy*, *from*, and *thyself*, are at first sight more puzzling, not
least because they are grammatical items without transparent meaning out
of context. Consider this quotation:

> The sun not yet thy sighs from heaven clears,
> Thy old groans yet ring in our ancient ears;
> Lo! Here upon thy cheek the stain doth sit
> Of an old tear that is not washed off yet.
> If e'er thou wast thyself and these woes thine (2.3)

Friar Laurence is not only the play's agony aunt, he is also an emotional
mirror: he articulates the traumas Romeo and Juliet are suffering. Comment
on the fact that he uses *thy* and *thyself*, as opposed to *your* and *yourself*, is

delayed until the following section. His other keywords, notably, *Mantua*, *letter*, relate to the role he plays in facilitating the plot, particularly in the fourth and final acts where those specific keywords occur.

2.5.3 Pronominal Patterns in the Keywords

In table 2.3, pronouns were revealed as keywords, both positive and negative, for each character. Table 2.4 displays the rank-ordered pronominal keywords for each of the six characters. Some interesting trends are apparent in these pronominal keywords. Table 2.5 summarizes these trends.

For both Romeo and Juliet, the two most key pronominal keywords are both first-person singular, while the third most key pronoun is the second person. It is no surprise that the protagonists Romeo and Juliet use first and second pronouns: they are at the heart of the social interaction in the play. Interestingly, the subjective first-person pronoun *I* appears in Juliet's list, but not in Romeo's, where instead we find the possessive *mine*, along with the objective first-person pronoun *me*. Although this is not conclusive evidence, it is consistent with the idea that Juliet spends much time in the play baring her soul (cf. instances in the examples above for Juliet), whereas Romeo has a much more external consciousness of his own role as a lover and of

Table 2.4 Rank-ordered pronominal patterns in the speech of six characters in *Romeo and Juliet*

	Romeo	Juliet	Capulet	Nurse	Mercutio	Friar L.
Positive keyword	mine	I	you	he's	he	thy
pronouns	me	my	her	you	us	thyself
	thine	thou	we	it		her
			tis	your		thou
			our	she		
Negative keyword	he	you	thou	thou	I		you
pronouns	you	her			my		I

Table 2.5 The pronominal preferences of six characters in *Romeo and Juliet* (parentheses indicate minor preferences)

	Romeo	Juliet	Capulet	Nurse	Mercutio	Friar L.
Person	1st (2nd)	1st (2nd)	2nd / 3rd / 1st	3rd (2nd)	3rd (1st)	2nd (3rd)
1st person singular / plural	S	S	P	–	(P)	–
Thou / you	T	T	Y	Y	–	T

the effect of circumstances upon him. Consider the following examples of Romeo's speech (in the examples given in this section, only pronominal keywords are underlined):

O, wilt thou leave me so unsatisfied? (2.2.)

O sweet Juliet!
Thy beauty hath made me effeminate,
And in our temper soft'ned valour's steel! (3.1.)

Thou canst not speak of that thou dost not feel:
Wert thou as young as I, Juliet thy love,
An hour but married, Tybalt murdered,
Doting like me, and like me banished (3.3.)

In faith, I will. Let me peruse this face:
Mercutio's kinsman, noble County Paris!
What said our man when our betossed soul
Did not attend him as we rode? I think
He told me Paris should have married Juliet:
Said he not so? or did I dream it so?
Or am I mad, hearing him talk of Juliet,
To think it was so? O! give me thy hand,
One writ with me in sour misfortune's book:
I'll bury thee in a triumphant grave (5.3.)

This pattern of usage fits the earlier suggestion that Romeo has an egotistical streak.

Capulet also uses first, second, and third-person pronouns, but importantly *you* is most key, followed by *her* and then *we*. This supports the idea that Capulet's major role in the play is to direct other people. When Capulet does use first-person pronouns, note that they are plural (that is, *we, our*). This relates to the fact that Capulet, the head of the household, often speaks on behalf of other people, as well as for himself. In the following instance of *we*, he refers to Montague and himself:

But Montague is bound as well as I,
In penalty alike; and 'tis not hard, I think,
For men so old as we to keep the peace. (1.2)

In the first and second instances of *we* below, Capulet is probably referring to Lady Capulet and himself as they both encounter Paris, while the third refers to all people:

Things have fall'n out, sir, so unluckily,
That we have had no time to move our daughter:

> Look you, she lov'd <u>her</u> kinsman Tybalt dearly,
> And so did I: well, <u>we</u> were born to die. (3.4)

In this example the reference of the plural first-person pronouns is unclear:

> All things that <u>we</u> ordained festival,
> Turn from their office to black funeral;
> <u>Our</u> instruments to melancholy bells,
> <u>Our</u> wedding cheer to a sad burial feast,
> <u>Our</u> solemn hymns to sullen dirges change,
> <u>Our</u> bridal flowers serve for a buried corse,
> And all things change them to the contrary. (4.5.)

The pronouns could refer to (1) Capulet alone (what we would call the "royal we"), (2) Lady Capulet and himself, or (3) the Capulet household. Overall, what is clear is that Capulet steadfastly avoids pronouns signaling individual reference to himself alone. This is consistent with the idea that Capulet does not have much of an identity of his own: he largely exists as a set of limited functions orientated towards other characters.

Third-person pronouns appear as most key for the Nurse and Mercutio, and of secondary keyness for Friar Laurence. (Note that *he* appears as a negative keyword for Romeo: he avoids this third-person pronoun). This reflects the fact that these characters tend to discourse *about* third parties, rather than *with* second parties. This is clear in the quotation given for Mercutio above, and in such discourse as this from the Nurse, as she recounts Juliet's youth:

> Yet I cannot choose but laugh,
> To think <u>it</u> should leave crying, and say "Ay."
> And yet, I warrant, <u>it</u> had upon its brow
> A bump as big as a young cockerel's stone;
> A parlous knock; and <u>it</u> cried bitterly:
> "Yea," quoth our husband, "fall'st upon thy face?
> Thou wilt fall backward when thou com'st to age;
> Wilt thou not, Jule?" <u>it</u> stinted and said "Ay." (1.3.)

The Nurse's strongly key keyword *he's* is localized: it is a reaction to Romeo's death; for example, "he's dead, he's dead."

The fact that Friar Laurence has a second-person pronoun as his most key pronominal keyword merits comment. But note that it is the possessive form of the second-person pronoun, *thy*, that is most positively key, followed by the possessive reflexive form, *thyself*. Friar Laurence's role is not to interact with the others, but to describe them, as can be seen in the quotation at the end of the previous section ("thy sighs," "thy old groans," and so forth). Also, we might observe that for both Friar Laurence and Mercutio

I appears as a negative keyword. These are the most minor characters of the six. As was argued above, they are not in the play to volunteer information about themselves, but to describe others and facilitate the plot.

Finally, we shall briefly comment on the second-person pronominal variants. Elizabethan English offered a choice between two forms for the second-person pronouns: the plural forms *ye, you, your, yours*, and *yourself*, and the singular forms *thou, thee, thy, thine*, and *thyself*. The variant chosen could have significant social or pragmatic implications. The usage of these variants is a matter of great controversy—a controversy that cannot be engaged here. What can be noted, however, from the keywords analysis is that certain characters prefer you-forms and avoid thou-forms, while others do the opposite. Romeo and Juliet prefer thou-forms. Contrary to this, Brown and Gilman (1960) predict that high-status social equals use you-forms. However, other researchers consider you-forms as dispassionate and emotionally unmarked, and thou-forms as expressive of negative emotions (for example, anger and contempt) or positive emotions (for example, affection and love) (for example, McIntosh 1963, and Mulholland 1987). This is consistent with the idea that the thou-forms favored by Romeo and Juliet mark the discourse of intimacy, or, more specifically here, love talk. This would also explain why Friar Laurence has a preference for thou-forms, since he engages in intimate and emotionally charged discourse. Both Capulet and the Nurse prefer you-forms. Capulet's usage would fit Brown and Gilman's (1960) prediction that social superiors use you-forms. Regarding the Nurse, Brown and Gilman (1960) predict that low status individuals use you-forms to social superiors. The Nurse mostly interacts with people of much higher social status (for example, Juliet, Romeo, Lady Capulet): hence her preference for you-forms. It may be objected that the Nurse is an emotional character, as already observed, and consequently this should, if the above arguments are correct, weight the Nurse's usage in favor of thou-forms. However, when the Nurse is at her most emotional (for example, in act 4, scene 5, when she finds Juliet apparently dead), she tends not to address anybody but to give personal vent to her own emotions. Also, it would be socially dangerous for the Nurse to use thou-forms to her superiors, whether in emotional contexts or not.

2.5.4 Reflections on the Analysis and Characterization

Interestingly, characters vary according to whether, to use Scott's terms, "aboutness" or "stylistic" keywords predominate. Romeo is characterized by guessable aboutness keywords, most notably *love*, and this captures his function as the lover in the play. Aboutness keywords also construct Capulet, although they also have an important grammatical dimension—the imperative mood. His keywords (for example, *go*) characterize not only his social position as "director" of the household but also his dramatic one as a character set up for a tragic fall. Juliet, in contrast, is characterized by less guessable stylistic keywords, many of which are grammatical (for example, *if*, *or*, and *yet*). It is through these grammatical choices—though choices that are in fact often more accurately logical semantic choices—that Juliet is given meaning as the anxious target of love. Mercutio, even more than Juliet, is characterized by stylistic keywords, most being grammatical, including *a*, *very*, *of*, *the*, *an*. Unlike Juliet, Mercutio's keywords do not specify logical semantic relations, but reflect a rhetorical style that deploys lists of noun phrases. Mercutio is all style and no substance. The Nurse's keywords are not easily categorizable as even aboutness or stylistic keywords. Discourse markers such as *warrant*, *faith*, *marry*, *ah*, *o*, and *well*, and vocatives such as *god*, *madam*, *lord*, *lady*, and *sir* are the Cinderellas of language, as they are considered by some linguists not to be part of the grammar or the lexicon. Discourse markers, and to some extent vocatives, have little semantic content, but rather pragmatic import, and they tend to be peripheral to the syntax. Given problems with the use of the term "stylistic" for keywords (see section 2.5.2) and the fact that neither the terms "aboutness" nor "stylistic" do justice to the Nurse's keywords, we suggest, broadly following Halliday, the use of "ideational keywords" (encompassing Romeo in particular, but also Capulet and Juliet), "grammatical keywords" (encompassing Mercutio), and "interpersonal keywords" (encompassing the Nurse). These neatly correspond with character types: Romeo, Capulet, and Juliet enact the love tragedy, they give it meaning; Mercutio is involved in the plot but is nevertheless largely a carriage for rhetorical displays; and the Nurse is there as the emotional thermometer. Of course, these are generalizations: all characters have something of a mix of keyword types. In fact, Friar Laurence is a particular case in point. Some of his keywords are ideational, reflecting the way he facilitates aspects of the plot such as correspondence, marriage, and meeting (for example, *letter*, *married*, and *time*). Some, such as *from* and *in*, are grammatical, reflecting the style he uses to dramatize the events that afflict Romeo and Juliet. Others, such as *thy*, *thyself*, and *thou*, might be described as interpersonal, although *inter*personal might not be the best term here, as Friar Laurence steadfastly avoids presenting himself (hence we see *I* as a negative keyword).

Keywords analysis offers a way into analyzing grammatical words. The sheer quantity of grammatical items in texts can make it difficult to see patterns. In particular, the keyword analyses exposed the pronominal patterns that helped construct the various characters. The protagonists, Romeo and Juliet, gravitate towards *I*, as they divulge their thoughts; Capulet's sense of his social position is reflected in his usage of *you*, directing others, and his use of the plural *we*; the Nurse's and Mercutio's use of the third person *he*, *she*, and *it* reflect their talk about other people—they are commentators in the play; similarly, Friar Laurence's usage of second-person forms *thy*, *thyself*, and *thou* reflects the fact that he comments on the feelings of his addressees. The analyses also reveal different preferences for thou-forms as opposed to you-forms, a distinction that carried sociopragmatic meaning in the early modern period.

2.6 CONCLUSION

This chapter started by discussing the notions of "style markers" and "keywords." It argued that the notion of style markers is synonymous with that of keywords, but that the term keywords links in with corpus linguistics research in general and the computer program Wordsmith Tools (Scott 1999) in particular. It then noted that the notion of keywords has a long history in stylometry, and seems to have been first labeled as such by Pierre Guiraud, and discussed keyword parameters, and in particular the choice of reference corpus, concluding that the choice primarily affected the specificity of the keyword results.

Keyword analysis has a relatively recent history, though it appears to be gaining steam, and not least in the analysis of literary texts, for example, Tribble (2000) on Romantic fiction; Scott and Tribble (2006) on Shakespeare's *Romeo and Juliet*; Mahlberg (for example, 2007) on Dickens; Fischer-Starcke (for example, 2009) on Jane Austen; Archer, Culpeper, and Rayson (2009) on Shakespeare's "love" plays; Archer and Bousfield (2010) on Shakespeare's *King Lear*; McIntyre (2010) on film dialogue; McIntyre and Archer's (2010) on mind style in a play; and Ho (2011) on John Fowles' *The Magus*. (For keyword related publications, see Mike Scott's comprehensive bibliography available at http://www.lexically.net/publications/publications.htm). An important aim of this chapter was to show how a keywords analysis offers an empirical way of establishing lexical or grammatical character patterns in dialogue. Specifically, it aimed to reveal such patterns in Shakespeare's *Romeo and Juliet*. It argued that the kind of results obtained do not easily fit the categories of "aboutness" and "stylistic" keywords. Instead, it proposed a three-way distinction among ideational, grammatical, and interpersonal keywords. Furthermore, it is important to remember, as Baker (2004, 348) points out, that keyword analysis is but the first step: the resultant keyword list provides the linguistic patterns that need to be interpreted in order to both validate them and to address specific research questions. Hence, keyword analyses are as much qualitative as quantitative, as demonstrated here where we see keywords motivated by characterization, plot function, rhetorical style, or some dramatic event.

As with any study, there are a number of limitations that need to be borne in mind (in no particular order):

- No attempt was made to lemmatize the word forms in the data, so that, for example, *loves* would form part of the word count of *love*. This was not done because (a) lemmatization programs tend to be inaccurate, and (b) lemmatization can obscure shades of difference in meaning.

- Contractions were counted separately, so that, for example, the first-person singular pronoun in the contraction *I'll* would not have been counted along with individual instances of the pronoun.
- Keywords involve statistical deviation from a relative norm. This is only one kind of deviation. Levin (1963), for example, distinguishes between "determinate" and "statistical" deviation, or, similarly, Leech (1985) distinguishes between an "absolute norm" and a "relative norm." For example, spelling an English word *ndfjh* breaks an absolute norm (a structural rule of English). Of course, there is an intimate relationship between these two types of norms: deviations from absolute norms tend to occur relatively infrequently. The point here is that a keyword analysis focuses squarely on statistical deviations from a relative norm, and ignores the significance of relatively infrequent deviations from absolute norms.
- Related to the above, keywords analysis does not consider *hapax legomena*—one-off occurrences of words.

A general issue for any keyword analysis is that each individual study tends to use its own settings (the frequency cut-off, the type of statistical test, the probability value). This, of course, raises issues of comparability. However, in practice, studies tend to focus on the most key keywords, which would arise in the context of most normally used settings. Perhaps a more substantial issue is whether keywords analysis is the best technique for capturing the stylistic characteristics of texts. Some scholars have suggested that Douglas Biber's (1988) multidimensional analysis does a better job. In a nutshell, multidimensional analysis involves statistical operations on the frequency counts of linguistic features, mostly grammatical, and identifies statistical relationships of co-occurrence between those features. Features that co-occur or group together constitute a bipolar "factor" or "dimension," which can be labelled according to the kind of features that constitute it. So, for example, Biber's dimension one is labelled "involved versus informational." Involved, interactive features include, for example, first and second pronouns, contractions, while informational features include longer words, attributive adjectives, and prepositions. Xiao and McEnery (2005) compared multidimensional analysis of three genres (conversation, monologic speech, and academic prose) with a keyword analysis of those genres. The results they obtained were "similar" (2005, 76) for both methodologies. Also, keyword analysis was "less demanding" (2005, 77), for the reason that multidimensional analysis first involves some complex algorithms for the extraction of certain grammatical features from the corpus, and then sophisticated statistical analysis. One could add the following benefit of keyword analysis. Whereas multidimensional analysis involves a priori decisions about what to count, keyword analysis does not. Interjections, for example, were not considered discourse markers and thus not counted in Biber's multidimensional analysis. Yet interjections turn out to be important features of both conversation and monologic speech in Xiao and McEnery's (2005) analyses. They also appear among the Nurse's keywords: *ay*, *a* (as an interjection), *ah*, and *o* help create her colloquial style. This would not have been identified with a multidimensional analysis. Discussion of further issues to do with keyness can be found in Bondi and Scott (2010).

The possibilities for further research are numerous. One area to consider is relationships between keywords. Scott (for example, 1997, 1996; also, Scott and Tribble 2006) has developed, for example, the notion of "key keywords" (keywords that are keywords in a number of different files; that is, they are generally key across the body of data), and "associates" (keywords that have a statistical association with other keywords). These notions could not be pursued in the data of this chapter, on account of the small number of words in each character file. More generally, it should be noted that keyword analysis need not be restricted to words; anything that can be counted can be considered for keyness. This could be punctuation features, multiword units, or grammatical tags added to the corpus. The idea of investigating key multiword units has particular appeal, as a keyword analysis might be misleading because it treats each lexical item in isolation. Language does not work like this: words cohabit with other words and give meaning to each other. Again, this issue cannot be adequately pursued in relation to the individual characters of *Romeo and Juliet*, because they do not speak enough for statistical analyses to be undertaken. Scholars who have undertaken such key multiword analyses in relation to literary characters include Mahlberg (for example, 2007), who shows how they contribute to some of the characters in Charles Dickens' novels.

The next chapter will extend the notion of keyness by examining grammatical and semantic categories.

NOTES

1. The switch-on tag can be introduced automatically by doing a "find and replace" operation on the original speaker identification in the text (for example, FIND Sam. + REPLACE WITH <SAM>). The switch-off tags are a little more problematic. We introduced them manually, since the total data set is not large. However, it should be possible to devise a program to introduce them automatically, since their position can be identified by the fact that they precede the switch-on tag for a different speaker (this does not apply where stage directions appear, so some way of identifying stage directions would be required).
2. To clarify, each of the six characters was compared with the rest of the play, excluding the particular character in question. This was so that the comparative data would be an independent variable.
3. In studies in corpus linguistics, ten seems to be a favorite minimum frequency. We experimented with various settings. Our character data sets are relatively small, and so five seemed to work best.

4. The keywords facility in WordSmith Tools automatically separates positive keywords from negative, each rank-ordered according to keyness (that is, how statistically unusual they are compared with the reference corpus). The raw frequencies of occurrence are supplied in round brackets. There is no simple correlation between these raw frequencies and whether a word is a positive or negative keyword, or how the items are ranked. Indeed, the rankings are likely to be influenced by the size of the raw frequencies, and thus not too much trust should be placed in the precise rankings, especially if there is a relatively low raw frequency. Furthermore, raw frequencies may give some indication as to how "general" the particular keywords are. However, one cannot assume an even dispersion throughout the play. We will draw attention to the importance of dispersion in our discussion.

5. Scott's example of *already* as a stylistic keyword is a borderline open/closed class word. Adverbs are a varied and thus problematic category, which is considered open class by some linguists and closed by others.

6. In fact, items such as *if* and *or* relate very clearly to the "logical" subcomponent of Halliday's ideational metafunction—they are not devoid of "content."

7. Readers may wonder what Capulet's keyword *t* is supposed to represent. In fact, it is a reduced form of *to*. Not much significance can be attributed to the fact that Capulet has this graphological oddity. Also, we should remember that this reduced form would almost certainly have been put there by a compositor or editor, not by Shakespeare.

8. In fact, WordSmith Tools lists negative keywords in ascending order of keyness.

3 Developing Keyness and Characterization
Annotation

Jonathan Culpeper

3.1 INTRODUCTION

This chapter builds on the last by extending the notion of keyword analysis to other phenomena apart from words. For this reason, it is more appropriate to refer to keyness analysis rather than key*word* analysis. More specifically, it applies grammatical and semantic annotation to the words of the data, and then analyses that annotation for keyness. This taps into fundamental issues about where the meanings of texts reside. One might argue that a keyword analysis is misleading because the grammatical functions of words are not explicitly taken into account in the analysis. However, as demonstrated, one can analyze the grammatical functions of the keyword results. Nevertheless, one cannot escape the fact that those results were selected on the basis of (graphological) word form. Furthermore, perhaps a keyword analysis is misleading because the semantic similarities between words are not explicitly taken into account in the analysis. Again, as demonstrated, one can analyze the semantic similarities of the keyword results, but those results were not selected on the basis of semantic similarities. This chapter undertakes analyses of the keyness of grammatical and semantic tags, and then compares the results with those of the keyword analyses in the previous chapter. In order to constrain the task within the confines of a chapter, the focus will be on just three characters, Romeo, Mercutio, and the Nurse. It may be remembered that the keyword results for these characters are diverse: Romeo's are characterized by ideational keywords, Mercutio's by grammatical keywords, and the Nurse's by interpersonal keywords.

This chapter begins by briefly noting some approaches to the grammar and semantics of characters within literary stylistics and literary studies. In order to incorporate grammar and semantics explicitly into the following keyness analysis, the data needs to be annotated, so there follows an outline of what annotation is in general and also an indication as to why it is controversial. Then, the software that was used is introduced, and some of the problems in treating historical data are discussed. Finally, after introducing grammatical annotation, the grammar of the three characters is analyzed for keyness, and then, after introducing semantic annotation, the semantics of the same characters is analyzed for keyness.

3.2 A NOTE ON GRAMMATICAL AND SEMANTIC ASPECTS OF CHARACTERIZATION

As pointed out in the previous chapter, the grammatical aspects of characterization have attracted little attention from scholars, and the same can be said of the grammatical styles of real-life people. What studies there are tend to focus on a link between syntactic complexity and cognitive organization. For example, in psychological and medical research, syntactic complexity is seen as an index or symptom of cognitive function, such that decreasing syntactic complexity correlates with progressively severe conditions such as Alzheimer's disease (see for example, Rondal et al. 2003 and references therein; note that not all the evidence supports this correlation at all stages of Alzheimer's disease). In the field of literary studies, similar assumptions are made. Brook, for example, points out that the old men in Shakespeare tend to speak in "short, jerky sentences, as though out of breath" (1976, 183), as is exemplified by the shepherd's speech in *The Winter's Tale*:

> Good lucke (an't be thy will) what haue we heere? Mercy on's, a Barne? A very pretty barne; A boy, or a Childe I wonder? (A pretty one, a verie prettie one) sure some Scape; Though I am not bookish, yet I can reade Waiting-Gentlewoman in the scape. (3.3.65–71)

Toolan (1985), however, explores the syntactic styles of characters in Faulkner's novels in a rather more sophisticated way, using Halliday-inspired grammatical concepts to demonstrate that distinct syntactic styles are linked to distinct (and varied) aspects of character.

Literary scholars, particularly of the structuralist variety, are no strangers to the semantics of characterization. Barthes ([1970] 1975), for example, attempts to capture characters by specifying a list of features or "semes" that distinguish one character from another. This approach was taken up by stylisticians in the 1980s (for example, Fowler 1986, 33–38; Pfister 1988, 166–70; Toolan 1988, 99–101). The use of semic analysis to tackle characterization is not surprising. Semic analysis is analogous to the componential analysis of meaning developed within linguistic semantics (Goodenough 1956), and componential analysis of meaning had already been allied with trait psychology for real life people (D'Andrade 1965). Typically, the semantic features considered in characterization form binary opposites (for example, male/female, adult/child, good/bad, beautiful/ugly). This can help highlight the structural similarities and contrasts between characters, as here in Fowler's analysis of characters in *The Great Gatsby*:

> Tom "overlaps" with Jordan Baker in respect to some semes (athleticism, competitiveness, hardness), with Daisy in other respects (handsomeness,

selfishness, restlessness). The three of them share some semes with Gatsby (wealth, ostentation, selfishness) but are polarised from him by others (Gatsby's romantic idealism). Gatsby's "extraordinary gift for hope, a romantic readiness"

. . . sets him apart from the other major protagonists in the novel. The semes "idealism, romanticism, purposefulness" excuse his materialism and criminality; the Buchanan set and the Wilsons, dissimilar in most other attributes, are all distinguished from Gatsby by a pointed lack of any seme of spirituality like the idealism that Nick attributes to Gatsby; they are all classified as purposeless, hopeless, spiritually dead. (1986, 37–38)

A number of criticisms could be made of the grammatical and semantic approaches briefly outlined above, with respect to their application both to real people and to literary characters. For example, grammatical choice is also a social choice, not just a cognitive reflex. This is most obvious when one considers that grammatical choices construct particular social dialects. Regarding semic analysis, the problem here is that it is founded on classical Aristotelian categories, which cannot cope with the dynamics and fuzziness of meanings. Linguistic semantics has moved away from componential analysis and deploys, for example, prototype categories, and trait psychology has undergone a similar move. Over the last ten years or so, literary scholars and stylisticians have been making similar changes to the way they approach characterization (see, for example, Culpeper 2001). However, there is still a serious methodological deficit. The study of characterization in a particular text proceeds through the analysis of short textual examples, chosen because they contain foregrounded features. Indeed, even Toolan (1985) follows this route, for all its sophistication. But as noted at the beginning of the previous chapter, other features, though less obvious and less easily observable, may affect our impressions—the accumulative effect of grammatical or semantic features may be decisive. Indeed, a key thrust of this book is to argue for the holistic analyses of texts.

3.3   WHAT IS CORPUS ANNOTATION AND WHY IS IT CONTROVERSIAL?

Annotating texts is not at all a mysterious practice. Many a university library book is covered with the annotations of past students. Similarly, annotating electronic data happens regularly when we switch on "track changes" in Microsoft Word, annotate a document, and pass it on to a colleague, or when we add comments to somebody's e-mail and send it back. The technicalities of adding annotation to a corpus are equally mundane: with a simple editor, such as Microsoft's Notepad or Wordpad, open up the text file to be annotated and type in the annotations. What makes corpus annotation stand apart from these more general annotations is the kind of information that gets added, as well as the format of the annotations themselves.

Corpus annotation of whatever kind involves associating chunks of language with a category chosen from a set, which could be predefined or derived from preliminary analyses of the data. Leech describes corpus annotation as "the practice of adding *interpretative, linguistic* information to an electronic corpus of spoken and/or written language data" (1997, 2). The type of annotation Leech has in mind involves the interpretation of some chunk of the language within the corpus: the categorization of that chunk within a particular linguistic category, and then the addition of an appropriate code or tag to that chunk. The linguistic categories typically relate to grammatical parts of speech or syntactic function, prosodic form, or, more recently, semantic field. There is no reason why "linguistic information" should not include information about language functions, such as speech act functions, though in practice not much annotation of this kind has taken place. However, there is another type of corpus annotation that does not involve the addition of linguistic information, but the addition of contextual and/or social information relating to the language—information that can be used to pursue, for example, pragmatic or discoursal research. In fact, the latter type of annotation was demonstrated in section 2.3. There we saw how chunks of the play-text—a mixed register text—can be explicitly associated with different characters by adding annotation that encloses their speech. There is no reason why more contextual/social information could not have been added with further codes associating the language chunk with, for example, the sex, social rank, role, or age of the character (Archer and Culpeper 2003 demonstrate how this can be done).

As for format, codes or "tags" are comprised of short strings of letters and/or numbers (for example, "NN1"), each unique and usually part of a logical sequence (for example, there is also "NN2"), and attached or tagged to the end of the unit to which it pertains. The tags are usually distinguished from the text under analysis in some way: they may be in capitals, as in the examples in the previous sentence, and they may (also) be attached to the language chunk they categorize in a distinctive way; for example, by using an underscore: "table_NN1." Sometimes, and particularly if more extensive information (for example, social/contextual information) is required in the annotations, a way of supplying it in brackets is used. Not any old way will do: computers need standardization. Individual corpus linguists could devise their own systems and apply them consistently (just one incorrect keystroke and a computer will not recognize the tag), but then they would not be able to do much with them. Indeed, corpus linguists have realized that if electronic documents or corpora are going to be assembled from different sources, if they need to be interrogated by a particular program, or even if they simply need to be displayed in the same way on computer screens, then there has to be some standardization. In fact, people in information technology have long been concerned with the management of electronic texts, inventing what was to be called the Standard Generalized Markup Language (SGML) in 1969.[1] A markup language is a metalanguage, a series of instructions about, for example, how the text is to be structured and presented. The most common example of a markup language is HTML (which is consistent with SGML). This underlies all web pages. A tag in this context contains a command for the computer about what to do with the text, and the markup system is a standardized way of (or syntax for) organizing the tags. Corpus linguists could draw upon these ideas. The fact that in section 2.3 character names—the metatext telling us how to attribute characters' speech—were put in angle brackets, that they touch the text to which they pertain, and that there is a beginning (a "switch on") and an end (a "switch off") tag is derived from SGML. The Text Encoding Initiative (see http://www.tei-c.org), which had at its core people interested in electronic text collections (for example, the Oxford Text Archive), was particularly important in suggesting ways forward for corpus linguists.

The key difference of whether the annotation is linguistic or not has implications for whether the annotation can be added automatically. Grammatical and semantic information has an explicit presence in the language form: there are formal traces that a computer can use to work out the category in which to place a chunk of language.[2] For example, words ending *-ness* are likely to be nouns, as are the word(s) following (though not necessarily immediately) the word *the*. Complex probabilistic rules can be built up in order to achieve fairly accurate tagging. Conversely, social or contextual information is less explicitly there in the language form: it must be added manually. A good example of this is a key work in corpus stylistics: Semino and Short's (2004) study of speech, writing, and thought presentation. Speech presentation categories do have formal correlates, but these correlations are not sufficiently strong to enable the precise prediction of a particular speech presentation category (even direct speech proves problematic). Bearing in mind the dialogic data of chapters 2 and 3 of this book, it is important to note that dialogue presents difficulties for annotation, and particular difficulties for automated annotation. The Expert Advisory Groups for Language Engineering Systems (EAGLES; see http://www.ling.lancs.ac.uk/eagles/) surveyed dialogue annotation practices and produced a set of guidelines (see also Gibbon, Mertins, and Moore 2000). Although this work contains important and useful insights, the notion of the "addressee" is conspicuously absent. This is because work in this area focuses almost exclusively on dyadic interactions, which means that the addressee is the other speaker by default, and hence relatively easy to identify automatically. Much language data, however, is multiparty talk, as indeed is frequently the case in play-texts. Automatically identifying the addressee in multiparty talk is well beyond the capabilities of current tagging programs.

In some ways, the idea of adding interpretative annotations—especially when those language annotations concern functional aspects, such as speech acts—to language data sounds more like a practice associated with qualitative research, and rather alien in the context of a quantitative methodology like corpus linguistics. However, such a view is based on a false dichotomy and stereotypes. Qualitative research frequently involves the exploration of patterns in data, and sometimes those patterns are quantified in programs such as NUDIST or ATLAS. Conversely, corpus linguistics is not just about counting things (we repeat the quotations from p. 4):

> both qualitative and quantitative analyses have something to contribute to corpus study. Qualitative analysis can provide greater richness and precision, whereas quantitative analysis can provide statistically reliable and generalisable results. There has recently been a move in social science research towards multi-method approaches which largely reject the narrow analytical paradigms in favour of the breadth of information which the use of more than one method may provide. Corpus linguistics could . . . benefit as much as any field from such multi-method research, combining both qualitative and quantitative perspectives on the same phenomena. (McEnery and Wilson 2001, 76–77)

> It is important to note that corpus-based analyses must go beyond simple counts of linguistic features. That is, it is essential to include qualitative, functional interpretations of quantitative patterns. In each chapter of this book, you will find that a great deal of space is devoted to explanation, exemplification, and interpretation of the patterns found in quantitative analyses. The goal of corpus-based investigations is not simply to report quantitative findings, but to explore the importance of those findings for learning about the patterns of language use. (Biber, Conrad, and Reppen 1998, 5)

Corpus annotation offers a way of tracking those "functional interpretations," or of correlating social and/or contextual features with the language. So why is it controversial?

Early grumbles about corpus annotation, particularly from historical corpus linguists, seemed to be based on assumptions that the annotations were damaging the integrity—even purity—of the text. Not so long ago this argument was still being voiced (Sinclair 2004, 191). This is not a serious objection, as one can have multiple copies of a corpus and just annotate one of them, or a computer can easily hide most forms of annotation. More significantly, some corpus linguists, particularly those in the John Sinclair tradition, argue that annotation is unnecessary, misleading, and fundamentally flawed. Although they refer to annotation generally, they seem to have in mind the particular type of annotation defined by Leech—the addition of interpretive linguistic information.[3] The key argument is that if grammatical and semantic information has an explicit presence in the language form, we should be analyzing that language form directly and not interpolating what they see as unstable and uncertain interpretative categories. This line of argument is reflected in the main title of Sinclair's book *Trust the Text* (2004; see in particular 190–91). It is this very argument that will be addressed in this chapter. A keyword analysis is based solely on word form, but as demonstrated in the previous chapter, it can reveal grammatical and semantic aspects of the language under consideration. In this chapter, the same data will be analyzed, but this time after it has been annotated for grammatical parts of speech and semantic categories. Key grammatical part-of-speech and key semantic categories will be extracted. If Sinclair's argument is right, we should see very little difference between the results presented in the previous chapter and the results to be presented in this. It is, however, by no means a foregone conclusion that the results will be similar. Rayson (2004) points out that "key grammatical categories and semantic classes are used to group together lower frequency words and those words which would, by themselves, not be identified as key, and would otherwise be overlooked."

3.4 SOFTWARE AND THE PROBLEM OF VARIANTS IN HISTORICAL TEXTS

It would have been possible to have produced annotated texts and then fed them into WordSmith for the analysis of keyness. However, a more convenient option was to use WMatrix, a web-based suite of tools developed by Paul Rayson at Lancaster University (see Rayson 2003, 2005, and http://www.comp.lancs.ac.uk/ucrel/wmatrix). Texts uploaded into WMatrix are automatically run through two programs that apply grammatical and semantic annotation (sections 3.5.1 and 3.6.1 will elaborate on these programs). Then WMatrix offers various options for considering the output: as well as the standard corpus linguistics techniques such a frequency lists and concordances, it allows you to analyze not only keywords but also key grammatical categories and key semantic categories. Sinclair claims that with annotation the "text becomes grossly overstuffed with tags, and the processing speed is affected" (2004, 191). This is partially true. It depends on whether one is considering the time it takes to annotate the text or the time it takes to interrogate the tags. Rayson (personal communication) estimates that WMatrix would take about four hours to apply both grammatical and semantic tagging to a million-word corpus. This is no problem for specialized corpora and texts (for example, Shakespeare), which tend to be fairly small. The application of the tags is a one-off operation and WMatrix can be set running overnight. But this *is* a problem for larger corpora. However, this is unlikely to be a long-term problem, considering both developments in computer processing power and in tagging techniques. As for interrogating the tags, WMatrix does this almost instantaneously and certainly as fast as (or faster than) currently available concordancing programs.

With standardized spelling, the computer has no problem in retrieving instances of a particular word form, and then particular word forms can be associated with particular lexemes. However, in the early modern English period, including the period in which Shakespeare was writing, each lexeme had word forms characterized by variable spellings. For example, for a computer to retrieve all instances of the word *would* (a form that in present-day English matches the lexeme one-to-one, not even allowing morphological variation), the computer would have to match an array of forms such as the following: *would, wold, wolde, woolde, wuld, wulde, wud, wald, vvould, vvold*, and so on. This means that any automated tagging program will fail, as such programs rely on matching words against lexicons, among other things. The Shakespeare edition used in this book has been modernized, and much of the spelling variation has been removed. However, there are still the problems of morphological variants (for example, *tellest, telleth*), grammatical variants (for example, *ye, thou, thine*), orthographic oddities (for example, *wing'd* instead of *winged*, the lack of an apostrophe for the s-genitive, and capitalization practices), and archaic/obsolete forms (for example, *becalmed*).

The solution was to use a program, the Variant Detector (VARD) (see Archer et al. 2003; Archer and Rayson 2004; Rayson, Archer, and Smith 2005; Baron and Rayson 2008). This program regularizes variation by matching variants to "normalized" equivalents using a search and replace script; the variant list now contains 45,898 entries.[4] Furthermore, it uses contextual information to tackle ambiguities such as—*(e)s* for the s-genitive or the plural, and has an additional lexicon, including both single and multiword items, in order to treat word forms that are specific to or have undergone semantic change since the early modern period. The original word is placed in a SGML tag that is attached to the regularized form (for example, "<reg o = "wolde">would"), and then that form can be retrieved or processed by a particular program. WMatrix includes the VARD program in its early modern English suite of tools.

3.5 KEY PARTS OF SPEECH IN THREE SHAKESPEAREAN CHARACTERS

3.5.1 Grammatical Annotation

Grammatical annotation simply means that grammatical information has been added to the corpus; linguistic items have been associated with particular grammatical categories. For example, *ball* might be represented as "ball_NN1": an underscore mark links the word to a tag representing, in this case, "a common noun" (a set of commonly used grammatical tags, the CLAWS tagset, can be found at http://www.comp.lancs.ac.uk/ucrel/bnc2/tagset_c7.htm). Part-of-speech (POS) tagging is perhaps the most common form of corpus annotation. Grammatical annotation can be useful in situations where you want to distinguish the grammatical functions of particular word forms, or identify all the words performing a particular grammatical function. For example, you may be interested in the usage of the word *house* as a verb (as in "the specimens are now *housed* in the British Museum"). The past participle of *house* (that is, *housed*) is tagged "housed_VVN," the *-ing* participle "housing_VVG," the -s form of the lexical verb "houses_VVZ," and so on. If you want *all* the verbal forms of *house* without doing separate searches, in principle some wildcards will do the trick; for example, "hous*_V*." In practice, the exact query syntax may be determined by the kind of corpus you are interrogating and the kind of software you are using (for example, some programs have difficulty with the underscore). Alternatively, one might wish to see what kinds of words perform particular functions and how many they are. Grammatical annotation could be used to retrieve all the verb forms in a particular text, and then one could compare these with the verb forms of other texts.

POS tagging software has been under development at Lancaster University since the early 1980s. The software is called CLAWS (the Constituent Likelihood Automatic Word-tagging System). In a nutshell, CLAWS works on the basis of (1) a lexicon, including words (or multiword units) and suffixes and their possible parts of speech and (2) a matrix containing sequencing probabilities (for example, the likelihood that following an adjective the word will be a noun), which is applied to each sentence to disambiguate words that could potentially be several parts of speech. Both the lexicon and the probability matrix are continuously updated in the light of new (and postchecked) tagged data (for descriptions of how CLAWS works, see Leech, Garside, and Bryan 1994, or Garside 1987). CLAWS is claimed to achieve 96 to 97 percent accuracy on written texts, and a slightly lesser degree of accuracy on spoken texts. Various POS classifications or tagsets have been developed; more comprehensive sets resulting in a more delicate analysis are more suited to smaller corpora.[5]

As pointed out in section 3.3, the spelling variability in early modern English texts presents a problem for automated tagging. By regularizing the spelling of the texts using the program VARD, one can reasonably expect the error rate to be at acceptable levels. Archer et al. (2003), explaining the development of VARD, note that the total error rates (that is, including variants spellings and/or POS errors) for two texts from 1654 were 1.7 percent and 2.6 percent. These figures are not as good, perhaps, as they may sound, since they represent errors reported by the program; it is possible that there were other errors that went unreported. One might also argue that by 1654 the standardization of spelling was well underway, and so the challenge for regularizing spelling is less than that represented by Shakespearean texts. However, it should be remembered that the texts used here have been modernized. Moreover, the VARD program has been improved since 2003, and it has been trained on early modern plays contemporaneous with Shakespeare. Archer et al. (2003, 28) demonstrate the importance of the VARD program being trained in the same text type as the text you wish to regularize. Nevertheless, caution must be exercised in the interpretation of results. All "key" results reported here have been scrutinized for tagging accuracy.

3.5.2 Grammatical Keyness Analysis

In order to contextualize the keyness analysis, figures for the top ten most frequent grammatical categories are provided for the three characters in table 3.1, followed by some brief comments.

Romeo and the Nurse have the first five highest ranking categories in common, and thereafter have two other categories in common. Differences between them relate to the presence of plural common nouns and definite articles for Romeo, and second-person pronouns (along with first) and modal auxiliaries for the Nurse. This fits their characterization: Romeo, unlike the Nurse, sometimes gives speeches in a high style with a more nominal quality, reflecting both his status in society and in the play, whereas the Nurse's speech is more interactive and colloquial, reflecting her role as the down-to-earth emotional busybody. Mercutio stands apart from both of them. The category of general prepositions appears slightly higher than the other two characters and the category of plural common nouns appears higher than it does with Romeo. But the striking difference is the presence of three categories of determiners—indefinite articles, definite articles, and possessive pronominal determiners—ranked fifth to seventh. This feature supports the idea proposed in the keyword analysis of chapter 2 that Mercutio has a highly nominal style.

Table 3.2 displays the grammatical categories that are key in Romeo's speech (the statistical criterion for all keyness tables in this chapter is the same as for the keyword results in chapter 2, namely, a log-likelihood value of 6.63 or higher, which is equivalent to $p < 0.01$, and a raw frequency value of five or more). Words that were identified as keywords in chapter 2 are emboldened, a convention that is also adopted in the remaining keyness tables in this chapter.

An important point to bear in mind is that the lexicon, the inventory of words, varies from more lexical items to more grammatical items. This distinction is sometimes couched in terms of "open-class" words versus "closed-class" words, but those terms only capture some of the characteristic differences. Other characteristics include, for example, the fact that grammatical items tend to be more frequent but less "contentful." Note that all the key grammatical categories are dominated by a particular word that is grammatical in nature, except the category General adjective (JJ). General adjective (JJ) is a more general category in the sense that it contains a wider and more even range of items, and also a more concrete category in the sense that most of its items are contentful. The more specific (that is,

Table 3.1   Rank-ordered frequencies of the top ten grammatical categories for three characters

Romeo		Nurse		Mercutio	
Singular common noun (e.g. book, girl) (NN1)	724	Singular common noun (e.g. book, girl) (NN1)	302	Singular common noun (e.g. book, girl) (NN1)	334
General adjective (JJ)	328	General adjective (JJ)	119	General adjective (JJ)	137
Do, base form (finite) (VV0)	240	Do, base form (finite) (VV0)		General preposition (II)	100
General preposition (II)	216	General preposition (II)	77	Plural common noun (e.g. books, girls) (NN2)	99
Possessive pronoun, pre-nominal (e.g. my, your, our) (APPGE)	197	Possessive pronoun, pre-nominal (e.g. my, your, our) (APPGE)	77	Singular article (e.g. a, an, every) (AT1)	96
Infinitive (e.g. to give . . . It will work . . .) (VVI)	169	Infinitive (e.g. to give . . . It will work . . .) (VVI)	76	Article (e.g. the, no) (AT)	91
Plural common noun (e.g. books, girls) (NN2)	157	2nd person personal pronoun (you) (PPY)	75	Possessive pronoun, pre-nominal (e.g. my, your, our) (APPGE)	70
Coordinating conjunction (e.g. and, or) (CC)	149	1st person sing. subjective personal pronoun (I) (PPIS1)	70	Do, base form (finite) (VV0)	70
1st person sing. subjective personal pronoun (I) (PPIS1)	144	Modal auxiliary (can, will, would, etc.) (VM)	69	Infinitive (e.g. to give . . . It will work . . .) (VVI)	59
Article (e.g. the, no) (AT)	134	Coordinating conjunction (e.g. and, or) (CC)	65	Coordinating conjunction (e.g. and, or) (CC)	58

constituted by a more limited set of items) a category is and the less content-ful the items by which it is constituted are, the more likely it is to be dom-inated by particular and frequent items. Is it the case that such categories are more likely to include items that appear in the keywords analysis? Of

Table 3.2   Romeo's parts of speech rank-ordered for positive keyness (that is, relatively unusual overuse)

Grammatical category (and tag code and frequency)	Items within the category (and their raw frequencies) up to a maximum of ten types if they are available (excluding clearly erroneous categorizations in square brackets)
Nominal possessive personal pronoun (e.g. mine, yours) (PPGE) (17)	**mine** (8), **hers** (4), **thine** (3), [his (1)], yours (1)
Comparative after-determiner (e.g. more, less, fewer) (DAR) (16)	**more** (15), less (1)
1st person sing. objective personal pronoun (i.e. me) (PPIO1) (73)	**me** (73)
General adjective (JJ) (328)	**fair** (14), **good** (10), **dear** (10), sweet (8), **rich** (7), dead (6), holy (5), true (5), heavy (5), **blessed** (4)
1st person sing. subjective personal pronoun (i.e. I) (PPIS1) (144)	I (144)
Than (as conjunction) (CSN) (16)	than (16)

the most frequent words for each of the six categories, four are indeed also keywords. However, this *includes* the general and contentful category General adjective (JJ), although we should add that the status of this category is called into question by the fact that the bulk of instances of *good* and *dear* appear in vocative expressions. Conversely, the highly specific and contentless categories first-person singular subjective personal pronoun (that is, *I*) (PPIS1) and *Than* (as conjunction) (CSN) do not. Clearly, there are more complex dynamics at work here: with keywords one is comparing single words with single words, whereas with the grammatical categories one is comparing units that may be composed of varying numbers of types and frequencies of words.

Despite Romeo being a character generally characterized by ideational keywords, a total of eight of his keywords listed in table 2.3 also occur amidst the grammatical categories in table 3.2, although four are in the less grammatical and more ideational category General adjective (JJ). This reminds us that the description of Romeo's keywords being characterized by ideational keywords is a generalization: his keywords also contain clues to his grammar. In section 2.5.3, it was suggested that Romeo's keyword pronouns of *mine* and *me* and Juliet's *I* might be symptoms of the fact that he reflects upon himself rather than, like Juliet, simply bearing his soul. The presence of the first-person pronoun *I* category in table 3.2 suggests that that conclusion may need to be refined. It would, nevertheless, support our general idea of Romeo being egotistical. Four of the general adjectives listed are also keywords. However, there is not a preponderance of adjectives among Romeo's keywords listed, and so this feature of his style could easily have been overlooked. Consider again Romeo's most famous lines with their high density of adjectives (adjectives are underlined):

If I profane with my <u>unworthiest</u> hand
This <u>holy</u> shrine, the <u>gentle</u> sin is this;
My lips, two <u>blushing</u> pilgrims, <u>ready</u> stand
To smooth that <u>rough</u> touch with a <u>tender</u> kiss. (1.5)

Let us turn to the Nurse. Table 3.3 displays the grammatical categories that are key in the Nurse's speech. As with Romeo's grammatical categories, we see a pattern whereby the word dominating the category also appears in our keyword analysis. In the case of the third-person singular subjective personal pronouns, both *he* and *she* were keywords. This fits the argument above, as this grammatical category consists of a very small set of words; that is to say, it is not a general and more concrete category like General adjectives (JJ), with the consequence that words that constitute it stand a better chance of being key. The category Temporal noun, and so forth, seems to reveal a grammatical feature of style that was not apparent from the keywords analysis. However, note the dominance of *day*, a keyword that

Table 3.3 The Nurse's parts of speech rank-ordered for positive keyness (that is, relatively unusual overuse)

Grammatical category, including the tag code and frequency	Items within the category (and their raw frequencies) up to a maximum of ten types if they are available (excluding erroneous categorizations in square brackets)
3rd person sing. subjective personal pronoun (he, she) (PPHS1) (46)	he (24) she (22)
Singular letter of the alphabet (e.g. A,b) (ZZ1) (16)	[o (9)], [a (3)], [I (3)], r (1)
Temporal noun, singular (e.g. day, week, year) (NNT1) (31)	day (18), night (5), year (2), [well-a-day (1)], second (1), lammas-eve (1), hour (1), time (1), afternoon (1)
3rd person sing. neuter personal pronoun (it) (PPH1) (41)	it (40), 't (1)
Interjection (e.g. oh, yes, um) (UH) (42)	o (16), ah (6), ay (5), nay (4), alas (3), no (2), amen (1), ho (1), yes (1), [the-no (1)], fie (1), farewell (1)

is highly localized to where the Nurse discovers Juliet is dead ("o woeful day," repeats the Nurse). If this item were excluded, it is somewhat doubtful whether this grammatical category would turn out key. Interjections were clearly established as a feature of the Nurse's speech during the keywords analysis. The top three items in this category were also keywords. Interestingly, we see items that were not keywords (that is, *nay, alas, no, amen, ho, yes, fie,* and *farewell*), and, conversely, we do not see interjections that were keywords (that is, *well, marry, hie, God,* and *warrant*). The fact that some items were not also keywords is presumably a consequence of the fact that as individual items they are more evenly distributed among the characters. The fact that some of the keyword interjections are not also represented in the grammatical category above suggests a failure of the tagger (and most probably the lexicon) to identify items like *marry, hie,* and *warrant* as interjections. Table 3.4 displays the grammatical categories that are key in Mercutio's speech.

As above, less general and more abstract categories are dominated by particular words, which are also keywords. It is of no surprise to see the definite and indefinite articles and the *of* preposition as key grammatical categories. This had lead to the conclusion that Mercutio had a nominal style, on the basis that nouns tend to follow such items. This conclusion is supported by the appearance of plural common nouns in table 3.4. The grammatical category of noun is both very general and concrete, and consequently less likely to be dominated by keywords—and indeed no keywords appear in this category. The fact that the category of common nouns refers

Table 3.4   Mercutio's parts of speech rank-ordered for positive keyness (that is, relatively unusual overuse)

Grammatical category, including the tag code and frequency	Items within the category (and their raw frequencies) up to a maximum of ten types if they are available (excluding erroneous categorizations in square brackets)
Singular article (e.g. a, an, every) (AT1) (96)	a (82), **an** (14)
Plural common noun (e.g. books, girls) (NN2) (99)	houses (4), dreams (4), eyes (3), wits (3), ears (3), maids (2), wings (2), cats (2), bons (2), minstrels (2)
Of (as preposition) (I0) (57)	of (57)
Singular cardinal number (i.e. one) (MC1) (10)	one (9), [I (1)]
Article (e.g. the, no) (91) (AT)	**the** (84), no (7)

specifically to plural nouns is something not predicted by the keywords analysis, but seems consistent with the rhetorical generalizations that Mercutio has a taste for (see the textual examples in section 2.5.2).

In general, the results of the keyness analysis for grammatical categories reveal little more than had already been revealed in the keywords analysis. This seems to be because the grammatical categories are often dominated by a restricted set of frequently occurring grammatical items. The grammatical analysis is most revealing in the case of more general, contentful categories, as illustrated by general adjectives for Romeo and plural common nouns for Mercutio. Here it does seem to offer some refinements of the keyword analyses. The results for the Nurse, and specifically the interjections, remind us that automated annotation systems needed further development. This is not surprising, as interpersonal items are not well accommodated by the grammar.

3.6 KEY SEMANTIC CATEGORIES IN THREE SHAKESPEAREAN CHARACTERS

3.6.1 Semantic Annotation

At Lancaster University, and, more specifically, in the University Centre for Computer Corpus Research on Language (UCREL), while development of grammatical annotation has the longest history, it is semantic annotation that, over the last fifteen years or so, has attracted increasing attention from a wide variety of staff. Semantic annotation is closely related to "content analysis," which is "concerned with the statistical analysis of primarily the semantic features of texts" (Wilson and Rayson 1993, 2). Content analysis, according to Wilson and Rayson (1993), can be traced to eighteenth-century Sweden and a "careful" analysis of a Lutheran hymn book. After the Second World War, it was increasingly accepted as a research methodology in the social sciences, and finally in the 1960s computer technology began to be brought into play. Today, perhaps the most widespread application that relies on a kind of content analysis is the use of search engines, such as Google, to retrieve web pages with a particular content. Analyzing literary texts for meaning or content by adding annotations is no alien activity for the literary scholar. Those annotations added to library books mentioned earlier in this chapter are frequently designed to capture particular "themes." But note that content analysis involves statistical analysis, which suggests something altogether more systematic and rigorous. Moreover, such manual annotations are not highly empirical: they typically involve finding evidence for a particular theory or research hypotheses.

The UCREL Semantic Analysis System (USAS) is an annotation program designed for automatic dictionary-based content analysis. The input to USAS is POS tagged text as produced by CLAWS (see section 3.3.1). Then the program SEMTAG assigns a semantic tag (or tags in the case of ambiguities) to each word or multiword unit (for details see Wilson and Rayson 1993). SEMTAG works by matching the words of your data with two lexicons (which include semantic tagging information), one of approximately 44,668 single words and the other of approximately 18,553 multiword units. Piao et al. (2004) evaluated the coverage of these lexicons by testing it on the British National Corpus. They claim that 99.39 percent of the BNC spoken data and 97.6 percent of the written data is covered, though they acknowledge that the remaining uncovered items could always prove critical for corpus analysis. SEMTAG is claimed to achieve an accuracy rate of between 80 and 90 percent (Thomas and Wilson 1996, 96), although given that there have been changes made to SEMTAG since that claim was made one might expect an improvement on those figures. A submodule of SEMTAG, AUXRULE, deals specifically with disambiguating auxiliaries and main verb senses of *be*, *do*, and *have* on the basis of their collocation or lack of collocation with particular participial forms. A "high degree of accuracy" is claimed for this program (Thomas and Wilson 1996, 97). In addition, there are other disambiguation procedures based on POS information (for example, *spring*, the noun, has different meaning potential from *spring*, the verb), likelihood ranking (*green*, the color, is more frequent than *green* meaning inexperienced), as well as other contextually driven rules and heuristics (Rayson et al. 2004). The USAS programs are the final processing stages that WMatrix conducts on one's texts, once it is put them through the spelling regularizer VARD and the grammatical tagger CLAWS.

Originally, the semantic tagset used by SEMTAG was loosely based on Tom McArthur's *Longman Lexicon of Contemporary English* (1981), because it offered what seemed the most appropriate thesaurus-type classification of word senses, but the tagset has received significant revisions over the years.[6] The classification has a hierarchical structure with the twenty-one major semantic fields displayed in table 3.5 at the topmost level. A visual representation of the hierarchy, along with a guide to all the categories, can be found at http://www.comp.lancs.ac.uk/computing/research/ucrel/usas. As can be seen from table 3.5, each top-level category has a letter associated with it.

Category subdivisions are indicated by numerals, and sub-subdivisions by a point and further numeral, and so on. For example, "E Emotional actions, states and processes" is divided into a further six categories (E 1–6), and in the case of E4 there is a further subdivision thus:

E4.1 Happy/sad: Happy Terms depicting (level of) happiness PROTOTYPICAL EXAMPLES: AMUSED (+), BLISS (+), CHEERFUL (+), CHUCKLE (+), CONTRITION (–), CRINGE (–), DEJECTED (–), DESPAIR (–) BUNDLE OF LAUGHS (+), BURST INTO TEARS (–), CLOUD NINE (+), DOOM AND GLOOM (–), DOWN IN THE DUMPS (–)

Table 3.5 The semantic tagset top-level domains

A General and abstract terms	B The body and the individual	C Arts and crafts	E Emotional actions, states, and processes
F Food and farming	G Government and the public domain	H Architecture, buildings, houses, and the home	I Money and commerce
K Entertainment, sports, and games	L Life and living things	M Movement, location, travel, and transport	N Numbers and measurement
O Substances, materials, objects, and equipment	P Education	Q Linguistic actions, states, and processes	S Social actions, states, and processes
T Time	W The world and our environment	X Psychological actions, states, and processes	Y Science and technology
Z Names and grammatical words			

E4.2 Happy/sad: Contentment Terms depicting (level of) contentment PROTOTYPICAL EXAMPLES: AGGRIEVED (–), CHUFFED (+), CONTENT (+), DISMAY (–), DISAPPOINTED (–), FRUSTRATED (–), HUMOUR (+) BROWNED OFF (–), CHEESED OFF (–), FED UP (–), GUILT TRIP (–), HAD ENOUGH OF (–), SICK TO THE BACK TEETH (–), TICKLED PINK (+) (Archer 2002, 10–11)[7]

The twenty-one semantic fields have up to three subdivisions each, and the whole scheme expands into a total of 232 category labels.[8]

There are, of course, problems for historical data. The lexicon changes over time. Piao et al. (2004) report 94.4 percent coverage of the words in the Lancaster Corpus of Seventeenth-Century Newsbooks. However, this is *without* the intervention of the regularizing program VARD and its historical lexicon, and so the prospects for our Shakespearean data may be better. A more fundamental problem relates to the nature of the classification.

The classification has been designed for the present-day world. One consequence of this is that words can be attributed to incorrect semantic categories; that is to say, "incorrect" according to the worldview contemporaneous with the text. For example, the word *cousin* is ascribed to **S4** *Kin*, but in Shakespeare's period simply denoted a 'friend,' and should therefore be in **S3.1** *Relationship: General*. Some of these specific problems have been corrected by the historical lexicon. However, one might go on to argue that the very structure of the semantic categories would be somewhat different. For example, the present-day view of intimacy implying a sexual relationship is reflected in the category **S3.2** *Relationship: Intimate/sexual*. However, the sexual mores of the Elizabethan world were rather different, with the consequence that intimacy was possible without such strong sexual implications. The word *lover*, ascribed to **S3.2** by SEMTAG, is a case in point, as in this period it had the sense of *friends* or *intimates*, but no strong implications of sexual relations. A counter argument in support of USAS might be that reading Shakespeare through the prism of the present-day worldview is the majority experience today. Few—if any—of us are sufficiently steeped in Elizabeth social history in order to be able to transcend our own milieu.

3.6.2   Semantic Keyness Analysis

In order to contextualize the keyness analysis, we provide figures for the top ten most frequent semantic categories for the three characters in table 3.6, followed by some brief comments.

All three characters share the same three semantic categories. The Grammatical bin (Z5) contains items such as conjunctions, (some) prepositions and (some) adverbs; Pronouns (Z8) contains all kinds of pronouns (for example, personal, relative, interrogative); and Being (A3+), although it can include items such as *nothingness* or *exist*, in practice the results it contains are all part of the verb "to be" as a main verb. Given the outstanding frequency at which the items that populate these categories occur in English (see, for example, Leech, Rayson, and Wilson 2001), it is not surprising that they dominate each character.[9] In contrast, the fact that Romeo and Mercutio have eight of the ten categories in common is not something that one would readily predict. Let us consider differences between them. The appearance of Living creatures generally (L2) reflects Mercutio's frequent references to animals in his rhetorical flights, as here, when he has been fatally wounded: "Zounds, a dog, a rat, a mouse, a cat, to scratch a man to death!" (3.1). Mercutio's other distinctive category, Moving, coming and going (M1), would have ranked somewhat lower, had it not been for the miscategorization of three to five instances of the discourse marker *come* (instead, it was treated as a main verb denoting locomotion). Turning to Romeo, he is a much more interactive character than Mercutio, and this seems to be supported by the presence of the category Speech acts (Q2 .2).

Table 3.6 Rank-ordered frequencies of the top ten semantic categories for three characters (excluding the "unmatched" Z99 category)

Romeo		Nurse		Mercutio	
Grammatical bin (Z5)	1192	Grammatical bin (Z5)	503	Grammatical bin (Z5)	606
Pronouns etc. (Z8)	793	Pronouns etc. (Z8)	398	Pronouns etc. (Z8)	298
Being (A3+)	150	Being (A3+)	90	Being (A3+)	66
Anatomy and physiology (B1)	107	Discourse bin (Z4)	48	Anatomy and physiology (B1)	64
Negative (Z6)	91	Personal names (Z1)	43	Living creatures generally (L2)	34
Speech acts (Q2.2)	86	Time: Period (T1.3)	41	Personal names (Z1)	33
Personal names (Z1)	69	Time: General: Future (T1.1.3)	38	Moving, coming and going (M1)	29
Time: General: Future (T1.1.3)	60	Anatomy and physiology (B1)	34	Negative (Z6)	29
General actions, making etc. (A1.1.1)	57	Speech acts (Q2.2)	34	Time: General: Future (T1.1.3)	25
Location and direction (M6)	56	Negative (Z6)	32	Location and direction (M6)	23

Also, the idea of Romeo being generally a more active character than Mercutio is supported by the presence of the category General actions, making, and so forth (A1.1.1), although this category is affected by the incorrect inclusion of some auxiliary usages of *do*. The Nurse has two distinctive categories. High in fourth position we predictably see the category Discourse bin (Z4), populated by interjections and discourse markers. The Nurse's other distinctive category is Time: Period (T1.3), but the presence of this category seems to have been influenced by the Nurse's frequent and localized usage of *day*.

Now let us turn to key semantic categories. For Romeo's speech, table 3.7 displays the semantic categories that are key:

The cut-off frequency for these analyses was five, just as it was for the keywords analyses. However, categories with fewer instances than fifteen (legitimate) words are noticeably less robust and well motivated than the others. For example, in Education in general (P1), the connection between "philosophy" and "school" is rather tenuous (even more so when these words are read in context). The notion of a semantic category is more abstract than that of a word. Before semantic category commonalities can be clearly seen, the categories need a certain weight of both word types and

Table 3.7   Romeo's semantic categories rank-ordered for positive keyness (that is, relatively unusual overuse)

Semantic category (and tag code and frequency)	Items within the category (and their raw frequencies) up to a maximum of ten types if they are available (excluding clearly erroneous categorizations in square brackets)
Relationship: Intimate/sexual (S3.2) (48)	love (34), kiss (5), lovers (3), kisses (2), paramour (1), wantons (1), chastity (1), in love (1)
Liking (E2+) (38)	love (15), **dear** (13), loving (3), precious (2), like (1), doting (1), amorous (1), [revels (1)], loves (1)
Color and color patterns (O4.3) (33)	light (6), bright (4), pale (3), dark (3), green (2), stained (2), black (2), golden (1), white (1), crimson (1)
Education in general (P1) (9)	teach (3), [course (2)], philosophy (2), school (1), schoolboys (1)
Business: Selling (I2.2) (19)	sell (4), [bid (4)], shop (2), hire (2), buy (1), sold (1), [stands (1)], [bade (1)], [stand (1)], [store (1)], merchandise (1)
Thought, belief (X2.1) (26)	think (7), feel (3), devise (2), believe (2), [take thence (1)], thinking (1), thought (1), engrossing (1), dreamt (1), [found (1)], in thine eyes (1), in mind (1)
Affect: Cause/connected (A2.2) (20)	[hence (7)], reason (2), [spurs (2)], depend (1), for fear of (1), provoke (1), excuse (1), effect (1), consequence (1), to do with (1), appertaining (1), prompt (1)
Avarice (S1.2.2+) (7)	envious (3), [mean (1)], tempt (1), jealous (1), sparing (1)
The universe (W1) (21)	world (8), [word (6)], **stars** (5), moon (2)
Money: Affluence (I1.1+) (7)	**rich** (7)

tokens. Also, semantic categories with fewer than fifteen instances tend to be localized. For example, regarding the category Business: Selling (I2.2), all instances of *sell*, *buy*, *sold*, and *shop* occur in act 5, scene 1, where Romeo purchases poison. Consequently, the discussion below will focus on categories that have more than fifteen tokens.

As can be seen from table 3.7, very few words constituting the semantic categories are also keywords. This suggests that Rayson (2004) was right to say that semantic categories group together words whose low frequencies will prevent them from being identified as key by themselves. As suggested in section 3.4.1, the first two categories, Relationship: Intimate/sexual (S3.2) and Liking (E2+), are not separated according to semantic categories that accurately reflect the historical context. Even in the present-day context, they are, of course, very closely related categories, and some argue that *liking* stands in a metonymic relationship with *love* (cf. Barcelona Sánchez 1995, 675, who argues that "a part of love stand[s] for the whole concept of love"). Taken as a whole, the identification of these categories as most key is very well motivated, a predictable finding that confirms Romeo's role as the lover of the play.[10]

The third top-most category, Color and color patterns (O4.3), is much less predictable. Sometimes Romeo is describing literal light: "But, soft! what light through yonder window breaks?" (2.2). But, more often, the terms are used metaphorically, as in for example, "More light and light; more dark and dark our woes" (3.5); "Be not her maid, since she is envious; / Her vestal livery is but sick and green" (2.2); "Death . . . Hath had no power yet upon thy beauty: Thou art not conquer'd; beauty's ensign yet / Is crimson in thy lips and in thy cheeks, / And death's pale flag is not advanced there" (5.3). These are all fairly conventional metaphors: light/dark for happiness/unhappiness, greenness for envy, and redness/whiteness for life/death. The semantic tagger cannot yet distinguish between literal and metaphorical meanings.[11] However, some of the semantic categories it picks out are metaphorical patterns. Archer et al. (2009), for example, analyzed three Shakespearean "love" tragedies and three "love" comedies, and showed how the key semantic categories were often metaphorical. They included, for example, LOVE IS WAR, LOVE IS PAIN and LOVE IS FOOD. Metaphor is often used to express emotions in more concrete terms, and Romeo's color terms often do just this. Note that this contributes to his characterization: the Nurse gives it to you straight with the repetition of expressions like "O woeful day," whereas Romeo uses metaphor: "more dark and dark our woes." This helps mark Romeo as the more complex character playing a more central role in the play.

The semantic category Thought, belief (X2.1) is like the above category in that it is not strongly predictable but seems well motivated. Examples of this category include the following:

This love feel I, that feel no love in this. (1.1)

What said my man when my betossed soul
Did not attend him as we rode? I think
He told me Paris should have married Juliet:
Said he not so? or did I dream it so?

Or am I mad, hearing him talk of Juliet,
To <u>think</u> it was so? (5.3)

All of the instances of this category relate to cognition, and usually the items are "private verbs" or verbs of cognition. This finding is consistent with the idea that Romeo is a self-reflective, even egocentric, character. In fact, verbs of cognition are a well-known indicator of point of view, and, as McIntyre (2004) argues, the issue of point of view is just as applicable to the study of drama as it is to prose fiction. McIntyre (2004, 157) states that point of view is an "integral part of the characterization process," assisting "readers and audiences in 'constructing' the various dramatic characters as they read or watch a play." Moreover, Hochman (1985) argues that whether authors give access to the character's "inner life" is an important dimension of characterization, and Culpeper (2001, 56) explicitly associates the presentation of a character's "inner life" with—to use E. M. Forster's terms—round characters. Thus it is not in fact surprising to see Thought, belief (X2.1) as a key semantic category for Romeo. The ability of the semantic annotation system USAS to reveal characters' point of view indicators, such as verbs of cognition, suggests a future research direction (see McIntyre and Archer 2010, for preliminary steps).

Table 3.8 displays the semantic categories that are key in the Nurse's speech. A rather larger number of keywords appear in the Nurse's semantic categories compared with either Romeo or Mercutio. In part, this may be due to the fact that the Nurse's speech is characterized by a high degree of repetition.[12] Importantly, however, not as many semantic categories include keywords as it might seem at first sight. Two interjections, *faith* and *warrant*, incorrectly appear in the categories Worry, concern, confident (E6+) and Obligation and necessity (S6+), respectively; they should be in Discourse Bin (Z4). Similarly, *well* in Evaluation: Good/bad (A5.1+) is also nearly always a discourse marker and thus should also be in Discourse Bin (Z4). Had these items been correctly tagged it is somewhat doubtful whether the categories in which they currently appear would still be key. Furthermore, the categories People: Female (S2.1) and Power, organizing (S7.1+) overlap. The vocatives *lady* and *madam* clearly also have implications of power, and thus should also appear under that category. Conversely, *mistress* also has the sense of female, and so should also appear under that category.

A characteristic of both the items in People: Female (S2.1) and Power, organizing (S7.1+) is that they contain vocatives. They indicate the kind of social network of which the Nurse is a part: she interacts with women such as Juliet and Lady Capulet, and also powerful individuals in the family such as Capulet. Words of this kind constitute a relatively restricted set that can potentially be used frequently, and so it is not surprising that there is overlap with the keyword results. The same can be said of the second-most key semantic category, Discourse Bin (Z4), which is well stocked with keywords—discourse markers were revealed in our keyword analysis as a

Table 3.8 The Nurse's semantic categories rank-ordered for positive keyness (that is, relatively unusual overuse)

Semantic category (and tag code and frequency)	Items within the category (and their raw frequencies) up to a maximum of ten types if they are available (excluding clearly erroneous categorizations in square brackets)
People: Female (S2.1) (31)	lady (15), **madam** (10), girl (2), gentlewoman (2), women (1), woman (1)
Discourse bin (Z4) (48)	God (11), ah (6), ay (5), nay (4), no (2), alack (2), as I said (2), [neer (2)], [forget it (2)], you know (2), fie (2), as they say (2)
Time: Period (T1.3) (41)	day (18), night (5), years (3), days (3), [stinted (2)], awhile (2), year (2), [second (1)], for a week (1), nights (1), hour (1), [mar (1)], afternoon (1)
Time: Old, new and young; age (T3) (6)	age (2), fourteen (2), twelve year old (1), eleven (1)
Happy/sad: Happy (E4.1–) (27)	woeful (6), alas (3), lamentable (3), weeps (2), crying (2), piteous (2), pitiful (1), woe (1), sorrows (1), weeping (1)
Entirety; maximum (N5.1+) (25)	all (16), any (5), every (2), full (1), [gross (1)]
Worry, concern, confident (E6+) (8)	[faith (8)], confidence (1)
Obligation and necessity (S6+) (23)	[warrant (7)], [should (6)], must (6), needs (3), need (1)
Power, organizing (S7.1+) (31)	sir (13), **lord** (10), mistress (4), [beats (1)], nobleman (1), [say (1)], lead (1)
Being (A3+) (90)	is (28), 's (20), be (15), were (8), was (7), are (6), am (6)
Generally kinds, groups, examples (A4.1) (9)	case (4), kind (2) [side (1)], [come to (1)], [coming to (1)]
Evaluation:- Good/bad (A5.1+) (21)	[well (10)], good (8), excels (2), great (1)

strong feature of the Nurse's style. In contrast, the category Being (A3+) contains no keywords at all, although we can note that the keyword *he's* also contains part of the verb "to be." This is despite the fact that it is populated by a restricted set of word types. The category is well motivated: it reflects the

Nurse's role as the irrepressible commentator in the play. She freely gives her opinion ("my mistress <u>is</u> the sweetest lady," "Paris <u>is</u> the properer man," "He <u>is</u> not the flower of courtesy," "I <u>am</u> the drudge"); states what is happening ("Your lady mother <u>is</u> coming to your chamber"); predicts what will happen ("Come Lammas-eve at night shall she <u>be</u> fourteen," "This afternoon, sir? well, she shall <u>be</u> there," "Hark ye, your Romeo will <u>be</u> here to-night"); and expresses doubts ("If you be he, sir, I desire some confidence," "Marry, that, I think, be young Petruchio"). Turning to the categories Time: Period (T1.3) and Happy/sad: Happy (E4.1–), both are highly localized. Fifteen of the eighteen instances of *day* occur in act 4, scene 5, when the Nurse discovers Juliet, apparently dead, as do all of *woeful, alas, lamentable, pitiful, woe,* and *weeping*.[13] Finally, the category Entirety; maximum (N5.1+) contains no keywords, but seems well motivated. It captures the Nurse's tendency to dramatize events she narrates, as in the following example:

> I saw the wound, I saw it with mine eyes,
> God save the mark! here on his manly breast:
> A piteous corse, a bloody piteous corse;
> Pale, pale as ashes, <u>all</u> bedaub'd in blood,
> <u>All</u> in gore blood; I swounded at the sight. (3.2)

Table 3.9 displays the semantic categories that are key in the Mercutio's speech. Mercutio speaks fewer words than Romeo or the Nurse, and so it is not surprising that only three semantic categories are above our cut-off point of fifteen. All three categories, Living creatures generally (L2), Grammatical bin (Z5), and Anatomy and physiology (B1), contain at least one keyword and were also listed in our raw frequency table. The Grammatical bin (Z5), like the Discourse bin (Z4) for the Nurse, contains three keywords as the most frequent items. For Living creatures generally (L2) and Anatomy and physiology (B1), the semantic analysis suggests that the keywords *hare* and *eye* are part of larger semantic categories, and that those categories are a significant distinctive feature of Mercutio's style. Mercutio's category Living creatures generally (L2) has been illustrated above already; the category Anatomy and physiology (B1) is closely related. Together, they suggest a focus on the physical and animate, as can be seen in the following example (words relevant to the two categories under discussion are underlined):

> Thou! why, thou wilt quarrel with a man that hath a <u>hair</u> more or a <u>hair</u> less in his beard than thou hast. Thou wilt quarrel with a man for cracking nuts, having no other reason but because thou hast hazel <u>eyes</u>. What <u>eye</u>, but such an <u>eye</u>, would spy out such a quarrel? Thy <u>head</u> is as full of quarrels as an <u>egg</u> is full of meat, and yet thy <u>head</u> hath been beaten as addle as an <u>egg</u> for quarrelling. Thou hast quarrelled with a man for coughing in the street, because he hath wakened thy <u>dog</u> that hath lain <u>asleep</u> in the sun. (3.1)

Table 3.9 Mercutio's semantic categories rank-ordered for positive keyness (that is, relatively unusual over-use)

Semantic category (and tag code and frequency)	Items within the category (and their raw frequencies) up to a maximum of ten types if they are available (excluding clearly erroneous categorizations in square brackets)
Living creatures generally (L2) (34)	hare (5), [bawd (3)], egg (2), dog (2), cats (2), mouse (2), wings (2), flies (1), herring (1), goose (1), rat (1)
Grammatical bin (Z5) (606)	the (82), a (82), of (58), and (52), to (31), in (28), for (26), with (21), 's (s-genitive) (16) as (16)
Shape (O4.4) (9)	straight (4), [row (1)], sharp (1), round (1), shape (1), circle (1)
Food (F1) (14)	meat (3), [hams (1)], [sauce (1)], [peppered (1)], pie (1), dinner (1), nuts (1), [grub (1)], bakes (1), fruit (1), pear (1), butcher (1)
Clothes and personal belongings (B5) (12)	wearing (2), worn (1), wear (1), livery (1), tailor (1), doublet (1), shoes (1), ribbon (1), [suit (10)], collars (1), button (1)
Anatomy and physiology (B1) (64)	eye (4), face (3), asleep (3), hair (3), ears (3), eyes (3), ear (3), bosom (2), head (2), nose (2), flesh (2)
Arts and crafts (C1) (15)	[art (10)], [draws (1)], [joiner (1)], coachmakers (1), [draw (1)], [drawn (1)]
Health and disease (B2–) (14)	plague (3), scratch (3), faints (1), faint (1), hurt (1), blisters (1), plagues (1), mad (1), [black eye (1)], pox (1)

In general, the semantic analysis also worked rather better for Romeo than the other characters, as one might expect from the characterization of his keywords as ideational. Apart from identifying categories such as Relationship: Intimate/sexual (S3.2) and Liking (E2+), which were already flagged up in the keywords analysis, the analysis picked out a relevant metaphorical pattern, as well as a relevant set of point of view indicators. The Nurse's categories had generally been indicated in the keywords analysis already. However, this was not the case with Being (A3+), which, upon examination, seemed well motivated. Mercutio's results matched the keyword results as far as the Grammatical bin (Z5) is concerned, but with

Living creatures generally (L2) and Anatomy and physiology (B1) the analysis revealed a wider semantic set lying behind single keywords. Finally, it might be noted that whether or not a category was comprised of a more or less restricted set did not seem to determine either whether the semantic category was key or whether keywords were part of it.

3.7 CONCLUSION

Where does the meaning of the text reside? Do we follow Sinclair and "trust the text"? Or do we follow the annotators and annotate the text for grammatical and semantic categories, so that lower frequency words that are not key in themselves can be grouped and taken into consideration (cf. Rayson 2004)? To answer these questions, we must consider grammatical annotation and semantic annotation separately. Regarding the analysis of key grammatical categories for the three characters, ten of the fourteen reliable grammatical categories were dominated by keywords.[14] Nine of those categories consisted of a relatively specific set containing contentless items— typically what are called closed-class words. None of the key grammatical categories were verbal or involved singular common nouns. Verbs and nouns are central open-class categories, and verb forms and singular nouns occurred in the keywords results, the latter with particular frequency. The generalization one might form, then, is that a keyword analysis matches the analysis of grammatical categories fairly well, and particularly so if those grammatical categories consist of more grammatical closed-class words. The main value of doing a key grammatical category analysis is in lending certain refinements to the keyword analysis, such as revealing Mercutio's taste for plural common nouns or highlighting a wider range of adjectives for Romeo. It should be added that the above is but a generalization. In particular, it does not account for the appearance of the categories First-person singular subjective personal pronoun (that is, *I*) (PPIS1), *Than* (as conjunction) (CSN), and Singular cardinal number (that is, *one*) (MC1). As we pointed out, all these categories are based on single words (*I*, *then*, and *one*), and so their dynamics are likely to be different from grammatical categories that are composed of more word types. It is worth noting, however, that only the first of those categories, *I*, is well motivated as part of Romeo's character; the others seem isolated and spurious.

Regarding semantic annotation, it became rapidly clear that the categories were more abstract and less stable than the grammatical ones. A consequence of this was that it was necessary to raise the cut-off frequency point to more than fifteen for a category to be eligible for scrutiny. Eleven of the total of fourteen semantic categories contained keywords—a very similar proportion to the grammatical analysis.[15] The distribution, however, was not even: two of Romeo's four categories, five of the Nurse's six categories, and all three of Mercutio's categories contained keywords. The strength of the semantic annotation is plugging the gap left by the grammatical annotation—the gap being the contentful or ideational patterns, the stuff of Romeo's speech. Moreover, where the key analysis of semantic annotation seems to have an advantage over grammatical annotation is that the semantic categories revealed as key and not consisting of keywords are also well motivated and difficult to predict. The metaphorical color patterns and point-of-view verbs of cognition for Romeo and the 'entirety' words (or boosters) and verbs relating to "being" for the Nurse are illuminating and fit their characters. Given that the analyses here have engaged relatively small data sets, it may be the case that these more abstract semantic categories can be more effectively revealed in larger sets of data, and, indeed, early work suggests that this is the case (for example, Archer, Culpeper, and Rayson 2009).

The results discussed here need, of course, to be replicated on larger sets of data. Nevertheless, a preliminary answer to the questions with which this section opened can be posited: generally we can trust the text, as a straight keyword analysis revealed most of the conclusions arrived at in this chapter. This general finding is not surprising, at least as far as grammatical analysis is concerned. Traditional grammatical perspectives and transformational grammars see a separation between the grammar and the lexicon. However, more recent (and varying) approaches see no such separation: the lexis is the grammar (for example, Brinton and Traugott 2005, and references therein). Such approaches tend to focus on the combinatory possibilities of particular words, and often recognize a continuum in the lexicon, the inventory of words, varying from more grammatical items to less. If there is no separation between grammar and the lexis, one would expect an analysis of keywords to produce results that are very similar to an analysis of key grammatical POS categories. And, indeed, this is the case. Of course, the analysis of grammatical annotation can contribute to traditional approaches to grammar. Traditional POS categories dominate grammar books, discussions of dialects, and language change, to mention but a few. But a more radical view—and one that Sinclair (1991, 2004) would take—would be to say that the whole basis of POS is wrong: we should be looking at how actual words combine and not imposing a particular set of abstract categories. Examples of grammars pursuing this agenda are "pattern grammar" (for example, Hunston 2002; see also Hunston and Francis 2000) and "lexical priming" (Hoey 2005). A final note of caution should be added here. The focus here has been on parts of speech, not broader syntactic rules and generalizations, the former being obviously more accessible via the word forms.

What about style and characterization? The fact that the analysis of POS and semantic tags did not add very much to the characterization of Romeo, Juliet, and Mercutio does not mean, of course, that those characters have no particular grammatical or semantic style. What it means is that the distinctive grammatical and semantic patterns of those characters can largely be found by focusing on the words. So, are studies like Toolan (1985) and

Fowler (1986, 37–38) worth doing? Toolan focused on foregrounded grammatical features and Fowler on *semes*. Our study would suggest that had they focused on foregrounded word patterns instead, many of the same conclusions could have been drawn. And, if those word patterns had been explored using a corpus-related methodology, such as keywords, a much more robust and systematic basis would underlie those conclusions. So, annotation is not worth doing? Whether or not annotation is worth doing depends very much on one's research agenda. In order to capture "style," whether of a character or some other entity, the words should be the first port of call. However, during this discussion, some significant fringe benefits of annotation were noted. The identification of metaphorical patterns is important for characterization (Semino and Swindlehurst 1996), just as is the identification of point of view indicators, even for drama (McIntyre 2004). Recent work has used key semantic categories to investigate these very areas (see McIntyre and Archer 2010 on mind style; see Archer, Culpeper, and Rayson 2009, Koller et al. 2008, and Deignan and Semino 2010 on metaphor). So, apart from sometimes refining or highlighting patterns that one might not have noticed looking solely at the words, key semantic analyses do sometimes reveal well-motivated results not predicted by keyword analysis.

NOTES

1. The invention of SGML is often credited to Charles Goldfarb, along with Edward Mosher and Raymond Lorie.
2. Prosodic annotation is something of a special case. It does have an explicit formal presence in the original spoken language data, but not in the transcribed orthographic computer corpus. Hence, prosodic annotation is not added on the basis of what is in the transcribed corpus, as is the case for grammar and semantics, for example, but on the basis of manual (with perhaps some instrumental assistance) analysis of the original data.
3. To have condemned social/contextual annotation would have meant excluding the topic of literary characterization and its real-life counterpart of sociolinguistics from the corpus approach, as characters/speakers create mixed texts and cannot be distinguished without annotation.
4. This refers to the first version of VARD. For VARD2, developed in large part by Alistair Baron; see http://www.comp.lancs.ac.uk/~barona/vard2/.
5. More information about CLAWS tagger can be found at http://www.comp.lancs.ac.uk/ucrel/claws. A free web-based tagging service is available (though with a few restrictions).
6. The full tagset can be found at http://www.comp.lancs.ac.uk/computing/research/ucrel/usas/.
7. The antonymity of conceptual classifications is indicated by +/– markers on tags.
8. This is rather different from MacArthur's original lexicon, which had 14 major codes, 127 group codes, and 2,441 set codes (Archer and Rayson 2004).
9. The results for three Shakespearean comedies and three Shakespearean tragedies revealed the same top three most frequent semantic categories.

10. The appearance of *love* in both categories is not an error. As we pointed out, the semantic tagger also uses POS information. Verbal usages of *love* are generally assigned to 'Liking' (E2+).
11. The use of the semantic tagger for metaphor identification is being investigated by Elena Semino and Veronika Koller at Lancaster University.
12. Culpeper (2001, 188–190) undertook a type-token ratio analysis and compared the Nurse with Capulet and Mercutio. The Nurse used significantly more repetition.
13. The Nurse's usage of the Latinate word *lamentable* is not at all characteristic of her preference for colloquial Germanic words (see Culpeper 2001, 184–86). Perhaps this is a slip by Shakespeare in the creation of a consistent idiolect.
14. The excluded categories are Singular letter of the alphabet (for example, A, B) (ZZ1) and Temporal noun, singular (for example, *day, week*, and *year*) (NNT1).
15. These figures assume that the categories People: Female (S2.1) and Power, organizing (S7.1+) are combined because of their overlap.

4 *The Moonstone* and *The Coquette*
Narrative and Epistolary Style

David L. Hoover

4.1 INTRODUCTION

In his seminal work on Jane Austen, *Computation into Criticism*, John F. Burrows demonstrates that Austen's characters can be distinguished from one another successfully on the basis of the frequencies of the most frequent words of their dialogue—that the dialogue of each character can be treated as if it were written by a different author (1987). His approach focuses attention on style variation of a very local nature—that within a single work. Chapters 2 and 3 above have used keywords and keyness to investigate characterization in drama, also focusing on style variation within a single work and also treating fictional characters as if they were real people. Much more work needs to be done on the styles of character dialogue in fiction and character speech in drama in a range of authors, but here I address two additional kinds of local intratextual style variation, the styles of multiple narrators of Wilkie Collins's *The Moonstone* (1868) and the styles of multiple letter writers in Hannah Webster Foster's epistolary novel *The Coquette* (1797).

The mysterious story of *The Moonstone* is told successively by several narrators whose styles seem intuitively very different. The task Collins sets himself is similar to that which any author faces in creating a distinctive narrative voice in a novel, but it is made more difficult by the fact that the narrators all tell parts of the same story, so that their narratives share many elements of plot, character, and physical and cultural setting. Narrative also has generic constraints that, while flexible, seem more restrictive than those of dialogue, which has additional complications of situation, purpose, and addressee. That is, it seems easier to individualize characters' voices through their dialogue than through their narration. *The Coquette* is a late eighteenth-century American epistolary novel that consists entirely of letters to and from the various characters. The coquette, the evil seducer, the virtuous friends, and the disappointed suitor seem intuitively as if their voices should be distinct. Like the multiple narrators of *The Moonstone*, the letter writers of *The Coquette* tell parts of the same story and their letters share many of the same elements, but they also exhibit some of the complications of dialogue. Treating the narratives and letters of these two novels as if they were texts by different authors will test how successful Collins and Foster are in distinguishing the voices within their texts and will also shed light on some practical and theoretical issues important to the study of authorship and style and on the styles of these authors, texts, and narrators.

4.2   NARRATIVE STYLE IN COLLINS AND NINE OTHER VICTORIANS

The Moonstone seems an appropriate place to begin an examination of narrator's style because its repeated shifts of narrative point of view were innovative and even daring in his time. This novel is often cited as the first mystery novel, which also gives it a unique claim to attention. The techniques of authorship attribution and computational stylistics that will be used to investigate the styles of the narrators are founded upon the premises that each author's style is distinguishable from that of every other author, and that at least some elements of authorial style are so routinized or habitual as to be outside the author's control. Style variation within the works of a single author or a single text seems to threaten the validity of the entire enterprise. Yet the problem is more apparent than real, for the consistency in style required for successful authorship attribution is perfectly compatible with style variation within an author's works. All that is required is that the author's substyles be more like each other than they are like the style of any other author.

The techniques of authorship attribution and computational stylistics cannot be used to investigate the narrative voices in *The Moonstone*, however, unless they can be shown to distinguish effectively between Collins and other roughly contemporary British authors.[1] Any technique that cannot reliably tell Collins from other authors can hardly be expected to characterize his substyles minutely enough to distinguish multiple narrators within a single novel. The demonstration that Collins is distinguishable from other authors begins with a specially created corpus of seventy Victorian novels by Collins and nine of his contemporaries (described more fully below). The novels were downloaded from online collections, usually Project Gutenberg (http://www.gutenberg.org/), and have been only lightly edited to remove extraneous material like Gutenberg information, prefaces, introductions, tables of contents, and so forth. Although this corpus is in no sense representative of Victorian novels, it is large enough and varied enough to test whether Collins can be distinguished from his contemporaries.

4.3   DISTINGUISHING COLLINS FROM OTHER AUTHORS: DELTA

The large number of long texts suggests that Delta, a relatively new measure of textual difference developed by John F. Burrows (2002a, 2002b, 2003), should be appropriate for this analysis. Delta is designed to determine which of a set of possible authors is most likely to be the author of a text of uncertain authorship. Like many other authorship methods, Delta is based on differences among the frequencies of the most frequent words of the texts. Burrows's discussion of his new measure of authorial difference analyzes selections of English Restoration poetry on the basis of the frequencies of the 150 most frequent words (MFW, below) of the entire set of texts (2003, 10). Delta is a relatively simple measure of textual difference, but working through an example, using frequencies from the corpus of novels described above and testing Delta on texts of known authorship will clarify its nature and derivation.[2]

Delta operates on a sample of text by each primary author (those against whom other texts will be tested for authorship) and a group of test texts, typically some by the primary authors and some anonymous texts. For these Victorian novels, the analysis begins with a set of ten primary authorial samples, each consisting of two long novels. The word frequencies for the two novels have been averaged. The logic of using multiple novels in a primary authorial set is that it reduces the effect of any unusual fluctuations in frequencies among the author's novels; averaging the frequencies across the novels rather than combining the novels and taking the frequency for the combined text allows novels of different sizes to have equal influence. The test set includes fifty novels by twelve authors. Forty-seven of these are by one of the ten primary set authors and three are by other authors. Because one of the primary authors (Hardy) does not have any texts among the test texts and three of the test texts are not by any of the primary authors, these tests will show whether Delta can correctly attribute those texts with authors in the primary set to their actual authors while also avoiding strong incorrect attributions.

The two sets of novels in the corpus are as follows:

Primary Samples

Besant	*Dorothy Foster* + *The Ivory Gate*
Brontë	*Jane Eyre* + *Vilette*
Collins	*The Moonstone* + *Law and the Lady*
Dickens	*Dombey and Son* + *Little Dorrit*
Eliot	*Middlemarch* + *The Mill on the Floss*
Hardy	*The Return of the Native* + *The Mayor of Casterbridge*
Meredith	*The Adventures of Harry Richmond* + *The Egoist*
Reade	*Hard Cash* + *Never Too Late to Mend*
Thackery	*Pendennis* + *Vanity Fair*
Trollope	*The Small House at Allington* + *The Prime Minister*

Test Set

Besant	*A Fountain Sealed, In Luck at Last, The Rebel Queen, The Revolt of Man*
Brontë, C.	*The Professor*
Brontë, E.	*Wuthering Heights*

Chesterton	*The Wisdom of Father Brown*
Collins	*Hide and Seek, The Dead Secret, The Woman in White, No Name, Armadale, Man and Wife, Poor Miss Finch, The New Magdalen, The Two Destinies, Fallen Leaves, Jezebel's Daughter, The Black Robe, Heart and Science, I Say No, The Evil Genius, The Legacy of Cain*
Conrad	*Almayer's Folly*
Dickens	*The Old Curiosity Shop, Martin Chuzzlewit, David Copperfield, Bleak House, Great Expectations, Our Mutual Friend*
Eliot	*Adam Bede, Silas Marner, Daniel Deronda*
Meredith	*The Ordeal of Richard Feverel, Evan Harrington, Beauchamp's Career, Diana of the Crossways, One of Our Conquerors*
Thackery	*The Luck of Barry Lyndon, Henry Esmond, The Newcomes, The Virginians*
Reade	*Christie Johnstone, The Cloister and the Hearth*
Trollope	*Barchester Towers, Doctor Thorne, Can You Forgive Her, Phineas Finn, He Knew He Was Right, The American Senator*

Essentially, Delta compares the word frequencies in each test text with those of each primary authorial sample, but it does so by way of their average frequencies in all of the primary authorial samples combined. That is, each word's frequency in each test text and in each primary authorial sample is compared with its average frequency in all of the primary authorial samples combined. These differences are then compared with each other to find which primary authorial sample most closely matches each test text in its distance from the average. The amount of difference between the frequencies, rather than which one is larger and which smaller, is the focus here, so Delta is based on the "absolute" or positive value of each difference. Table 4.1 shows partial results for a test of Collins's *Man and Wife*, treated as if it were a text of unknown authorship. In the top half of the table are figures for *the*, the most frequent word in this corpus, with an average frequency of 4.916 percent.[3] It is easy to see that Collins's primary sample shows the least difference from the test text, so that this identification based on only the word *the* is correct. As the bottom half of the table shows, however, we cannot simply add the figures for the differences for all the words to create an overall measure of difference. The frequency of *asked*, the 169th most frequent word, is so low that any differences between its frequencies in various texts would have an insignificant effect on any such measure. One very effective way to allow the differences in smaller frequencies to have an appropriate effect is to turn the "Sample minus Avg." and "Test minus Avg." differences into z-scores. This is done by dividing each difference by the standard deviation of the frequency for the word.[4]

Table 4.1   Frequencies of *the* and *asked* in *Man and Wife* and three primary samples

Test text	% freq. of *the*	Avg. freq. in primary samples	Test minus avg.		
Man and Wife (Collins)	6.446	4.916	1.530		
Primary sample			Sample minus avg.	Test minus avg.	Absolute difference
Collins	6.106	4.916	1.190	1.530	0.340
Besant	5.186	4.916	0.270	1.530	1.260
Thackeray	5.535	4.916	0.619	1.530	0.911

Test text	% freq. of *asked*	Avg. freq. in primary samples	Test minus avg.		
Man and Wife (Collins)	0.121	0.061	0.060		
Primary sample			Sample minus avg.	Test minus avg.	Absolute difference
Collins	0.118	0.061	0.057	0.060	0.003
Bronte	0.066	0.061	0.005	0.060	0.054
Thackeray	0.075	0.061	0.014	0.060	0.046

Table 4.2 shows the results of using z-scores rather than frequencies on the same two words for the same texts. Here we can see that Collins's use of *the* is far above average. Normally, more than two-thirds of all texts would be expected to fall within one standard deviation from the average on the basis of chance (z-scores between −1 and 1), so his use of *the* in his primary sample is quite unusual, as the z-score of 1.739 suggests (the score for *Man and Wife*, at 2.236, is even higher). His z-score for *asked*, however, is even larger, at 2.060, so that we can say that *asked* is a word that Collins strongly favors, in spite of the fact that the difference between its frequency in the Collins primary sample and the average of all the primary samples is only 0.057 percent.

The calculations shown for *the* and *asked* are performed for all of the words being analyzed, until each test text has been compared sequentially with each of the primary samples. The result is a list of z-score differences between the differences of each pair of texts from the mean. Finally, Delta is calculated by taking "the mean of the absolute differences between the z-scores for a set of word-variables in a given text-group and the z-scores

Table 4.2   Frequencies and *z*-scores of *the* and *asked* in *Man and Wife* and three primary samples

Test text	% freq. of "*the*"	Avg. freq. in primary samples	Test minus avg. *z*-score		
Man and Wife (Collins)	6.446	4.916	2.236	Standard deviation: 0.684	
Primary sample			Sample minus avg. *z*-score	Test minus avg. *z*-score	Absolute difference
Collins	6.106	4.916	1.739	2.236	0.497
Besant	5.186	4.916	0.395	2.236	1.842
Thackeray	5.535	4.916	0.905	2.236	1.332

Test text	% freq. of "*asked*"	Avg. freq. in primary samples	Test minus avg. *z*-score		
Man and Wife (Collins)	0.121	0.061	2.167	Standard deviation: 0.028	
Primary sample			Sample minus avg. *z*-score	Test minus avg. *z*-score	Absolute difference
Collins	0.118	0.061	2.060	2.167	0.106
Bronte	0.066	0.061	0.194	2.167	1.973
Thackeray	0.075	0.061	0.507	2.167	1.659

for the same set of word-variables in a target text" (Burrows 2002a, 271). Once the difference between the test text and each of the primary samples has been calculated, the primary author whose sample shows the smallest mean difference from the test text, the smallest Delta, is identified as the likeliest author of the test text.[5]

The Delta tests for these texts have been modified from Burrows's initial method. First, the calculation of Delta has been limited to words that have relatively large *z*-scores in the test text, a method called DeltaLz (see Hoover 2004b for details). Second, personal pronouns have been deleted, to limit the effects of different points of view and different numbers of male and female characters. Finally, any words that are frequent in the word list simply because they are very frequent in a single text have been removed, typically names of characters and places. For example, *Florence*, the 908th most frequent word in the corpus, is the first name of Dombey's daughter in Dickens's *Dombey and Son*. It appears 1,154 times in that novel and a few times as a place name in about twenty of the other novels. Even though the city is mentioned 105 times in Trollope's *He Knew He Was Right*, it would not be among the four thousand

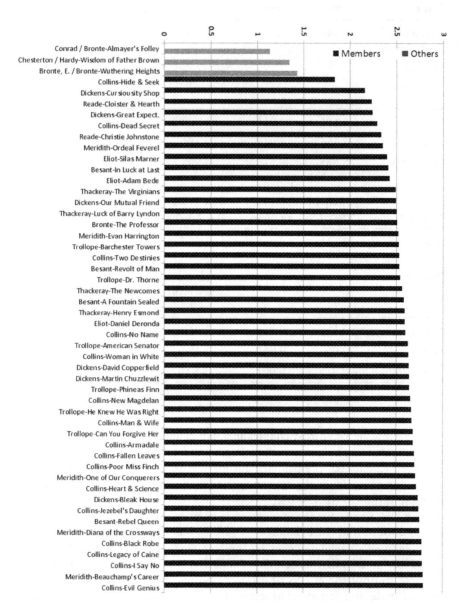

Figure 4.1   DeltaLz analysis of fifty Victorian novels: Nine hundred MFW, no pronouns, culled at 70 percent

MFW without its high frequency in *Dombey and Son*. It would seem inappropriate to analyze such words as authorship indicators because the extremely high frequency in one text gives them an importance they do not have overall. A "culling" percentage is indicated in some analyses below; if an analysis is "culled at 70 percent," for example, that means that any word with 70 percent of its occurrences in a single text has been removed.[6]

Delta does an excellent job of identifying the correct authors of the forty-seven novels in the corpus above that are by one of the ten primary authors. It gives completely correct results in all forty analyses from the 100, 200, . . . 4,000 MFW. A representative analysis based on the 900 MFW is shown in figure 4.1; note, near the top of the graph, how much stronger even the weakest correct attribution is (for Collins's *Hide and Seek*) than the strongest attribution of a novel not by any of the primary authors (for Emily Brontë's *Wuthering Heights*).

4.4   DISTINGUISHING COLLINS FROM OTHER AUTHORS: CLUSTER ANALYSIS

Cluster analysis is an inductive statistical method of classification that has often been used in authorship and stylistic studies. Its results are normally presented as dendrograms like that shown in figure 4.2, which shows an analysis of the seventy novels in the corpus described above, based on the 990 MFW with personal pronouns removed and the word list culled at 70 percent. Cluster analysis has many different forms with varied results, and there is no space here to discuss this topic fully. The crucial point is that the closer to the left of the graph that items or groups join together, the more similar they are to each other in their use of the words analyzed. Conversely, the farther to the right that two items or groups join, the more different they are.

The cluster analysis in figure 4.2 is extremely accurate, in spite of the large number of texts. In all cases of multiple novels by a single author, all the novels are correctly clustered. Furthermore, the three novels not by any of the primary authors all form distinctly separate clusters of their own. All analyses based on the 400–990 MFW give completely accurate results. The fact that Collins's eighteen novels form one of the two main clusters reflects his distinctive style and strongly suggests that cluster analysis should be useful in analyzing his style. Finally, the titles of the novels in figure 4.2 begin with the publication date, so that it is easy to see that the novels of Meredith, Dickens, Eliot, Trollope, and Collins (though not Besant or Thackeray) tend to group by publication date. This suggests that cluster analysis is sensitive enough to authorial style to be appropriate for analyzing the voices of the multiple narrators of *The Moonstone*.

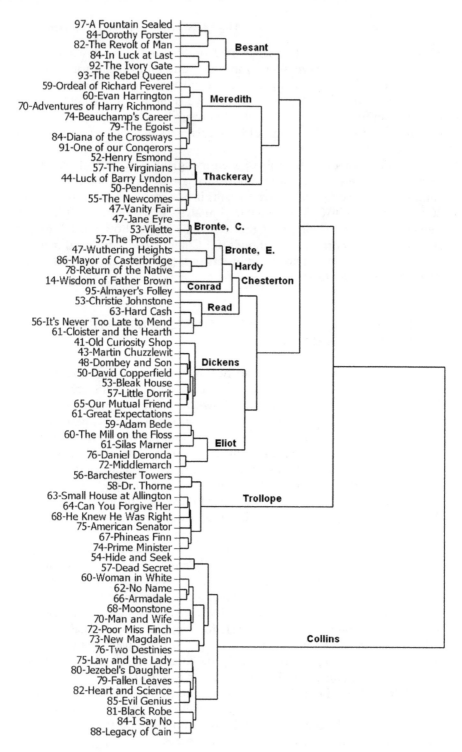

Figure 4.2 Seventy novels by thirteen Victorians: 990 MFW, no pronouns, culled at 70 percent

4.5 THE STYLES OF THE MULTIPLE NARRATORS
OF *THE MOONSTONE*

The literary and historical reasons for selecting *The Moonstone* for a study of intratextual style variation seem compelling, but the internal structure of the novel makes it an especially appropriate test case. Most of the narration comes from a small number of narrators who seem intuitively very diverse. The old servant Betteredge, with his veneration of *Robinson Crusoe* and his obtuseness; Franklin Blake, the upper-class young lover; the obnoxious and hypocritical Miss Clack; Mr. Bruff, the careful and sagacious family lawyer; the humble, wronged, and mysterious Ezra Jennings; and the famous and canny detective, Sergeant Cuff, have such different personalities and backgrounds that it would seem odd if their dialects were not different. The novel would hardly have remained so popular for so long if these narrators all sounded alike.

Collins also makes the analyst's job easier by presenting the narrators of *The Moonstone* to us serially and giving them clearly demarcated segments, most of which are quite long. After editing the entire novel to remove extraneous material such as section numbers and chapter titles, and checking for consistency in hyphenation, dashes, apostrophes, and single quotation marks, I separated the various narratives and removed all dialogue and speech markers from them. (Speech markers are phrases that identify part of the text as a character's speech and sometimes characterize it; for example, "He said," "she quietly responded.") Retaining the speech of other characters within a narrator's section would be equivalent to retaining quotations by other writers in an authorial sample in an attribution problem. It could be argued that some of the speech markers should have been retained. For example, Miss Clack's, "I said, in my most winning way," helps to create her hypocritical, self-congratulatory style. Nevertheless, I have removed the speech markers to prevent any odd effects that might arise from large differences in the amount of reported speech in the various narrations. This seems the most conservative procedure, but it raises what is actually a complex question about whether the amount of reported speech is a matter of content (some narrators have more speech to report) or a matter of style (some narrators choose to report more speech).

Once this editing is done, the six narrators named above emerge as the logical choices for analysis (their narratives are much longer than the next longest narrative). To these explicitly designated narrators I have added the despairing, lovesick Rosanna, whose letter and memorandum are found after her suicide and are included by Franklin Blake among the other narratives. The function and nature of Rosanna's account seem quite similar to those of the other narratives, which Franklin Blake has commissioned under the assumption that each part of the story should be narrated by the person who was in the best position to observe the events. The edited narrative of Sergeant Cuff is the shortest of the seven at about forty-three hundred words, followed by Rosanna and Bruff at about six thousand, Jennings at about ten thousand, Clack at about nineteen thousand, Blake at about twenty-one thousand (in two separate narratives combined), and Betteredge at about fifty-one thousand (in two separate narratives combined, the second very short). For my first analysis, I have divided Jennings into two parts, Clack and Blake into three parts, and Betteredge into eight parts, a process that results in nineteen sections that range from forty-three to sixty-nine hundred words.

Cluster analysis suggests that, in general, Collins does an excellent job of writing his narrators' parts distinctly. In almost all analyses based on more than the four hundred MFW, all eight of Betteredge's sections cluster together, and, joined with Rosanna's section as a distant neighbor, form one of two large clusters. Within the other large cluster, Blake's three sections and Clack's three sections form distinct clusters, so that fifteen of the nineteen sections regularly and consistently cluster correctly. The remaining three narrators do not cluster so perfectly, however. Jennings's second cluster usually forms a larger cluster with Blake's sections, but his first section clusters with Bruff up to about the seven hundred MFW, and then with Cuff. What this means, practically, is that all of the narrators except Jennings strongly tend to cluster correctly. (The second section of Jennings's narration is his account of the night when he drugs Franklin Blake in an attempt to uncover the mystery of the theft of the moonstone, and so seems more clearly narrative than the earlier section, but such after-the-fact explanations are always suspect.)

When a modified technique that I have developed especially for investigating style variation within a text or author is used, the results are even better. This method, which I will refer to as the "style variation method" below, abandons the culling procedure I have described above. In an authorship test, words that are frequent overall because of a very high frequency in a single text are typically proper names that can skew the results, but a word that is frequent because it is heavily used by a single narrator seems important to retain as a possible narrator's style marker. The style variation method also changes the method of creating the word frequency list on which the analysis is based. Instead of listing all the words of the corpus (here the corpus consists of the six narrative parts described above) in order of their total frequency in the corpus, the words are selected on the basis of their frequency in the narrative part in which they are most frequent. This has the effect of placing words with wide variations in frequency among the narrators—words that seem likeliest to be markers of a single narrator's style—closer to the top of the word frequency list (see Hoover 2003c for further discussion).

As figure 4.3, based on the 900 MFW, shows, all of the sections by all of the narrators except Jennings cluster correctly, and his two sections are near neighbors (analyses based on the 870–895 MFW correctly cluster all the narrators). In addition, every two-section cluster consists of contiguous sections. The fact that the analysis captures narrative structure so well

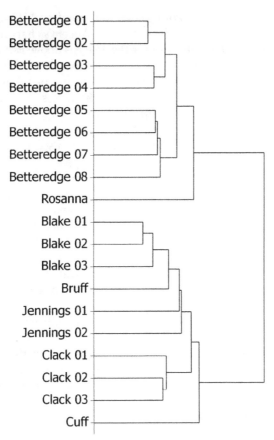

Figure 4.3 *Moonstone* narrators: Nine hundred MFW, no pronouns, style variation method

provides further evidence that it is accurately characterizing the narrators' styles. However, results such as these risk an appearance of circularity that must be addressed briefly. The "best" results, which are the ones I have just presented, are best in the sense that they validate the assumption that Collins has written the parts of different narrators with sufficient variety so that they can be treated as if they were written by different authors. Yet that is one of the questions that the analysis was designed to answer in the first place.

The basic assumption has long been that authors can and do separate characters within their texts on the basis of character style within their overall authorial styles, so that, as Burrows found, there is an Austen style and an Austen dialogue style, but there is also a Mr. Darcy style, a Mr. Collins style, an Elizabeth Bennet style (1987). Burrows generally found the character separations and groupings satisfying and appropriate, but, as in most of his work, he focused on a single analysis of less than one hundred MFW. Given the relatively small amounts of speech from some of Austen's characters, this was a reasonable approach. The difficulty for the analysis above is that there are no obvious criteria for selecting a word list of any specific size. Unlike Burrows, I use a large span of different numbers of frequent words, and the different analyses often separate and cluster different characters. As is typical in such analyses, many of the different groupings seem appropriate after the fact.

On what basis can one decide which analyses are giving the "true" picture of narrator differentiation? The method normally used in authorship attribution problems is to perform preliminary analyses on known samples and select the type and range of analyses that most accurately attribute a set of texts by known authors, but that method is obviously not applicable here. Another possibility is to use the same range of analyses that give the best results in distinguishing Collins from other Victorian authors, but the narrators' sections in *The Moonstone* are so much shorter that this is not appropriate. The consistency of the results can be used as a basis for selecting a range of analyses, as I have done rather uncritically above. Any narrators whose sections are clearly distinguished throughout a large range of analyses may fairly be characterized as different from the other narrators. Conversely, any narrators whose parts consistently cluster together must be characterized as relatively similar, compared to the other narrators in the analysis.

Another criterion that seems reasonable is based on the pattern that is typical when authorship attribution methods are tested on texts by known authors: very small numbers of the most frequent words fail to group the texts accurately, but the accuracy improves steadily, if sometimes cyclically, as more and more words are included, until a maximum accuracy is reached. There is often a plateau of consistent results at this point, followed by a decline in accuracy as even more words are included. This pattern is very general, though the plateau occurs with word lists of different sizes for different sets of texts, and there are sometimes secondary plateaus. Results like those shown in figure 4.3 occur over a relatively narrow range of analyses of *The Moonstone*, but the pattern of improvement in accuracy from small numbers of words to the nine hundred MFW is very clear, and the few results in which all of Jennings's sections cluster are also those in which the clustering for the sections of the other narrators is most distinct and accurate. The assumption that different narrators within a novel can be treated appropriately as if they were different authors thus seems true for Collins, and it can safely be taken as a working hypothesis for other authors, so long as its contingent nature is kept in mind.

4.6   THE STYLES OF THE MULTIPLE NARRATORS OF *THE MOONSTONE*: FURTHER TESTS

A more fine-grained investigation of *The Moonstone* that includes two more narrators will put Collins's ability to differentiate his narrators to a sterner test. For this analysis, I have included all nine of the narrators' parts that are longer than 1,000 words and have divided them into very nearly equal sections. All of the narratives except those of Cuff (4,329 words), Mr. Murthwaite (1,390 words), and Sir John Verinder (2,000 words—like Rosanna's, his is an independent narrative inserted by Franklin Blake) divide neatly into sections of approximately 3,000 words, resulting in a total of thirty-eight sections. The word lists for this analysis have been prepared using the style variation method that produced superior results in the analysis above. I have also used DeltaLz to analyze these thirty-eight sections, and have combined four of Betteredge's sixteen sections (one, six, eleven, and sixteen), three of Clack's six sections (one, three, and six), and two of Blake's five sections (one and five) and two of Jennings's three sections (one and three) to create their primary samples. For Bruff and Rosanna, with only two sections each, I have used the first section as the primary sample. Cuff's single section is included among the primary samples, and the single sections of Murthwaite and Verinder among the secondary samples. In twenty-five analyses based on the 100, 200, . . . 1,000, 1,200, 1,400, . . . 4,000 MFW, DeltaLz correctly identifies the narrator of all twenty-two sections by one of the primary narrators in analyses based on the 600 and 700 MFW, and makes only one incorrect attribution in 8 other analyses (based on the 300, 500, 800–900, 1,400–2,000 MFW). There are just 2 incorrect attributions in each of the other fifteen analyses, for a total of 512 correct and 38 incorrect attributions (all but 4 errors attribute one of Blake's sections to another narrator). This is an overall accuracy rate of 93 percent and a rate of more than 97 percent for the analyses based on the 500 to 900 MFW. Clearly Collins seems to have created distinctive narrative voices for his narrators.

Cluster analysis confirms this conclusion. Analyses based on a wide range of numbers of words (using the style variation method and with pronouns removed) show only a single error (Jennings's third section forms a separate cluster with Blake as nearest neighbor). A few analyses, based on the 800–990 MFW are completely correct. Although the cluster membership changes frequently in these analyses, the most accurate results also tend to reflect the narrative structure, with sequential sections frequently occurring in order, as figure 4.4, based on the 880 MFW, shows.[7]

For *The Moonstone*, then, the intuitive feeling that the narrators have very distinct styles can be substantiated with authorship attribution tools. The novel's long, distinct narrative parts, which describe different events from different perspectives, behave very much as if they were written by different authors, so that there is a Betteredge style, a Rosanna style, a Clack style, a Bruff style, a Cuff style. The Blake and Jennings styles are slightly more problematic, but there is a consistent early Blake style and a consistent early Jennings style. The fact that these two characters have similar styles also resonates with wider social themes in which Collins is interested. Further research would be needed to determine if their similarity marks the limits of Collins's skill in differentiating characters who are, after all, closely

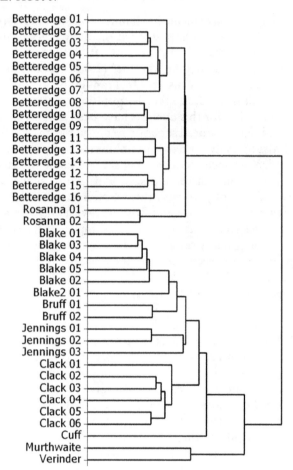

Figure 4.4   Moonstone narrators: 880 MFW, no pronouns, style variation method

connected by the plot, or if it should rather be seen as a suggestive interpretive connection. Given the length of the novel, the generic constraints of narrative, and the inherent similarities of plot, setting, and characters, this is a remarkable achievement on Collins's part. It is even more remarkable considering that, among the six Victorian authors shown in figure 4.1, Collins's style is the most distinct from the styles of his contemporaries, in spite of the fact that it encompasses the styles of all the narrators and characters in ten of his novels (see Hoover 2010b for further discussion of Collins's style and a study of his final novel, *Blind Love*, completed by Walter Besant).

It is worth pointing out, however, that the task of creating separate voices for narrators or characters is quite difficult, and not all authors can manage it. In Collins's earlier (1860) attempt at multiple narration, *The Woman in White*, the various narrative voices do not separate nearly as well as they do in *The Moonstone*. Bram Stoker's *Dracula* (1897) has quite a complex structure in which speech and letters are mingled with narratives. Unlike in *The Moonstone*, the narrative voices in this novel are not very well delineated, though the foreign voice of Van Helsing and the "journalism" of an article from *The Daily Globe* are nicely distinct. In *As I lay Dying* (Faulkner 1930, 2005), however, Faulkner does a very good job of creating separate voices for a group of characters that intuitively seem like they should be more similar than those of *The Moonstone* (see Hoover 2010a for details).

4.7 EPISTOLARY STYLE IN *THE COQUETTE* AND FIVE OTHER NOVELS

Hannah Webster Foster's *The Coquette* (1797) is, to say the least, a very different kind of novel from *The Moonstone*. In addition to its radically different content, it is much shorter (only about 53,000 words, compared to *The Moonstone's* 195,000), it was written seventy years earlier, and it is American rather than British (though before 1800 this is not very important). Finally, it is an epistolary novel, so that the various voices take the form of letters rather than long, connected narrative segments. My initial comparison here departs from my usual practice of testing a large group of novels by contemporaries. The techniques are so successful on the Victorian novels discussed above that another test hardly seems necessary, and similar contemporaneous epistolary novels are not widely available as electronic texts. Instead I compare some of the letter writers in the following small corpus of six epistolary novels:

> Hannah Webster Foster's *The Coquette* (1797)
> Anna Maria Bennett, *Agnes De-Courci: A Domestic Tale* (1789)
> Fanny Burney, *Evelina* (1778)
> Maria Susanna Cooper, *The Wife; Or, Caroline Herbert* (1813; a revision of a 1762 novel)
> Maria Edgeworth, *Letters for Literary Ladies* (second edition, 1798)
> Tobias Smollett, *The Expedition of Humphrey Clinker* (1771)

This kind of comparison will show whether authorship attribution methods can successfully attribute the various letter writers to their authors in spite of the intentional differentiation that their fictional identities imply.

The six novels above present several challenges for computational stylistics. The dates of the texts raise the question of regularization; eighteenth-century spelling conventions were different from and not as regular as modern conventions, and may have been altered by later editors or by the creators of the electronic versions. Fortunately, this problem seems manageable: selecting the one thousand MFW of the combined sections of all the authors, sorting them alphabetically and reading down the list reveals only a few variations. For example, *honor* and *honour* both occur at about rank three hundred, *favor* and *favour* at ranks seven hundred and five hundred, and *connection* and *connexion* at about six hundred and nine hundred. In the case of *choose* (rank eight hundred) / *chuse* (rank forty-eight hundred), only one of the pair ranks in the one thousand MFW, and I may have missed a few others of this sort. Running a spell-check on the rank-ordered word frequency list for all of the novels uncovers a few other words in -*our* / -*or* among the two thousand MFW, such as *endeavour, behaviour, humour, labour, endeavoured, honoured, favourite, neighbourhood, neighbours*. Among the *in*- /*en*- words, I found only the modern *en*- spelling of *intreat/entreat* and *intirely/entirely* among the two thousand MFW. Other early spelling variations, such as -*l* / -*ll* (*travelling*), -*ise* / -*ize* (*surprize*), -*o* / -*oa* (*cloaths, doat*), -*ea*- / -*ee*- (*chear, chearful*) occur rarely, typically not within the two thousand MFW. My usual practice of culling words that are frequent in only a single text will, in any case, eliminate any true idiosyncrasies, and the use of large numbers of frequent words should mask any remaining small effects.

Another difficulty is that many of the letters are short, so that several must often be combined to produce samples long enough for reasonable computational analysis. This means that, in some cases, the letters that are combined occur quite far apart in the novel, so that they address different topics and concerns and are written in different settings and circumstances. This problem is similar to but less severe than the problem of dialogue, which typically occurs in even shorter segments. Furthermore, in these epistolary novels, an event may be described by more than one letter writer in turn, creating similarities of content that could affect the vocabularies of the sections.

The characterization of a letter writer's style is also complicated by the fact that a single writer may have more than one addressee. One would expect, for example, that, in Fanny Burney's *Evelina*, Evelina would write very differently to her friend Miss Mirvan than she does to her adoptive father Reverend Villars, and that the rather formal letter genre might constrain letters from a daughter to a parent differently or more seriously than those from one friend to another. I have controlled for this to some extent by combining into a single section only letters between a single writer and a single addressee. In spite of the fact that some writers have more than one addressee, I have also, for the initial experiment, included only letters to one addressee for any given writer, though I have sometimes included sections by more than one writer to a single addressee.

Finally, it is not clear to what extent one should expect the letters written by different characters in a single novel to cluster together and separate from the letters written by all of the characters in other novels. Even if novels typically separate well from each other when analyzed as wholes, it seems possible that very distinct characters might sometimes be less similar to the other characters in their own novels than to one or more characters in other novels. This seems especially likely if two novels feature characters of a similar age, gender, and class (an upper-class ingénue, for example) and if the letters chosen for analysis are also addressed to a similar person (her mother, for example). This situation might more closely resemble a genre question than an authorship question, and genre effects are so powerful that they sometimes overwhelm authorship effects (see Burrows 1992b for an excellent early discussion). Although it seems reasonable to expect individual writers to have a single recognizable style throughout their letters, it might also be true that different circumstances, such as growing up, a trauma, a marriage, a breakup, or a conversion, might make some letters by a writer quite different from others. A further question for investigation is whether in this latter case we should expect the two or more groups of letters by a single writer to remain distinct from the letters of other writers, even if they do not all group together. The lack of any clear a priori answers to questions such as these suggests that an open-ended, inductive inquiry is appropriate.

The Coquette and Edgeworth's *Letters for Literary Ladies* are both quite short (the latter only about twenty-two thousand words), so I have taken samples from the longer texts, concentrating on writers with multiple long letters. I have removed any quotations from the letters—mainly lines of poetry and reported dialogue—and have removed any enclosed messages, notes, and letters. I have also removed formulaic greetings and closings. (Although different writers may typically use different characteristic formulas, such formulas also seem likely to involve generic constraints, and the relatively small number of letters included in each sample reduces any importance this effect might otherwise have.) I begin with forty sections of roughly thirty-five hundred words: Bennett—eight sections by three writers; Burney—three sections by two writers; Cooper—four sections by four writers; Edgeworth—five sections by three writers; Foster—ten sections by five writers; and Smollett—ten sections by three writers.

In spite of the large number of varied sections, the sections of letters from individual novels can be grouped together quite effectively by cluster analysis. In analyses based on the 890–990 MFW (no personal pronouns, culled at 70 percent), all of Cooper's, Edgeworth's, Foster's, Bennett's, and Smollett's sections cluster correctly, but one of Burney's sections is a nearer neighbor to Bennett's cluster than to Burney's. This is McCartney's letter to Evelina (the shortest section in the analysis, at 2,385 words). Analyses based on fewer words show a less accurate pattern. As figure 4.5 shows, many of the sets of letters by a single writer to a single addressee group together within an author's cluster, but note that, among the letters from *The Coquette*, the first three sections of Eliza's letters to Lucy cluster with Boyer's letters to Selby and the last section clusters with Lucy's letters to Eliza. Julia's sections form their own cluster within the Foster cluster. These patterns are quite regular over a large number of analyses based on different numbers of words. Delta also does a very good job with these sections when

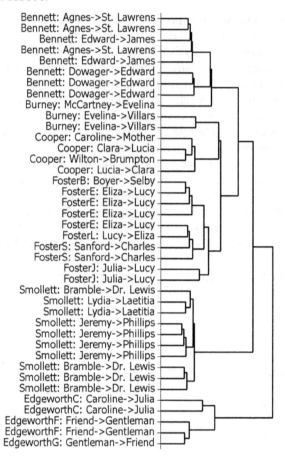

Figure 4.5   *The Coquette* and five other novels: 990 MFW, no pronouns, culled at 70 percent

the word frequencies of two or more sections are averaged to produce the primary sets, where possible, with all analyses correctly attributing all the sections in analyses based on the 200 to 1,100 MFW.

4.8   EPISTOLARY STYLE IN *THE COQUETTE*

Turning now to an analysis of *The Coquette* alone, I have added three sections to the ten included in the six-novel analysis above. These thirteen sections by six writers are approximately 3,000 words each, as in fine-grained *Moonstone* analysis, though there is more variation in size here and more short sections (1,309, 1,400, and 1,628 words). In two cases, there are separate sections by a single writer to two different addressees (Eliza to her mother and to Lucy, and Boyer to Eliza and to Selby). Although these thirteen sections by six writers should be considerably easier to attribute successfully than were the thirty-eight sections by nine narrators in the fine-grained analysis of *The Moonstone* above, the results, using word lists created using the style variation method, are not very encouraging (using the standard method gives even weaker results). DeltaLz gets five of six correct using the style variation method word list once; for this set, standard Delta does a bit better, with five of six correct twice.[8]

Cluster analysis works better using the standard method, with pronouns retained, and produces results that are quite similar to those of the analysis of the six novels above. In analyses based on large numbers of words (six hundred to nine hundred), only the sections of Sanford, Julia, and Selby cluster correctly: Julia's two appear in one of the two large clusters and Sanford's two in the other; the Selby section forms its own cluster within one of the two large clusters. For smaller numbers of words (two hundred to five hundred), the pattern is similar except that the Selby section switches to the other large cluster. In all of these analyses, letters by Boyer and Eliza appear in both large clusters. Boyer's letters to Eliza appear in the same cluster as Eliza's letters to her mother and her last section of letters to Lucy, and his letters to Selby appear in the same cluster with Eliza's other three sections of letters to Lucy. In addition, Lucy's letters to Eliza cluster with the last section of Eliza's letters to Lucy in all of these analyses, making this wrong identification as strong as any of the correct ones.

In analyses based on the two hundred MFW or fewer, the clustering changes frequently, with only Julia's and Sanford's clusters remaining stable. The most accurate clustering, found only in a very narrow range around one hundred MFW, is shown in figure 4.6. In this analysis Sanford, Julia, and Selby cluster correctly, Eliza's last section to Lucy clusters with the section to her mother, and Boyer's letters to Eliza cluster with Lucy's letters to Eliza. Letters by Boyer and Eliza continue to appear in both of the two main clusters, however, as they do in all analyses I have performed, and, in Eliza's case, letters in both main clusters have the same addressee (Lucy). In an authorship attribution problem, results like these would not support the conclusion that all of the letters by Boyer or all of the letters by Eliza were written by a single author. Finally, the fact that the "best" results are found in analyses using small numbers of words and do not match the very consistent results based on larger numbers of words suggests that this is a chance effect.

It may seem intuitively reasonable that Boyer should sound different when he is writing to his friend than when he is writing to Eliza, and it may seem suggestive that the last section of Eliza's letters includes only letters written after Boyer has rejected her. Yet such special pleading is almost always possible after the fact, and it can in any case only explain

why Boyer's and Eliza's voices are not consistent, leaving without explanation the fact that other authors *do* create characters with consistent voices.
And if we accept such arguments, we are left wondering why the early and
late letters of Sanford, the villainous seducer, consistently cluster together
in spite of the fact that he shows remorse in the later letters. If his early
and late letters had not clustered together, it would have been reasonable
to ascribe this to his remorse. Furthermore, any suggestion that Boyer's
letters to Eliza should be distinct from his letters to Selby is impossible
to reconcile with the fact that the former cluster consistently with Eliza's
early letters to Lucy. And any suggestion that Eliza's early letters to Lucy
should be distinct from her later despairing letters to her is impossible to
reconcile with the fact that the former consistently cluster with Boyer's letters to Selby, and the latter almost as consistently cluster with Lucy's letters
to Eliza. Foster has simply not created distinct voices for her characters in
The Coquette.

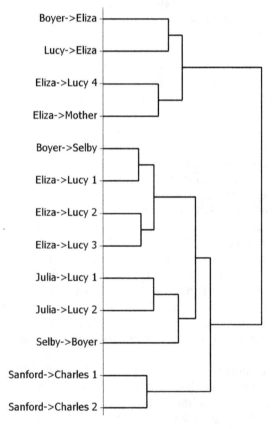

Figure 4.6   *The Coquette*: One hundred MFW, standard method, with pronouns

4.9   A CONTRAST: EPISTOLARY STYLE IN *EVELINA*

A brief comparison with the letters of Fanny Burney's *Evelina* should help
to clarify the situation. *Evelina* has only four writers with parts long enough
for reasonable analysis, but there are interesting complications: Evelina
writes to both her adoptive father Reverend Villars and to her friend Miss
Mirvan, and Reverend Villars writes to both Evelina and Lady Howard. In
both cases, it would not be surprising if there were significant differences in
style between the letters to the two addressees. Furthermore, Evelina herself
might be expected to show some style variation between her letters describing her innocent but awkward coming-out and those that describe Lord
Orville's proposal and Sir John Belmont's acknowledgment of her as his
daughter. Mr. Macartney's letter to Evelina and Lady Howard's to Reverend
Villars are both about twenty-five hundred words long, and the sections

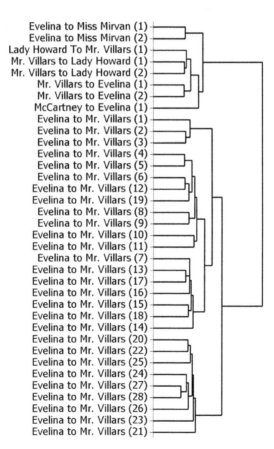

Figure 4.7   Epistolary voices in *Evelina*: 990 MFW, standard method, with pronouns, not culled

of Evelina's letters to Miss Mirvan, Reverend Villars to Evelina, and Reverend Villars to Lady Howard can each be divided into two sections of about twenty-four to twenty-seven hundred words. I have therefore divided Evelina's letters to Reverend Villars into sections of about twenty-four hundred words (twenty-eight of them). Analyses of all thirty-six sections of letters from *Evelina* show that the styles of the characters in *Evelina* are much more distinct than are those of *The Coquette*, in spite of the larger number of shorter sections. As figure 4.7 shows, all of the writer-addressee pairs cluster together. The largest cluster contains all of Evelina's letters to Reverend Villars, and the other contains all of the other letters. Within the smaller cluster, Evelina's letters to Miss Mirvan form a distinct cluster, the letters from Reverend Villars form a single cluster within which the letters to his two addressees separate into distinct clusters, and the single sections of Macartney and Lady Howard form their own separate clusters. As is normal in the most accurate authorship attribution results, the graph strongly reflects the narrative structure of the novel. (Note that these excellent results are based on the simplest method: the standard list, not culled, and with pronouns retained.) It is clear that Fanny Burney, like Wilkie Collins, is much more successful in creating distinctive voices for her characters than is Foster.

4.10   CONCLUSION

Criticism of Foster's novel has paid very little attention to the styles of the different voices of the characters, and the following comment about *The Coquette* and four other early sentimental novels seems apposite: "Clearly, many critics have turned away from examining the surface structure of these novels and are delving into the subtexts instead. The contemporary women's movement, rediscovery of women writers, and the practice of reading against the grain all contributed to the uncovering of the sophisticated subtexts in these novels" (White 1995, 296). What commentary there is about the characters in the novel, however, does not suggest that the patterns shown above should have been predictable.[9] Praise for Foster's relatively complex characterization and her handling of the epistolary form (Petter 1971, 259–63; Wenska 1977, 243–44) suggests that the voices of the characters should be distinct, though "Mrs. Foster showed discretion . . . in the use of stylistic embellishments; if the result was a rather dry manner of writing, it compares favorably with most novels by her contemporaries" (Petter 1971, 263). Finseth suggests that Boyer has a noticeably tepid style that is ill suited to captivate Eliza (2001, 138). Wenska suggests possible similarities between Sanford and Eliza, both of whom think of marriage as a necessary evil, and both of whom "are attractive, strong-willed, willful characters who see in each other the qualities they prize most in themselves" (1977, 249–50).

Carroll Smith-Rosenberg suggests a difference between Eliza's voice and "the feminized Greek chorus of Richman, Freeman, and Eliza's widowed mother, who, at the end, can only mouth hollow platitudes" (2003, 35). Several other critics have endorsed the idea of a chorus or have discussed these characters as a relatively monolithic group that voices "opinions about 'woman's place' as advocated by the dominant culture" (Harris 1995, 9; see also Finseth 2001, Baker 1996, and Mower 2002). Although it has been suggested that Julia is the heroine of the novel (Evans 1995), a comment that might suggest a different voice for her, Julia is usually included in this group. For example, Brown, who omits Eliza's mother from the group, argues that "Mrs. Richman and Lucy and Julia appear most often as annoying exponents of gender and class proprieties rather than as advocates of the rights of individual women" (1997, 643). Several critics also suggest some variation in Eliza's own style over the course of the novel. Petter suggests that there is a change in Eliza's style in the second half of the novel when her affair with Sanford makes her secretive (1971, 263). A similar division is proposed by Baker, who suggests that Eliza uses a false new voice full of maxims after Boyer's rejection of her, but that her aphoristic bent soon wanes (1996, 61–64). This division is at letter thirty, however, roughly at the beginning of Eliza's third (of four) sections. A conflicting suggestion is that Eliza's fall takes place not with her seduction, but at letter forty-eight, after Boyer's second rejection (in Eliza's fourth section) (Mower 2002, 335–38). Perhaps this question should take into account the fact that Foster seems to compress the events of the last thirteen years of Eliza Whitman's life (the real woman upon whom the novel is based) into a much shorter (though unspecified) time in the novel (Bontatibus 2000, 188–90). This compression is most startlingly revealed when we read the inscription on Eliza's tombstone and realize that this "coquette" is thirty-seven when she dies.

The critical views just discussed, it must be reemphasized, are not suggestions about stylistic characteristics of the voices of the various characters, so that my findings do not specifically contradict them. On the other hand, critical intuitions have clearly not been very congruent with the patterns revealed by computational analysis. Given the consistency of some of those patterns, it might be fruitful to reexamine the notion of a univocal "chorus" of Republican voices and the related issue of how and why Julia's voice is so distinct, especially from Lucy's, and whether this difference is related to more significant differences of opinion, character, or principle. The similarity of Boyer's letters to Eliza and her letters to Lucy, a possible connection between Eliza and Sanford, especially near the end of the novel, and the position and nature of the change in Eliza's style might also repay a closer investigation based on the language of the letters. Given that Foster's novel is of interest chiefly on cultural, historical, and political grounds rather than literary ones, however, such further investigation would be more likely to advance the theory and practice of computational stylistics than the criticism of *The Coquette*. It is clear, at any rate, that the techniques of computational stylistics are adequate to the task of distinguishing the voices of the letter writers of epistolary novels, if the authors are adequate to that same difficult task.

NOTES

1. For an excellent and authoritative overview of the field of authorship attribution, both traditional and computational, see Love 2002.
2. The following is a small varied sample of articles featuring Delta, which has become one of the most widely used authorship attribution methods: Burrows 2012; Rybicki and Eder 2011; Rybicki and Heydel 2013; Eder 2013; Hoover 2004a, 2004b, 2009a, 2012; Jockers, Witten, and Criddle 2008; van Dalen-Oskam 2012; van Dalen-Oskam and Joris van Zundert 2007.
3. That is, 4.916 percent of the tokens in all of the primary samples combined are occurrences of *the*. A "token" is an occurrence of an individual word form, or "type"; in all of the analyses below, each unique spelling is single type. For example, in "to be, or not to be" there are just four types (*to, be, or, not*) but six tokens (*to*: 2, *be*: 2, *or*: 1, *not*: 1), and both *to* and *be* have frequencies of 33.33 percent in this tiny sample.
4. The standard deviation measures how much the frequency of the word varies around the average; because the difference is divided by the standard deviation, the z-score assures that a large difference counts more if the word does not vary much and less if it varies a great deal. For *the*, with an average frequency of 4.916 percent, the standard deviation is 0.684, about one-seventh of the average frequency. For *miss*, with an average frequency of 0.106 percent, the standard deviation is 0.101, very close to the average frequency. Because the frequencies of *miss* generally vary much more than do those of *the*, a very high or very low frequency of *the* is thus more likely to indicate a strong individual difference in style, and this is captured by the use of the z-score.
5. Recently, Argamon (2008) has shown that Delta can be calculated as a nearest neighbor measure without using the mean frequency in the corpus. This refinement simplifies the calculation of Delta without affecting the results.
6. Removing personal pronouns nearly always improves the results of analyses based on the one hundred to three hundred MFW (there are too few pronouns to influence analyses based on larger numbers of words). Culling the word list by removing any words that are frequent overall because of very high frequencies in one or two texts also regularly improves the results quite markedly (see Hoover 2002 and 2003b for discussion). As Burrows has pointed out, this automated method seems preferable to manual culling, which may unintentionally bias the results (2006, 20; 2005, 443)
7. The dialogue of the eleven characters with at least one thousand words of dialogue in *The Moonstone* is not so distinct as the narrative. The variation in length of parts is greater than for the narrative, though the average length of sections of dialogue remains approximately three thousand words. Only the sections of dialogue by Bruff, Clack, Godfrey, Jennings, Lady Verinder, Penelope, and Rachel separate perfectly from other characters, and only three of these (Bruff, Jennings, and Rachel) involve more than a single section of dialogue. The remaining four characters cluster partially. The two sections of Betteredge's dialogue taken from his own and Blake's narratives cluster together, but the much shorter section taken from Jennings's narrative forms a separate cluster with Jennings's two sections as nearest neighbor. The second

and third of Blake's sections of dialogue cluster together, but his first section clusters with Murthwaite's dialogue. The first three sections of Cuff's dialogue cluster together, but his much shorter final section forms its own cluster. Further investigation would be required to show whether the narrative contexts of the sections of dialogue that fail to cluster correctly by speaker account for those failures.

8. The primary samples for the Delta and DeltaLz analyses consist of the first sections of the letters by Julia to Lucy and Sanford to Charles, the average of the frequencies of the first and third section of letters from Eliza to Lucy, and the single sections of letters by Boyer to Eliza and Selby to Boyer. The secondary samples are the remaining two sections by Eliza to Lucy, and one section each by Eliza to her mother, Boyer to Selby, Julia to Lucy, Lucy to Eliza, and Sanford to Charles. The nature and complexity of this problem will unfortunately make it impossible for other researchers to duplicate my analysis precisely, but the amount of detail that would be necessary to allow duplication seems excessive in the present context.

9. As is my usual practice, I postponed reading criticism of *The Coquette* until after I had completed my analysis to avoid any chance of unconsciously working toward what I thought should be true.

5   A Conversation Among Himselves
Change and the Styles of Henry James

David L. Hoover

Fanny herself limited indeed, she minimised, her office; you didn't need a jailor, she contended, for a domesticated lamb tied up with pink ribbon. This wasn't an animal to be controlled—it was an animal to be, at the most, educated. . . . This left, goodness knew, plenty of different calls for Maggie to meet—in a case in which so much pink ribbon, as it might be symbolically named, was lavished on the creature. What it all amounted to at any rate was that Mrs. Assingham would be keeping him quiet now, while his wife and his father-in-law carried out their own little frugal picnic; quite moreover, doubtless, not much less neededly in respect to the members of the circle that were with them there than in respect to the pair they were missing almost for the first time.

The Golden Bowl (1904)

5.1   INTRODUCTION

Stylistic studies typically focus on authors whose texts are marked by a distinctive style and characterize that style by describing its peculiarities, often by contrasting it with the style of one or more other authors. Even if no explicit contrast is offered, any characterization of an author's style implies some kind of contrast. The most neutral comparison is perhaps with the norms of the language in which the text is written, but an author's style might more appropriately be compared with other texts of the same genre and historical period and written by authors of broadly similar cultural backgrounds. Sometimes texts of the same genre and written by the same author display quite diverse styles, so that the style of one or more individual texts rather than the overall style of the author may also be an appropriate focus. In this case, the style of one or more of an author's texts may be contrasted with other works by the same author rather than with those of other authors. As we saw in chapter 4, the diverse voices of multiple narrators and multiple letter writers within a single work can also be contrasted.

Stylistic diversity among an author's works can arise in many ways and for many reasons, but here I will focus on the well-known change in the style of Henry James during the course of his long literary career (see Hoover 2007 for another approach to chronological changes in James's style). James's first novel, *Watch and Ward*, was published in 1871, and his last complete novel, *The Outcry*, in 1911. It would be surprising if any author's style showed no change over such a long period of time, but for James the change has long been considered an extreme one. Writing in 1921, just five years after James's death, Carl Van Doren alludes to the change in a way that has become a commonplace:

> Criticism must take account of the vast gulf across which those who like Henry James view with contempt those who do not, and in return those who do not like him view with incredulity those who do. Casual gossip says that his style by its obscurity has fixed the gulf there. While this indubitably operates with regard to certain of his later works, it can have nothing to do with *The American*, or *The Europeans*, or *Daisy Miller*, or *Washington Square*, or *The Portrait of a Lady*, which are all as pellucid as a clean spring. And even in the elaborate, maturer books the style is obscure only in the sense that it speaks of matters less blunt and tangible than those which most fiction deals with (18).

In his 1949 introduction to *The American*, Joseph Warren Beach adds a minor amplification in commenting that James's "characteristic features of style, technique, and content are all present, at least in embryo, in the early stories . . . ; but in the later work they appear in greatly intensified form, and critics divide his work into distinct periods, with the 1890's constituting a transitional stage" (1963, x).

A great deal of work has been done on James's style, and on his revisions of his early novels for his definitive, twenty-four volume collected edition, normally referred to as the New York Edition (1907–09). Many stylistic analyses naturally concentrate on the syntax, which is the locus of the obscure and elaborate nature of the later style that Van Doren mentions. R. W. Short remarks that James's "distortions" often "obliterate the normal elements of connection and cohesion. When he has undone the usual ties, his meanings float untethered, grammatically speaking, like particles in colloidal suspension" (1946, 73–74). Watt (1964) also memorably discusses syntax in his explication of the first paragraph of *The Ambassadors*. Ohmann (1970, 274–75) and Leech and Short (2007, 80–83) also focus on the syntax, as I have noted in my own discussion of the opening paragraph of the novel and some altered versions of it (2004c). Among the frequently mentioned nonsyntactic alterations that James made in his early novels for the New York Edition are a more explicit and precise lexis, an increased use of figures of speech, more varied and elaborated speech markers, an increased use of contractions and colloquialisms, and an increase in adverbial modifiers.

Many of these also characterize the later novels in comparison with the earlier ones. Although I will discuss these characteristics, I want to begin with an examination of James's novels using methods of authorship attribution and computational stylistics—an examination that will investigate both the distinctiveness of James's style and the traditional division of the novels into early and later styles as they are reflected in the frequencies of words.

5.2   DISTINGUISHING JAMES FROM OTHER AUTHORS

As I have pointed out above, the tools of computational stylistics cannot be used to investigate stylistic diversity within the works of a single author unless they can distinguish effectively between that author and other roughly contemporary authors. Only if a technique can reliably distinguish James from other authors can it be used to characterize his substyles minutely enough to distinguish early and late James. My examination of the chronological change in James's style begins with a corpus of 106 American novels by twenty-six authors—all 22 of James's novels and 84 others by James's contemporaries. As with the Victorian novel corpus used in chapter 4, the novels were downloaded from online collections and similarly edited to remove extraneous material.

5.2.1   Distinguishing James from Other Authors: Delta

Delta's effectiveness on the Victorian corpus might seem to make further testing superfluous, but it is a frustrating fact about computational stylistics that different techniques vary in effectiveness on different corpora (see Eder and Rybicki 2013 for a recent study). In light of this, it seems worthwhile to confirm Delta's accuracy in distinguishing James from his contemporaries before applying it to style variation within James's novels. The Delta tests begin with a set of twenty primary authorial samples. Eight of these consist of single novels, ten consist of two novels, one consists of three novels, one (James's) consists of four novels. For samples consisting of multiple novels, I have averaged the word frequencies for the novels. The test set includes seventy-one novels by twenty authors, sixty-five of these are by twelve of the primary set authors and six are by other authors. Including primary authors without any test texts and test texts that are not by any of the primary authors will show whether Delta can match test texts to the correct primary authors without strongly attributing test texts to incorrect primary authors.

Primary Samples

Barr, Robert	*A Rock in the Baltic* + *The Face and the Mask*
Bellamy, Edward	*Looking Backward*

Cable, George W.	*John March, Southerner*
Cather, Willa	*My Antonia + Death Comes for the Archbishop*
Chopin, Kate	*The Awakening*
Davis, Rebecca H.	*Frances Waldeaux*
Dreiser, Theodore	*Jennie Gerhardt + The Titan*
Eggleston, Edward	*The Hoosier Schoolmaster*
Frederic, Harold	*The Damnation of Theron Ware*
Glasgow, Ellen	*The Deliverance + Virginia*
Howells, William D.	*A Foregone Conclusion + A Modern Instance + The Kentons*
James, Henry	*Roderick Hudson + The Bostonians + The Spoils of Poynton + The Golden Bowl*
Jewett, Sarah Orne	*A Country Doctor + The Country of the Pointed Firs*
Lewis, Sinclair	*Main Street + Arrowsmith*
London, Jack	*Burning Daylight + Martin Eden*
Phillips, David G.	*The Deluge + The Conflict*
Rinehart, Mary R.	*The Circular Staircase*
Stratton-Porter, Gene	*Freckles*
Twain, Mark	*The Adventures of Huckleberry Finn + The Tragedy of Pudd'nhead Wilson*
Wharton, Edith	*The House of Mirth + The Age of Innocence*

Test Texts

Barr, Robert	*A Woman Intervenes; In The Midst of Alarms*
Cather, Willa	*O Pioneers!; The Song of the Lark; One of Ours; A Lost Lady; The Professor's House; Shadows on the Rock; Lucy Gayheart; Sapphira and the Slave Girl*
Chesnutt, Charles	*The House Behind the Cedars*
Crane, Stephen	*The Red Badge of Courage*
Dixon, Thomas	*The Clansman*
Dreiser, Theodore	*Sister Carrie; The Financier*
Fitzgerald, F. Scott	*The Great Gatsby*
Glasgow, Ellen	*The Voice of the People; The Battle-Ground; The Wheel of Life; Life and Gabriella; One Man in His Time*
Howells, William D.	*Their Wedding Journey; A Chance Acquaintance; The Lady of Aroostook; The Rise of Silas Lapham; A Hazard of New*

	Fortunes; Through the Eye of the Needle; The Leatherwood God
James, Henry	*Watch and Ward; The American; The Europeans; Confidence; The Portrait of a Lady; Washington Square; The Princess Casamassima; The Reverberator; The Tragic Muse; The Other House; What Maisie Knew; The Awkward Age; The Sacred Fount; The Wings of the Dove; The Ambassadors; The Outcry; The Ivory Tower; The Sense of the Past*
Jewett, Sarah Orne	*Deephaven; A Marsh Island; The Tory Lover*
Lewis, Sinclair	*Our Mr. Wrenn; Babbitt; Elmer Gantry*
London, Jack	*The Sea Wolf; White Fang; Adventure; The Valley of the Moon; The Star Rover*
Norris, Frank	*McTeague*
Phillips, David G.	*The Cost; The Fashionable Adventures of Joshua Craig; The Grain of Dust; The Price She Paid; Susan Lenox*
Sinclair, Upton	*The Jungle*
Twain, Mark	*The Adventures of Tom Sawyer; The American Claimant; The Prince and the Pauper*
Wharton, Edith	*The Valley of Decision; The Reef; Summer; The Glimpses of the Moon*

The results of forty analyses based on the 100, 200, 300, . . . 4,000 MFW (no personal pronouns, culled at 70 percent) show that DeltaLz is very effective for this group of texts. The 100 and 200 MFW do a creditable job, attributing sixty of the sixty-five secondary texts by primary authors to their correct authors (about 92 percent accuracy). In the analyses based on the 300 to 1,200 and the 1,400 and 1,500 MFW, sixty-two or sixty-three of the secondary texts are correctly attributed to their authors (95 to 97 percent accuracy). Most of the other analyses correctly attribute sixty-four of the secondary texts (98 percent accuracy), but eleven analyses based on the 2,000–2,700, 2,900, 3,100, and 3,200 MFW correctly attribute all sixty-five texts. Of the forty-four incorrect attributions in analyses with at least sixty-two correct attributions, seventeen are for Howells's *Their Wedding Journey*, ten are for his *The Leatherwood God*, and six for his *Through the Eye of the Needle*. The first two of these are his first novel and the last novel published in his lifetime, respectively; the other eleven errors are for Twain's *The Prince and the Pauper*.[1] A few of the correct attributions are no stronger than the attributions of texts with authors who are not in the primary set, as figure 5.1 shows, but none of the texts by other authors is strongly attributed to a primary author (I have retained all the James novels for this graph, but have removed some of the strong correct attributions for other

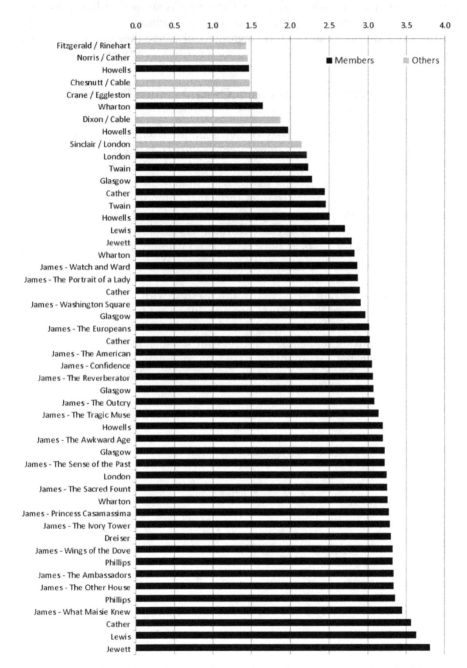

Figure 5.1 DeltaLz: forty-four members and six others: Thirty-two hundred MFW, no personal pronouns, culled at 70 percent

authors to make it more readable).[2] These results show that Delta does an excellent job of attributing these texts to their authors. Its effectiveness in attributing James's novels to him, regardless of where they fall in his career, confirms that it is an appropriate tool for a further investigation of his style.

5.2.2   Distinguishing James from Other Authors: Principal Components Analysis

Principal Components Analysis (PCA) is another widely used method of authorship attribution and computational stylistics. It is a statistical method for simplifying the description of a set of related variables. In authorship and stylistic studies, it groups words with similar distributions in a group of texts together into new variables (principal components), each of which accounts for a much larger proportion of the differences among the texts than do the frequencies of any one word. It has the advantage of being able to analyze all of the texts at once because no primary samples are needed. PCA results are usually presented as scatter graphs in which the distances between items reflect their how different they are.[3]

Minitab, my current software, is able to deal with about one thousand words at a time, and PCA graphs are difficult to read when large numbers of texts are compared. Even so, the twelve authors represented by multiple texts show a strong tendency to form groups, and James's texts are nicely separate. When the task is made easier by including only Cather, James, Lewis, London, and Wharton, PCA does a very good job of grouping the

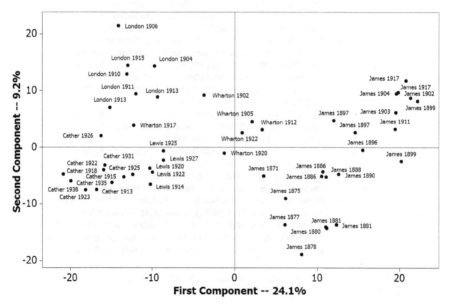

Figure 5.2   Five authors, fifty novels: Eight hundred MFW, no personal pronouns, culled at 70 percent

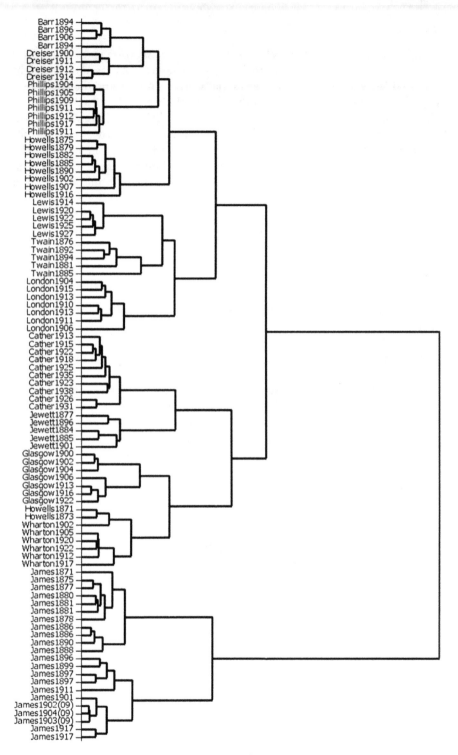

Figure 5.3 Twelve authors, ninety-two novels: 990 MFW, no personal pronouns, culled at 70 percent

texts by each author: Edith Wharton's 1917 novel *Summer* is the only novel that clearly falls outside its author's cluster, as figure 5.2 (based on the eight hundred MFW) shows. It also shows that Cather's novels and the late novels of James are the most different in their use of these eight hundred words and Cather's novels and Lewis's novels are the least different. James's texts also appear in roughly chronological order, with early texts lower and farther to the left, and later texts higher and farther to the right. The fact that the texts of London and Wharton also show a strong tendency to appear in composition order suggests that, for these authors, PCA should be useful in tracing the changes in their styles over time. Note that London's and Wharton's earlier texts tend to appear toward the top of the graph rather than the bottom, as James's did, which shows that these trends are not simply part of any general linguistic drift over time.

5.2.3   Distinguishing James from Other Authors: Cluster Analysis

Cluster analysis of all 106 novels is quite accurate, with errors only for Glasgow, Howells, and Wharton, in spite of the large number of texts and authors. James's novels form one of the two main clusters, reflecting his distinctive style. The cluster analysis of the ninety-two novels by the twelve authors with multiple test texts shown in figure 5.3 groups the texts very accurately, failing only for two of Howells's texts (97.8 percent accuracy). I have included the publication dates for the texts, so that it is easy to see that the early and late novels of Howells, Glasgow, Phillips, and James tend to group separately within each author's cluster. James's novels form four groups by date: 1871–81, 1886–90, 1896–99, and 1901–17, except for the anomalous 1911 *The Outcry* (a novelization of a 1909 play). This remarkable pattern suggests that cluster analysis, like Delta and PCA, should prove very useful in investigating style changes over time.

5.3   JAMES'S NOVELS: EARLY, INTERMEDIATE, AND LATE

These three proven techniques can now be applied to James's twenty-two major novels, including two incomplete novels that were posthumously published. The e-texts of three of the late novels represent the revised forms in which they appear in the New York Edition. All the other e-texts represent the original forms of the novels, including the seven major novels that James did not include in the New York Edition. *The American* and *The Portrait of a Lady*, two of the most heavily revised of the early works (McWhirter 1995, 7), along with *The Reverberator* (1888) and *What Maisie Knew* (1897) will be analyzed in both their early and their New York Edition versions, so that the effects of James's extensive revisions can be examined briefly.[4] On the basis of relatively large gaps in original publication dates, the novels divide reasonably into three groups—the editions and lengths are as indicated; novels published before 1910, but not included in the New York Edition (1907–09), are marked with asterisks, and years in brackets indicate New York Edition versions:[5]

Early novels (1871–81):

Watch and Ward 1871*	64,000 words
Roderick Hudson 1875	131,000 words
The American 1877	134,000 words
The Europeans 1878*	59,000 words
Confidence 1880*	76,000 words
Washington Square 1881*	64,000 words
The Portrait of a Lady 1881	226,000 words

Intermediate novels (1886–90):

The Bostonians 1886*	163,000 words
The Princess Casamassima 1886	209,000 words
The Reverberator 1888	53,000 words
The Tragic Muse 1890	206,000 words

Late novels (1896–1917):

The Other House 1896*	71,000 words
The Spoils of Poynton 1897	71,000 words
What Maisie Knew 1897	96,000 words
The Awkward Age 1899	131,000 words
The Sacred Fount 1901*	77,000 words
The Wings of the Dove 1902 [1909]	188,000 words
The Ambassadors 1903 [1909]	157,000 words
The Golden Bowl 1904 [1909]	207,000 words
The Outcry 1911	56,000 words
The Ivory Tower 1917	64,000 words
The Sense of the Past 1917	72,000 words

Novels before 1900 in NYE versions:

The American 1877 [1907]	143,000 words
The Portrait of a Lady 1881 [1908]	225,000 words
The Reverberator 1888 [1908]	55,000 words
What Maisie Knew 1897 [1908]	96,000 words

This division, though somewhat artificial, agrees fairly well with critical opinion: for example, Richard Poirier ends his *The Comic Sense of Henry James: A Study of the Early Novels* with *Washington Square* and

The Portrait of a Lady (both published in 1881), and, as noted above, *The Portrait of a Lady* is also the last mentioned by Carl Van Doren as preceding the obscurity of James's later works. Joseph Warren Beach's division into early and late with a transitional stage in the 1890s is somewhat different, and it does not map very well onto publication dates, given the short gap between *The Reverberator* in 1888 and *The Tragic Muse* in 1890 and the relatively long gap between the latter and *The Other House* in 1896. Dorothea Krook-Gilead suggests a slightly different division, with *The Awkward Age* (1899) as "the inaugural work of Henry James's late period" (1962, 135), and Burrows suggests a division much like the one above when he notes that, in contrast to *Washington Square* or *The Europeans*, "the James of the late 1890s had begun to play a different game" (1987, 159). In spite of some variation in critical opinion, then, there is reasonably solid consensus about which are the early and late novels.

5.3.1   Delta and James's Early, Intermediate, and Late Novels

To test these novels with Delta, I have used *Roderick Hudson*, *The Bostonians*, and *The Ambassadors* as representatives of the early, intermediate, and late styles. Given the lengths of the early novels and the fact that I want to examine both the early and the New York Edition versions of *The American* and *The Portrait of a Lady*, *Roderick Hudson* is the only reasonable choice for the primary early sample. I selected *The Bostonians* as the primary intermediate sample because it is closest in length to *Roderick Hudson*. It would seem odd to choose any late novel other than *The Ambassadors*, *The Wings of the Dove*, or *The Golden Bowl* as the primary late sample, given their centrality in the James canon, and length again pointed toward *The Ambassadors*. The other twenty-three novels, including both early and New York Edition versions of *The American*, *The Portrait of a Lady*, *The Reverberator*, and *What Maisie Knew*, comprise the test texts. Although, as I have suggested above, using a single novel as a primary sample is not ideal, it seems best to test the method on as many novels as possible rather than to combine novels to create primary early, intermediate, and late samples.

DeltaLz performs extremely well in forty analyses based on the 100, 200, 300, . . . 4,000 MFW (personal pronouns removed, culled at 70 percent), producing completely correct results for the nineteen unambiguously early, intermediate, and late novels in all analyses except the one based on the 100 MFW, in which the intermediate novel *The Tragic Muse* is classified as early. All but four of the analyses classify the four New York Edition versions according to their original publication date. The four "errors," based on the 2,300, 3,800, 3,900, and 4,000 MFW, identify the heavily revised New York Edition version of *The Portrait of a Lady* as intermediate (note also that this novel is the last of the early novels). These results demonstrate that, whatever other differences exist between early and late Henry James, these broad and widely accepted critical categories are compellingly correlated with the frequencies of the most frequent words of the novels.

5.3.2   PCA and Cluster Analysis and James's Early, Intermediate, and Late Novels

PCA and cluster analysis also give excellent results. PCA analyses like the one in figure 5.4, based on the 990 MFW with no personal pronouns and culled at 70 percent, is similar to those based on smaller numbers of words, and it clearly shows a remarkable trajectory in the development of James's style. Not only do the novels clearly form into the three periods identified above, there is even a tendency for them to appear in publication order within their groups. Furthermore, the New York Edition versions of the early novels move toward the later novels, though without leaving the early group, showing that James's extensive revisions made them significantly more similar to the later novels with respect to word frequencies, but without fully masking their dates of composition. The only anomaly is the position of James's final completed novel, *The Outcry* (1911), a novelization of a 1909 play. These results confirm Burrows's earlier work on the original and New York Edition version of *The American*, in which he briefly (but nicely) discusses James's remarkable ability to vary his style (1992b; he does not investigate the developmental of James's style throughout his career).

Finally, a cluster analysis, again based on the 990 MFW with no personal pronouns and culled at 70 percent, also produces quite striking results, shown in figure 5.5. Note the very fine-grained grouping of the novels by

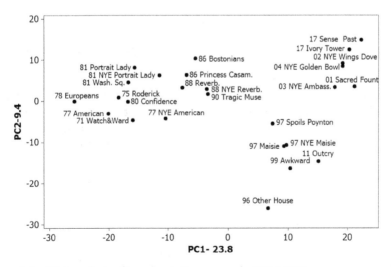

Figure 5.4   PCA analysis of twenty-six James novels: 990 MFW, no pronouns, culled at 70 percent

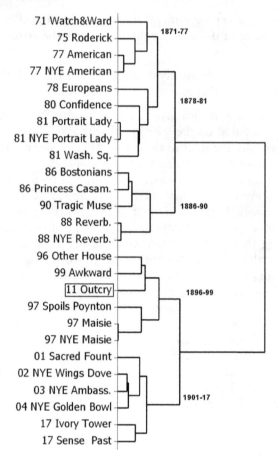

Figure 5.5   Twenty-Six James novels: 990 MFW, no pronouns, culled at 70 percent

date, with *The Outcry* again the only novel that is not correctly grouped. Many years of experience analyzing novels suggests that other authors' novels almost never fall into such neat chronological patterns: the novels of Henry James are characterized by an extraordinary unidirectional development over time.

5.4   CHARACTERIZING JAMES'S STYLES: THE DISTINCTIVENESS RATIO

Discovering and documenting the chronological development of James's style, however, does not go very far toward characterizing it, so it is time to look more closely at James's changes in word use over time. The increasingly long word lists that I and other researchers have been using lately have the unfortunate effect that the sheer number of words involved in the analysis pushes the researcher farther and farther from contact with individual words and from meaningful statements about the author's style. One of the beauties of Burrows's early work is the way he maps a PCA graph of texts onto the words that produce the grouping of the texts so that it is easy to refocus on the texts themselves by concentrating attention on words that are especially frequent or rare in the various texts (for example, Burrows 1992a, 175–82, 188–93). With nearly one thousand words involved in each PCA and cluster analysis, and as many as four thousand involved in a Delta analysis, the glut of information makes this kind of concentration impossible. To limit the sheer volume of information and assure that attention is focused on the words that best characterize James's style, we can concentrate on words with very different frequencies in the early, intermediate, and late novels, using the distinctiveness ratio (DR). This very simple but effective measure of variability, invented by Ellegård, is defined as the rate of occurrence of a word in one text divided by its rate of occurrence in another text, and only those words with a DR of 1.5 or more or of 0.67 or less are considered good discriminators (Kenny 1982, 69–70). The distinctiveness ratio was designed to compare just two texts, but a modified version can be used to identify those words with the widest range of frequency among the three periods of James's style.

The DR is a very simple measure of difference, but identifying the most distinctively used words in the three periods requires a good deal of care. First, I created samples of exactly equal length for each of the three periods. With unequal samples, the smallest sample will always produce the highest frequency for any words that occur the same number of times. Because James wrote only four novels during his intermediate period, I augmented this period with three novellas: *The Aspern Papers* (39,000 words), *A London Life* (44,000 words), and *The Modern Warning* (26,000 words). To make an almost equal early sample I dropped *Watch and Ward*, James's first novel, and replaced it with two novellas, *Daisy Miller* (21,000 words) and *An International Episode* (27,000 words). For the late sample, I used *The Awkward Age*, *The Wings of the Dove*, *The Ambassadors*, and *The Golden Bowl*, and filled out the sample with two novellas, *Covering End* (35,000 words) and *The Birthplace* (22,000 words).[6] These combined samples for each period were within 400 words of the same length, so I simply removed enough words from the ends of the longest intermediate and the longest late novel to make all the samples exactly the same length, 739,308 words.

To compare the vocabularies of the three periods, I created a word frequency list of all three samples combined (about thirty-one thousand different words). In previous work with James's novels I had noticed a substantial amount of spelling variation (mainly British versus American spellings), so I sorted this list alphabetically, read through it, and regularized the spellings by combining the frequencies for words like *colour/color*, *criticise/criticize*, *enquired/inquired*, *unmistakable/unmistakeable*, *traveled/travelled*, *goodbye/good-by/goodbye*, and so forth.

With three stylistic periods, the frequency of any given word can be different in all three periods, it can be the same in any two periods and different in the other, and it can be the same in all three periods (using samples of exactly the same length is clearly crucial). When the frequency of a word is different in each period, there are six possible patterns: HML, HLM, MHL, LHM, MLH, LMH ("H" = high, "M" = mid, "L" = low). When the frequency of the word is the same in two of the periods, there are six more possible patterns; any of the three periods can have the different frequency, and the two that are the same can be either higher or lower: HHL, LLH, HLL, LHH, HLH, LHL. Finally, all the frequencies can be the same: HHH (this is equivalent to LLL). Intuitively, it seems that the patterns with two or three identical frequencies should be rare, and those with three identical frequencies are indeed the least frequent. But those with two identical frequencies are the most frequent of all because of the very large numbers of words with low frequencies. That is, about one-third of the 31,000 total word types occur just once in the entire corpus, so that more than ten thousand of the patterns must be either LLH, HLL, or LHL (with frequencies of 001, 100, or 010). In my examination of chronological changes in James's style, I am interested only in words that show substantial change in frequency across the periods, however, so I first retained only the 16,262 words with a frequency of at least three (the minimum frequency that allows for different frequencies in all three periods), then culled the list at 70 percent, yielding 14,123 words for analysis. Finally, I removed some additional character names and a few designations like *ladyship*, which function almost like names, leaving 14,100 words, with the following frequencies in the thirteen possible patterns (the percentage of the 14,100 types with each pattern appears in parentheses):

HML	2,434
HLM	1,135
MHL	2,109
LHM	1,473
MLH	1,152
LMH	2,058
HHH	293
HHL	560
LLH	682
HLL	796
LHH	390
HLH	307
LHL	711

Obviously, removing words that occur only once or twice in the corpus has made words with different frequencies in all three periods much more frequent than those with the same frequencies in two or all three periods.[7]

One surprising fact about the patterns with three different frequencies is that three are substantially overrepresented (HML, MHL, LMH). Two of these are progressive decrease and progressive increase in frequency; in the other, the intermediate period is highest, with the early period next, and the late period lowest. The last of these is not easy to interpret, but the other two show that James had a strong tendency to progressively adopt and progressively abandon words over his long career. Surely this largely explains why it is so easy to divide his novels into three periods on the basis of word frequencies.

I entered the frequencies of the remaining 14,100 words in the early, intermediate, and late samples into an Excel spreadsheet that calculates two versions of the DR: one for the highest frequency divided by the lowest frequency, and the other for the highest divided by the second highest.[8] Because this modified calculation always divides lower into higher frequencies, the minimum possible DR is one. The spreadsheet also calculates the total DR (the sum of the two). Sorting the word list on either the Max/Min DR or the total DR gives a very interesting group of words with widely different frequencies in the three periods.

5.4.1   Function Words

Function words seem relatively uninteresting in their own right, and have been variously defined, but they clearly affect and help to create James's style, and many critics have noticed in his late style a high frequency of pronouns, especially personal pronouns; (expletive) *it*, and expletive *there* (Lee 1968, 243–44, Chatman 1972, 55–57, 72); prepositional phrases (Gettmann 1945, 281); cleft sentences and phrasal verbs (Chatman 1972, 65, 107); and adverbs, the most common of which are sometimes treated as noise words (Gettmann 1945, 281, Chatman 1972, 50). I can only glance briefly at these words here, but, like all of the groups of words to be discussed, function words would richly repay a full individual study.[9]

Many function word forms fall into multiple categories, so that a fully lemmatized corpus would be required for any precise statements about them, but an examination of 208 function words of all kinds shows that a progressive increase in frequency over the course of James's career—rather than a progressive decrease, consistency, or mere fluctuation—is the order of the day for function words in general. If the high, intermediate, and low frequencies were randomly distributed, each of the six patterns with three different frequencies should be found in about 17 percent (thirty-five) of the words. Instead, ninety-two words (about 44 percent) increase progressively from the early to the late novels, showing an LMH pattern, and thirty-one (15 percent) decrease progressively, showing a HML pattern (the other patterns are even more underrepresented, ranging from 5 to 12 percent). Given that many of these words are among the most frequent words in the entire corpus, the effect of very substantial increases in their frequency in the late novels is disproportionately great, so that it is not surprising that the very high frequency of function words in the late novels has been noticed by critics. Just seventeen of the progressively decreasing function words are among the one hundred MFW of the corpus, compared to twenty-seven of the progressively increasing ones. A few classes of function words deserve a brief individual mention.

Though critics have suggested that a high frequency of personal pronouns is characteristic of James's later style, my corpus does not confirm this. As a whole, the twenty-eight personal pronouns actually progressively decrease in frequency from 98,238 in early James, to 89,659 in intermediate James, to 88,468 in late James. The progressive increase in *him, them, their, herself, our, us,* and *themselves* is overwhelmed by the progressive decrease in *I, you, me, my,* and *yours,* mainly because of very large decreases in *I* and *you.* This issue is too complex to be investigated further here, as it involves narrative point of view, authorial commentary, and the ratio of dialogue to narration.

Many critics have noted a large increase in the frequency of contractions in James's later novels (for example, Gettmann 1945, 282, Krause 1958, 85–86). This is part of a tendency toward a more colloquial style. Of the sixty contractions among the 14,100 words above, all but six of which have a DR higher than 1.5, forty-two increase progressively from the early to the late novels. Only two (*don't* and *let's*) decrease progressively from the early to the late novels, and *can't, here's,* and *needn't* are more frequent in the early novels than in the late novels (*let's* and a few other contractions are not function words). Thus the presence of large numbers of contractions is a clear indication of a late date of composition for James, and would be a good indicator to examine for authorship attribution and dating purposes. Contractions, however, are not particularly interesting from a stylistic point of view.

About twice as many prepositions progressively increase as progressively decrease in frequency. The progressive decrease of *until, beneath,* and *upon* seem related to the progressive increase of *till, under,* and *on,* in a pattern that seems congruent with the increasing colloquialism of James's style over time. The progressive decrease of both *toward* and *towards* suggest that James sometimes abandoned small families of function words.

As with prepositions, about twice as many of what can conveniently be called common adverbs progressively increase in frequency (for example, *out, only, now, before, how, just, yet, without, really, almost, ever, further*) as progressively decrease (for example, *not, very, no, never, always, away, down, often, apparently, slowly, farther*). There is no obvious pattern, but some individual examples deserve comment. Though *further* is much more frequent than *farther* in all three periods, it completely replaces *farther* in the late texts. The progressive decrease of *no* is undoubtedly related to the very large increase in *nobody* and the decrease of *no one* in the late novels, and the progressive decrease of *not* is undoubtedly related to the progressive increase of contractions. There is also probably a connection between the progressive decrease of *very* and the tripling of the frequency of *quite*, from about four hundred in both early and intermediate texts more than twelve hundred in the late texts. Burrows's comments on the prevalence of *quite* and the scarcity of *very* in *The Awkward Age* could be applied to the later novels in general, especially if *wonderful* is added to the list of "artificial blooms":

> "Very", perhaps, is too shy a plant to flourish in the hothouse of *The Awkward Age*. But "quite", at the stage its degeneration had reached by the end of the last century, is not out of place beside such artificial blooms as the "beautiful" and "splendid" in which some of James's characters rejoice and behind which others of them shelter. (Burrows 1987, 67–69)

5.4.2   Speech Markers

As Royal Gettmann has pointed out, the change from the unremarkable "M. de Bellegarde asked, very softly" in the 1877 version of *The American* to the peculiar "M. de Bellegarde inordinately fluted" in the New York Edition is very noticeable, and amounts to "novelty-hunting" (1945, 282). And this verb is quite memorable, in spite of appearing only three times in the twenty-three novels being discussed here, twice in the New York Edition version of *The American* and once in the New York Edition version of *The Golden Bowl*. The novelty of *flute* as a verb is not as complete as Gettmann suggests, however. Among the novelists in the corpus examined above, Ellen Glasgow (who may have learned it from James) uses *fluted* as a speech marker in *Life and Gabriella* where a woman's laugh also *flutes*; in her other novels "the call of the street" *flutes*, as well as canaries and the whistles of partridges. Another example from *The American* is "she sweetly shrilled" (Gettmann 1945, 282), but it is even rarer, appearing only this once in *The American* and once more in the New York Edition version of *The Reverberator*. In the corpus of novels above, a character also *shrills* once in Edith Wharton's *The Reef*, once in her *The Glimpses of the Moon*, and twice in David Graham Phillips's *Susan Lennox*.)

Rather than multiplying these notable but rare examples, I have collected eighty-three speech markers, including those suggested by Gettmann in *The American*. Unlike contractions or function words, speech markers both progressively increase and progressively decrease more frequently than expected: sixteen progressively decrease and twenty-eight progressively increase, rather than the fourteen of each that would be expected by chance. All of those that progressively decrease and twenty-seven of the twenty-eight that progressively increase have a DR of 1.5 or higher. James's early characters more likely *said, asked, told, answered, cried, declared, began, murmured, observed, rejoined, promised, proposed, begged, urged,*

meditated, or *whispered,* but late characters more likely *took, put, continued, spoke, wondered, returned, showed, laughed, explained, pursued, produced, insisted, sighed, appealed, echoed, breathed, challenged, prompted,
maintained, quavered, winced, argued, conceded, wailed, subjoined, gasped,
contended,* or *asserted.* There is a general trend toward the unusual, the specific, and the colloquial in the later novels, and a decrease in the ordinary,
vague, and neutral words that tend to characterize the earlier novels. These
are not laws, but they are strong tendencies. A corollary is the increase in
multiword speech markers. All of the following are much more frequent
in the late novels: *wound up, brought out, bring out, broke out, went on,
made it out, make it out, bring it out, brought it out, worked it out, work
it out.* Finally, a trend that is not evident in these observations is a general progressive decrease in the frequency of speech markers overall. James
sometimes replaces ordinary speech markers with unusual ones and at other
times simply uses fewer of them.

5.4.3   Nouns

The three hundred nouns with the largest DR show a strong trend toward
progressively decreasing, with 27 percent (eighty-one) progressively decreasing, rather than the expected 17 percent. The DR for these words is very
high: the minimum for the three hundred most variable nouns is fourteen,
so that one of the periods has at least fourteen times as many occurrences as
another. The forty most variable progressively increasing and progressively
decreasing nouns are shown below. There seems to be a trend away from
formal, elevated diction: *physiognomy, portal, affectation,* and *epithet,*
decrease, along with *jocosity, bibelots, visage, imprecation,* and *rancour*
later in the list. Words related to courting and marriage also progressively
decrease: *ardor, matrimony, enchanting, deportment, coquetry,* and *flirta-
tion,* with *kisses* later in the list. Among the progressively increasing nouns,
there is a corresponding trend toward a more casual vocabulary: *doom,
gasp, queerness, flare, make-believe, score, blur, clue, gloss,* and *traps,* with
brim farther down the list. These short lists also clearly show the growing preference for abstract nouns that has often been noticed in James's
later style (Lee 1968, 246–47, Watt 1964, 471, Lodge 1966, 193), although
Chatman seems right in suggesting that "intangible" is a more accurate
designation (1972, 4–8). About half the progressively decreasing nouns are
concrete or tangible, and about three-quarters of the progressively increasing nouns are intangible.

> Progressively decreasing nouns: *grudge, toilet, nephew, ardor, dresses,
> matrimony, enchanting, bonnet, mockery, shrewdness, dwelling, moun-
> tains, foreigners, deportment, dollars, narrative, emotions, affectation,
> plants, peculiarities, metropolis, coquetry, perfume, flirtation, displea-
> sure, painting, physiognomy, expedition, epithet, jaw, meditations,*

spectacles, sarcasm, portal, keenness, candlestick, perplexity, talents, cure, slippers

Progressively increasing nouns: *connexions, doom, alternative, plea, gasp, straightness, detachment, pilgrim, seconds, arrest, nervousness, recognitions, necktie, affinity, queerness, glimmer, abysses, predicament, token, quantities, split, accommodation, flare, repudiation, make-believe, impunity, attenuation, score, glamour, blur, absurdity, initiation, clue, denial, evocation, satiety, austerity, gloss, traps, pomp*

5.4.4 Verbs

Of the three hundred verbs with the largest DR, both progressive increase and progressive decrease are overrepresented, with both patterns accounting for about 26 percent of these verbs, and again the distinctiveness ratios are large, with a minimum of eight for these three hundred words. The forty most variable progressively increasing and progressively decreasing verbs show trends that seem similar to those of the nouns. Among the decreasing verbs are the formal and archaic *strode, bestowed, bade,* and *deemed,* and among the increasing verbs are the more colloquial *echoed, cleared, squared, gasped, slipped, quavered, winced, wailed, wince, snatched, quit, prowling, dodge, blinked,* and *braced,* along with *chuck, humbugging, tackle, dash, fidget,* and *flared* farther down the list (note that some of these are unusual speech markers, which have been mentioned above). Another remarkable difference between the lists of progressively increasing and progressively decreasing verbs is in the behavior of past-tense verbs and verbs in *-ing*: fifty-two past-tense verbs progressively increase while only forty progressively decrease, and only nine *-ing* forms progressively increase while nineteen progressively decrease. I am unable at this point to offer an explanation for this pattern, and it remains to be seen whether they can be related to broader thematic or stylistic characteristics.[10]

Progressively increasing verbs: *echoed, cleared, squared, invoked, gasped, slipped, strained, happening, sufficed, imputed, discriminated, demur, brooded, named, controlled, quavered, winced, wailed, minded, intensified,* wince, *snatched, attenuate, glowed, fed, quit, asserted, prowling, precipitated, consorted, acclaimed, mused, tormented, glimmered, opined, sparing, dodge, blinked, explains, braced*

Progressively decreasing verbs: *scold, apologize, whispered, detest, displeased, insult, telegraphed, detested, ran, recommend, abused, abstained, ride, scratching, inherited, complied, motioned, contemplated, offended, offend, exclaiming,* strode, *aroused, bestowed, conversing, stroked, entreat, scorched, inspected, relating, stooped, laughing, bade, deemed, narrated, cried, fascinated, blushing, despise, cursed*

The presence of pairs like *detest/detested, offend/offended* (decreasing), and *wince/winced* (increasing) in these two short lists suggests that, as we will see in more detail below, James sometimes adopted or abandoned whole families of words during his career. In the three cases just mentioned, the words belong to a single lemma (base form), but the concept of word family is broader than this (see section 5.4.6 for more discussion).

5.4.5   Adjectives

A different pattern emerges for adjectives. The clear tendency for the three hundred adjectives with the greatest variability of frequency among the three styles is to decline in frequency. There are eighty-three progressively decreasing frequencies rather than the fifty that would be expected by chance, while forty-nine progressively increase in frequency, about as expected (the other patterns are significantly underrepresented, except for the MHL pattern, with seventy-seven words). This trend is correlated with an overall decline in the frequency of adjectives from the early to intermediate to late novels.[11] It supports the notion that late in life, James disliked adjectives: as his secretary Theodora Bosanquet quoted him as saying, "Adjectives are the sugar of literature and adverbs the salt" (Chatman 1972, 50). Curiously, there seems to be a reverse trend in James's revisions of early novels for the New York Edition, as Gettmann noticed in the case of *The American* (1945, 281), and a fuller study should lead to a better understanding of James's revisions of his early novels for the New York Edition.

Adjectives, like nouns and verbs, are so frequent that they are difficult to examine, but a simple list of the forty most variable progressively decreasing and increasing examples is instructive (the minimum DR for the three hundred most variable is nine).

Progressively decreasing *tranquil, demonstrative, miserable, desultory, heartless, habitual, joyous, gloomy, imperious, powerful, devilish, tremulous, manly, judicious, indefinable, mossy, puzzling, adjoining, polite, wooden, dishonorable, grassy, diminutive, rural, urbane, noticeable, scanty, defiant, fraternal, scandalous, conjugal, discontented, ornamented, glowing, childish, zealous, shrewd, second-rate, muscular, matrimonial*

Progressively increasing: *funny, sharper, sharpest, ironic, straighter, abject, expert, disconcerting, prompt, wondrous, peopled, workable, blest, specific, conjoined, fuller, recurrent, wan, sequestered, clearer, unmistakeable, congruous, unspoken, uncanny, gregarious, equivocal, clearest, occult, specious, well-nigh, thinkable, seasoned, firmer, stray, incredible, alien, dire, queerer, quicker, woeful*

The trends noted in nouns and verbs continue here, with the progressively increasing adjectives seeming less formal and more casual, and mostly intangible. The progressively decreasing adjectives are more tangible (*manly, mossy, adjoining, wooden, grassy, diminutive, scanty, ornamented, glowing, muscular*), and include another word from the marriage family, *matrimonial*. Also very noticeable is the large number of comparative and superlative adjectives in the progressively increasing list (nine in all) and their complete absence from the progressively decreasing list. Although adjectives drop steadily in frequency from the early to the late novels, as I have noted, superlatives and comparatives are most frequent in the late novels. It seems reasonable to include this trend as one aspect of the search for more precise diction noted by the critics.

5.4.6 Word Families

The presence of both *sharper* and *sharpest*, and both *clearer* and *clearest* in the progressively increasing list of adjectives and the appearance of *sharp* and *clear* a bit farther down, again point to families of words that James increasingly adopted. The *clear* family is one that James uses increasingly throughout his career. The most frequent members of the *clear* family, *clear, clearly, cleared, clearness, clearer, clearest,* and *clearing,* all progressively increase from the early to the late texts, *clearance* appears just once in the early texts and five times in the late texts, and *clearnesses, clearances, clear-browed, clarifying, clarify,* and *clarified* occur just once each in the late texts. The only significant exception to this trend is *clear-cut,* which occurs six times in the early texts and twice in both the mid and late texts. The word *clear-faced* occurs twice in each period, *clearing-up* and *clear-cheeked* occur just once in the mid texts, *clear-coloured* occurs just twice in the early texts, and *clear-voiced* and *clear-eyed* once each in the early texts. The fact that all of the exceptions are hyphenated compounds is part of a larger trend: James uses hyphenated words of all kinds much more frequently in the early than in the mid or late texts.

The progressively increasing *sharp* family can be profitably discussed along with its progressively decreasing synonym, *keen,* as table 5.1 shows. The adjectival forms and the abstract nouns show how strongly *sharp* characterizes late James and *keen* characterizes early James; only *sharply* shows a weak deviation from the pattern. The forms *sharpness* and *sharpened* also basically follow the pattern, leaving a residue of forms that occur only once in individual periods, with *sharply-cut* acting like a hyphenated adjective rather than a form of *sharp*; the hyphenated forms with *keen* conform to both trends.

It is easy to characterize the change in James's style simply by listing a few of the word families that predominate in the early and late periods (all these families contain at least three forms, and nearly all either progressively increase or decrease; the exceptions are almost always very rare words).

Table 5.1   The *sharp* and *keen* word families in early, intermediate, and late James

Sharp Family	Early	Inter.	Late	Keen Family	Early	Inter.	Late
sharp	58	66	145	keen	34	16	9
sharper	0	8	28	keener	7	2	0
sharpest	0	2	26	keenest	2	0	0
sharply	22	18	63	keenly	14	2	0
sharpness	12	17	49	keenness	10	3	0
sharpened	1	1	12	keen-faced	2	0	0
sharpen	1	0	0	keenly-narrowed	1	0	0
sharpening	0	1	0	keenly-glancing	1	0	0
sharpish	0	0	1				
sharply-cut	1	0	0				

From *rapid, rigid, serious, pretty,* and *young* in the early novels, we move to *abject, awful, obscure, odd, queer, sublime, vivid,* and *wide* in the late novels. And the early James is more likely to use *recommend, regret, suspect, tremble, venture, weep, sentiment,* or *anger,* the later James is more likely to use *recognise, stray, take, testify, wonder, worry,* or *yearn.* Early James favors *walk, stroll, travel, tread, wander,* and *trudge,* and later James favors *advance, pace, prowl,* or *dash.* There is even a kind of fitness in the distinction between early forms of *tell* and late forms of *show,* as many of the trends we have seen seem related to an increasing tendency for James to present rather than comment upon. Occasionally, a word family is associated mainly with a single text, and we can see the influence of topic or content. For example, all the forms of *abolitionist(s)* and *abolitionism* are found in *The Bostonians,* which deals with the Mississippian Basil Ransom among the abolitionists of Boston.

5.4.7   -ly Adverbs

Both Gettmann (1945, 282) and Chatman (1972, 50n1) note the high frequency of *-ly* adverbs in the late novels. An examination of more than fifteen hundred such adverbs confirms this tendency: more than 28 percent of these adverbs progressively increase in frequency, while only about 15 percent progressively decrease. The only other overrepresented pattern is MLH, in which the late period also shows the highest number of words (more than 21 percent).

The progressively decreasing adverbs among the forty with the highest DR are shorter and seem more ordinary than the progressively increasing adverbs, which gives support to the notion that James increasingly sought precision and nuance in his later novels. Both lists include about the same number of what might be called positive psychological adverbs: *ardently, imploringly, gallantly, passionately, lovingly, hopefully,* and *appealingly* progressively decrease, while *amusedly, pleasantly, obligingly, wonderingly, blissfully, yearningly, touchingly,* and *fondly* progressively increase. Note that *ardently, gallantly, passionately,* and *lovingly* seem loosely related to the vocabulary of court-ing and marriage that we saw among the nouns, verbs, and adjectives. The progressively decreasing adverbs, however, include far more negative psycho-logical adverbs (*doggedly, angrily, insufferably, unpleasantly, harshly, sternly, severely*) than do the progressively increasing adverbs (*abjectly, nervously*).[12]

One -*ly* adverb that neither progressively increases nor decreases deserves mention here: *scarcely* increases in frequency from the early to the intermedi-ate novels, but then declines sharply in favor of the progressively increasing form *scarce* as an adverb in the late novels (*scarce* has the highest DR of any word in the corpus at 177). To the modern ear this very frequent use often sounds peculiar, as in "It allowed her scarce an interval" (*The Golden Bowl*). Many of the novels in the large corpus discussed above contain a few examples of this usage, so it is not peculiar to James. The fact that the 2 occurrences of *scarce* in the early and intermediate novels are both adjectives and that all 177 occurrences in the late novels are adverbs (more than 50 in *Wings of the Dove* alone), however, makes this very much a late James word.

Chatman also notes James's use of unusual adverbs (1972, 50n1), and here the corpus provides strong confirmation. The simple if crude crite-rion of rejection by a spell-checker identifies the following seventy-five -*ly* adverbs as unusual among the approximately fifteen in the corpus (frequen-cies indicated parenthetically at the end of each group):

> Unusual -*ly* adverbs: *protestingly* (6); *assentingly, consideringly* (4); *preg-nantly, reasoningly, renewedly, shrinkingly* (3); *appointedly, compunc-tiously, conciliatingly, confoundingly, diviningly, hauntedly, pantingly, pecuniarily, remonstrantly, undivertedly, unperceivingly* (2); *applau-sively, attestedly, booklessly, confessingly, contrastedly, creepingly, dauntedly, defeatedly, deludedly, detectedly, discoverably, flashingly, inattackably, incidently, irreflectively, lumpishly, morganatically, need-edly, needfully, obstructedly, peeringly, persuadedly, ponderably, pre-concertedly, prelusively, protectedly, recordedly, rejoicingly, relievingly, revivingly, savingly, simplifyingly, smokingly, stammeringly, sustainingly, swingingly, thinkably, thumpingly, tinily, tormentingly, unchallenge-ably, uncomplacently, unconfusedly, unencouragingly, unexpectingly, unfrequently, unitedly, unmagnanimously, unmanfully, unpractically, unprotestingly, unresentfully, unsurpassably, untenderly, unwinkingly, vexatiously, wailingly* (1)

These adverbs, some of them (*savingly, wavingly, inattackably, need-edly, booklessly, smokingly*) more unusual than others (*protestingly, discoverably, deludedly, pregnantly*) to my ear, are overwhelmingly late (sixty-six late, twenty-three intermediate, and seventeen early occurrences). In addition to the examples above, there is another occurrence of *consideringly*, and one each of *aspiringly* and *unlightedly* in the New York Edition version of *The Portrait of a Lady*, and one occurrence each of *provokedly, protectingly, bullyingly*, and *perturbingly* in the New York Edition version of *The American*, showing that James added a few unusual adverbs during his revisions.

5.5   EARLY AND LATE WORDS IN EARLY AND LATE TEXTS

We have seen how consistently and unidirectionally James's style changes through the three periods represented by the corpus examined above, but it remains to be seen how well the changes and the distinctively early and late words discussed above characterize other James stories and novels. One simple way to answer this question is to graph the frequencies of all words with a DR of at least 1.5 in the texts above in other James texts. Figure 5.6 shows just how amazingly consistent James is in his use of these words. In the left margin of the graph are the publication dates for sixty-one novels and short stories that were not included in the corpus above (including only texts that have not been revised). On the right side of the graph are the percentage frequencies of 3,019 words favored by late James, with a DR of at least 1.5, and on the left side are the frequencies of 2,528 words favored by the early James, with a DR of at least 1.5. The frequencies for the early words have been multiplied by –1 to make them more clearly visible (I have included words with the frequency patterns LLH and HLL along with the progressively increasing and decreasing patterns LMH and HML). The texts shown in figure 5.6 had no influence on the list of words selected, but the early words decrease and the late words increase in frequency throughout James's career in a very consistent way. The trend lines are so similar that they look parallel (they are not, quite), in spite of the fact that there is no necessary connection between the frequencies of these two specific sets of words.

In figure 5.7, we can see that James's revisions for the New York Edition of his works removed many of the words he favored early in his career and added many of his favorite late words. It is easy to see as well that *What Maisie Knew* (1897) is already so characteristically late that he does not remove many early words or add many late words during his revisions of it. This close connection between the acts of composition and revision in the late period is hardly surprising, but neither is it completely predictable.

Finally, it is important to emphasize just how densely the characteristic words appear in stretches of James's fiction. In the two sentences below,

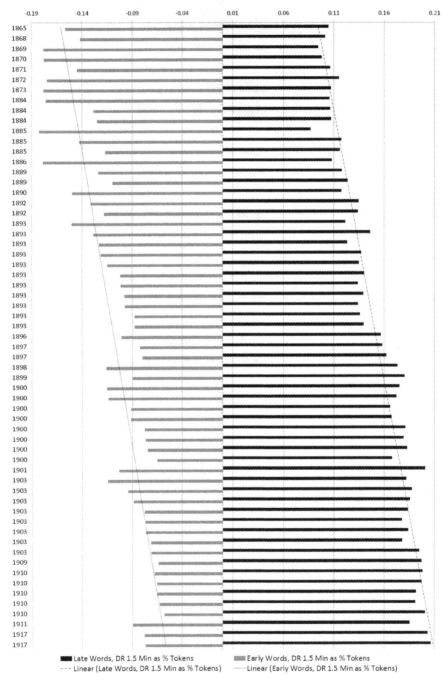

Figure 5.6 Early and late words in early and late texts

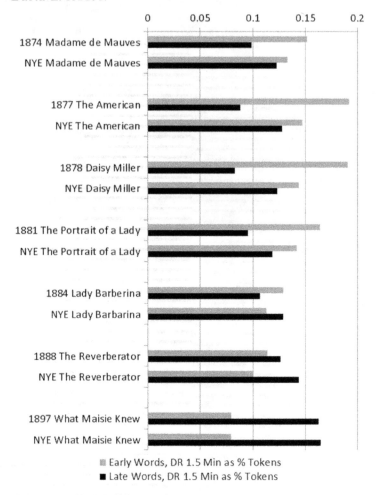

Figure 5.7   Early and late words in original and New York Edition versions

from *The Golden Bowl*, about 38 and 46 percent of the words are characteristically late words, respectively (in bold type):

> It **almost resembled** a return from a funeral—**unless indeed** it **resembled more** the **hushed approach** to a house of mourning.

> And she **showed how** the **question** had **therefore** been **only** of **their** taking everything as everything came, and all as quietly as might be.

Even in the longer sentence below, also from *The Golden Bowl*, about 30 percent of the words are characteristically late, and the sentence also amply demonstrates the self-interruptive nature of James's later style. Note the interrupting effect of "for her husband's general sense of her method," "whimsically enough," "in his corner," "especially in communion like the present," and "the aboriginal homeliness, still so delightful." Here there is more interruption than sentence.[13]

> **Touch by touch** her meditation had completed it, but with a cumulative **effect** for her husband's **general sense** of her **method** that **caused** him to overflow, **whimsically enough,** in his corner, into an ejaculation **now** frequent on his lips for the **relief** that, especially in **communion** like the present, it gave him, and that Fanny had **critically traced** to the **quaint** example, the aboriginal **homeliness, still so** delightful, of Mr. Verver.

5.6 CONCLUSION

My examination of James's style and how it changes throughout his career has only scratched the surface of a large and complex subject. The main conclusions reached by quantitative methods are in general accord with critical opinion: as David Lodge puts it, "There has never been any doubt that he had a 'style'" (1966, 189). Quantitative methods, however, show graphically how distinctly this style differs from the styles of his contemporaries on the basis of word frequencies, and show that his unusual style pervades the whole spectrum of word frequencies from the ubiquitous to the unique. James's novels manifestly do fall into the early and late phases that any critic, indeed any reader, can scarce avoid noticing. But quantitative methods can do more than bolster critical commonplaces. They can identify three distinct periods in James's style that correspond closely with gaps in publication dates and show that, even within the three periods, James's novels display an essentially unidirectional stylistic development. They can do this, moreover, without directly measuring the convoluted and interruptive syntax that has been the main focus of other discussions of his style.

Once the three periods of James's style have been established, an examination of some of the differences between the styles confirms some critical claims, produces some surprises, and suggests some fruitful avenues for further research. Presumably as a result of the increasing complexity of James's syntax, function words in general burgeon in frequency in the later novels, though this corpus does not support the claim that a higher frequency of personal pronouns is a mark of the late style. The trend toward unusual speech markers in the later James is confirmed, and the progressive decrease of the more usual ones and of speech markers overall again suggests that James was increasingly interested in exact nuances. The trend toward intangible nouns is easily perceptible, and the trend toward colloquial and past-tense verbs and away from archaic and progressive verbs again suggests the need for further investigation, as does James's adoption and abandonment of whole families of words. It will be very interesting to see whether this pattern, which seems natural enough, is found in the vocabularies of other authors.

James's increasing reliance on -*ly* adverbs, especially unusual ones, suggests a countertrend to his increasing colloquialism, and, along with the decreased use of adjectives in general but increased use of comparatives and superlatives, will need to be investigated further in conjunction with the nouns and verbs that are associated with them. Finally, the higher than expected proportion of steady increase and steady decrease, rather than steady state or simple fluctuation, in the frequencies of individual words and word families throughout James's career suggests a way of investigating the nature, growth, and decay of authorial vocabulary.[14] The topic seems much more significant than has been recognized, whether the patterns found for James are unusual (and perhaps related to the relatively small size of his vocabulary), or typical of other authors as well.

NOTES

1. First novels and late novels often tend to be somewhat uncharacteristic, and Twain's novels are more diverse than those of most authors.
2. The graph shows the *z*-score for the Delta score for each identification. Thus the Jewett novel at the bottom of the graph is extremely similar to the primary Jewett sample; its Delta score, its difference from the primary Jewett sample, is 3.5 standard deviations less than the average Delta score for all the primary authors.
3. For an interesting variation on the use of PCA that runs the analysis not on the most frequent words, but rather on a set of words already identified by t-tests as effective discriminators, see Craig and Kinney 2010.
4. Some analysts have assumed that any author with a moderately long career will show the kind of consistent stylistic development that James does, but a glance at the novels of Willa Cather in figure 5.2 casts some doubt on this assumption. Her early and late novels (1912–38) fall into patterns that are not chronological, and these patterns persist in analyses based on many different numbers of the most frequent words. The electronic text of the New York Edition of *The American* was kindly supplied by John F. Burrows, who created it to use in a comparison of James and Austen (1992b).
5. Long after I began working on this analysis, I discovered that C. B. Williams (1970, 111–13) had anticipated this idea of dividing an author's career into three periods for computational analysis. Williams's book deserves to be much more widely read.
6. James wrote many more novels in his late period, so I began with the 1899 *The Awkward Age,* rather than with any earlier late novels. I also omitted the two unfinished posthumously published novels, *The Sacred Fount* (James's only first-person novel), and the 1911 *The Outcry,* which, as we saw above, is unusual among the late novels.
7. Among the six patterns with two equal frequencies, the three with one high and two low frequencies are more frequent than those with one low and two high frequencies because of the large number of words with very low frequencies in each of the periods. For example, more than seventy-two hundred words in each period have a frequency of one, which naturally leads to many words with frequencies of one in two periods and two or three in the other.

8. The DR cannot be calculated normally for words that do not occur in one or more of the three periods because it would require dividing by zero. For such words, I divide by 0.5 (half the frequency of a word that occurs once), which seems a reasonable way of allowing the calculation of the DR without over-emphasizing words that are not present in one of the periods. I have since discovered that Clement and Sharp (2003, 430) also use half the frequency of a word that occurs once to avoid division by zero problems.

9. I collected the words for discussion by sorting the entire word list on the maximum/minimum DR, removing some forms when a concordance check showed that many of the occurrences belonged to a different word class.

10. Automatic part-of-speech taggers might eventually be used to make more precise statements about the frequencies of various verb forms in the early, intermediate, and late novels. Unfortunately, some are extremely inaccurate, and not all of them use the same set of tags, or divide verbs into the same or even the same number of forms, so it is difficult to compare results in order to assess their accuracy.

11. This claim is based on statistics for the nineteen novels discussed above from Qtag and NLP, two automatic part-of-speech taggers that agree closely on the frequencies of all forms of adjectives.

12. The categorization of adverbs throughout my discussion is not intended to be precise; a much fuller study would be valuable in tracing trends in James's thought and style.

13. For a discussion of the density of late and early words in James using somewhat different methods, see Hoover 2007, 186–92.

14. The idea of an author's total vocabulary is intricately related to measures of vocabulary richness, but there has been little discussion of vocabulary growth (see Holmes 1994, 97), or decay (Hoover 2003a, 157).

6   Corpus-Assisted Literary Evaluation

Kieran O'Halloran

6.1   INTRODUCTION

6.1.1   Fowler's Evaluation of "Street Song"

The aim of this chapter is to show how the use of a large corpus can assist in the evaluation of initial responses to a literary work. As data I use the poem, "Street Song," by Fleur Adcock. The corpus I draw on is the Bank of English, a corpus of 450 million words. I first encountered "Street Song" in an analysis of it by the stylistician, Roger Fowler (1996, 201–4). The poem (Adcock 2000, 141–42) can be seen below. Fowler (1996, 202–4) notes how the "shifts of register" in the poem "produce unsettling shifts of tone." For him the poem "feels dynamic and disturbing." So, for example, he observes that the first verse has a "four-beat pulse . . . associated with popular oral verse and, particularly, verse for children." For Fowler, the cheery childlike verse shows an ironic relation to the "menace and perversion of vocabulary that follows." This creates, as Fowler notes, double meanings for *waiting*, *hiding*, and *games* since the game is not only "hide and seek" but the "perverse ('peculiar') sexual play of the adult predator."

Street Song

> Pink Lane, Strawberry Lane, Pudding Chare:
> someone is waiting, I don't know where;
> hiding among the nursery names,
> he wants to play peculiar games.

> In Leazes Terrace or Leazes Park
> someone is loitering in the dark,
> feeling the giggles rise in his throat
> and fingering something under his coat.

> He could be sidling along Forth Lane
> to stop some girl from catching her train,
> or stalking the grounds of the RVI
> to see if a student nurse goes by.

In Belle Grove Terrace or Fountain Row
or Hunter's Road he's raring to go–
unless he's the quiet shape you'll meet
on the cobbles in Back Stowell Street.

Monk Street, Friars Street, Gallowgate
are better avoided when it's late.
Even in Sandhill and the Side
there are shadows where a man could hide.

So don't go lightly along Darn Crook
because the Ripper's been brought to book.
Wear flat shoes, and be ready to run:
remember, sisters, there's more than one.
© Fleur Adcock 2000

When Fowler makes these observations, he is not offering an *interpretation* of the poem, his own singular reading of it, which could well differ from what the poem means to other readers in different contexts. Instead, he is providing an *evaluation* that the poem "feels dynamic and disturbing." These are effects experienced in the first instance. By "in the first instance," I mean the initial stage of literary response before a reader goes to the effort of making an individual interpretation of the literary work, but has formulated some impressions—has noticed something about the work that attracts them into it. As with much literary evaluation, Fowler leaves it implicit that this judgment of the poem could apply to readers generally. While we can read what Fowler points to in the text to substantiate his evaluation, ultimately the judgment relates to his own cognition—the effects of the poem on his mind. Since, when we examine such an evaluation, we can have no direct access to a literary critic's mind, there is an inevitable "leap of faith" for the examiner of this kind of literary judgment. This leap is from the textual evidence, which is observable, to what the critic says is happening in their mind, which is not directly observable.

6.1.2 Aims

I agree with Fowler's evaluation that "Street Song" "feels dynamic and disturbing." For me, it feels this way because, in part, it is unclear whether intention to act malignly is being expressed. This initial effect is a little like walking down quiet streets at night and not knowing whether the footsteps behind are those of someone who is merely walking or someone who may also have malign intentions. What I want to do in this chapter is to show how the investigation of a large corpus can have a useful role to play in

1. helping to substantiate whether or not such initial evaluations of a literary work are likely to be experienced by readers generally; in this case, substantiating that the "dynamic and disturbing" effects of "Street Song" are likely to be stereotypical; and,

2. showing, where possible, where responses by a critic to a literary work are likely to be idiosyncratic and where others are likely to be shared by readers generally; in this case, where Fowler's responses to "Street Song" are likely to be stereotypical and where they are not.

To be clear, by "generally" or "stereotypical," I am referring to a broad spectrum of readers rather than readers universally.

The first aim is the main concern of this chapter. Work in corpus stylistics has on the whole focused on showing the power of large corpora in providing a systematic identification of a literary work's salient features (for example, Fischer-Starcke 2010, Ho 2011, Mahlberg 2013, Stubbs 2005) or assisting in the interpretation of a literary work (for example, Adolphs and Carter 2002, Louw 1997, O'Halloran 2007, Starcke 2006), that is, what the literary text means to an individual stylistician after some reflection. There has been some focus, too, on how corpora might provide evidence of underlying cognitive processes (for example, Deignan 2005, Stefanowitsch 2006). However, the focus has not been on using corpora to support initial literary impressions. Nor has it been to evaluate how a literary text works in the first instance to establish itself in readers' minds, by making us want to ponder it or to draw us in. (In other words, *before* we make an effort to provide an individual interpretation based on a fair degree of analysis.) To help me in this focus, I will draw on the corpus-informed concept of formulaic sequence.

6.1.3   Formulaic Sequence and Language Cognition

For Sinclair (1991), much language use is in line with the "idiom principle": the hearer or reader understands language in chunks, rather than as individual words in a grammatical sequence. Such chunks are difficult to define because they range from the long, "You can lead a horse to water; but you can't make him drink," to the short, "Oh no!" (Schmitt and Carter 2004, 3). To capture this variability, Wray (2002) refers to such chunks as "formulaic sequences": "*formulaic* carries with it some associations of 'unity' and of 'custom' and 'habit,' while *sequence* indicates that there is more than one discernible unit, of whatever kind" (Wray 2002, 9). On this broad definition, formulaic sequences can include both collocation and phraseology—phenomena that feature in the corpus analysis later in this chapter.

Underwood, Schmitt, and Galpin (2004) use measurements of eye movements to assess processing of formulaic sequences. They find that terminal words of sequences are processed more quickly than the same words in non-formulaic contexts. This is taken to indicate holistic storage and processing of formulaic sequences. Moreover, Wray (2002) finds both pausing and errors to be much less frequent inside formulaic sequences than outside them. There is some contention over whether or not formulaic sequences are always stored in a holistic way (see Schmitt, Grandage, and Adolphs 2004). Nevertheless, the evidence points to the fact that language processing takes place holistically. In other words, formulaic sequence meaning has cognitive reality. This has significant ramifications for the implicit or explicit evaluations that stylisticians make about how readers will perceive a literary work, such as Fowler's when he describes "Street Song" as "dynamic and disturbing." This is because such judgments are based on text-focused analytical practices (for example, Jakobson 1960), which do not take account of formulaic sequence meaning in relation to the processing of literary works (see section 6.3.2).

Since the link between formulaic sequence meaning and cognition is important in this chapter, I will need to ground corpus-derived formulaic sequence evidence, in relation to "Street Song," in cognitive theory. This will help us to see (where it is possible) whether what is activated in Fowler's mind in reading the poem (see section 6.2.2) is likely to be stereotypical or not. A cognitive theory that has been used in stylistics is schema theory (for example, Cook 1994, Semino 1997). A schema (plural schemata) is a packet of knowledge that is needed for processing of language and other (for example, visual) types of data. It is to schema theory that I now turn, linking it to the concept of formulaic sequence.

6.2 SCHEMA ANALYSIS AND FORMULAIC SEQUENCE

6.2.1 Scripts, Plans, Goals, and Themes

Cook (1994) makes a distinction between three types of schema: language, text, and world. Language schemata refer to typical knowledge of a particular language. So to understand a piece of text written in English, one requires schemata for English grammar, and so forth. But one will also need text schemata—knowledge of how a language is shaped for particular register purposes (for example, we need a text schema of a menu to understand what the waiter places in our hands when we are in a restaurant). And we also need world schemata, knowledge of the world, to help us to make sense of a text (for example, by selecting from a menu in a restaurant, we understand that the meal we choose will then be cooked for us). In common with the schema theoretical perspective of Schank and Abelson (1977), Cook (1994) separates world schemata into four subtypes: scripts, plans, goals, and themes. A "script" refers to knowledge of a stereotypical situation or activity; for example, we choose food from a menu in a restaurant. A "goal" relates to stereotypical purposes; for example, we want food when we are hungry. Another type of stereotypical schema is known as a "plan" and is often activated in advance of a goal schema. A plan is something that needs to happen so that a goal can be achieved; for example, for a cordon bleu restaurant we usually need to make a booking (plan schema) so as to eat there (goal schema). Lastly, other more abstract and evaluative schemata may be activated in a particular situation. If one hears that a friend spent 150 euros on a meal at a cordon bleu restaurant, one might evaluate this politically ("most of the world is impoverished—how can spending 150 euros on one meal be justified?"), aesthetically ("it's good for one's quality of life to experience the best"), and so on. Such schemata, which are less tied to specific situations but derive from our evaluations of our experience, are known as "themes." A theme thus carries a stronger element of subjectivity by contrast with scripts, plans, and goals, which are more stereotypical.

6.2.2   Schemata in Fowler's Response to the Poem

Below are extracts from Fowler (1996, 202–4) that provide other examples of his responses to "Street Song."

(a) *Loitering* is a uniaccentual word from the register of police observation. A person can only loiter with bad intent; and in this context the intent is sexual assault on children and young women (*verse 2, line 2*)

(b) gratification watching [children and young women]: "fingering something under his coat" is clear enough. (*verse 2, line 4*)

(c) vernacular, colloquial mode . . . as if some local people are talking about a voyeur or rapist (*verse 3*)

(d) "*stalking*", "*Hunter's Road*", and "*raring to go*" have connotations of animals and hunting. (*verse 3, line 3 and verse 4, line 2*)

(e) "Quiet shape", "cobbles", "Back", "Monk", "Friars", "Gallowgate" are sinister or medieval in their connotations; Chaucer's readers know all about the bad morals of the monks of olden times. (*verse 4, lines 3 and 4; verse 5, line 1*)

Fowler does not draw on schema theory or any other type of cognitive theory in his analysis.[1] I have indicated below how these responses in Fowler's reading could be related to respective schematal types. Having Fowler's response discriminated into these schematal types will, when I look later at corpus evidence in relation to "Street Song," allow us to see, where possible, whether these are likely to be stereotypical schematal activations or not (that is, in line with my second aim, stated in section 6.1.2):

World schemata

Script	*(b)*
Plan	*(a)*, *(b)*
Goal	*(a)*, *(b)*
Theme	*(a)*, *(e)*

Language schemata

Historical connotation	*(e)*
Hunting animals connotation	*(d)*
Intention	*(a)*
Negative connotation	*(a)*, *(e)*

Text schemata

Text schemata	*(a)*, *(c)*

Let me deal with the world schemata first. I place (a) and (e) into the schema category of theme because of the evaluation ('bad,' 'sexual assault,' 'bad morals'). (a) and (b) imply the activation of plan and goal schemata in Fowler's mind, and in the case of (b) a script, too. Aside from the world schemata, Fowler also implies language schemata that were activated in his reading. Fowler notes this with *loiter* (a) since he associates it with an intention. This is also regarded as having negative connotations, and the items detailed in (e) are regarded as having negative connotations or historical ones. The items detailed in (d) have connotations of hunting animals. There are text schemata for (a) and (c) as well. This is because in (a), for Fowler, *loitering* is from a particular linguistic register and for (c) he associates verse 3 with the vernacular and colloquial.[2]

6.2.3 Stereotypical World Schemata from Reading "Street Song"

Looking at the whole poem, it would be difficult to imagine that "Street Song" will not for most adult readers activate stereotypical world schemata, which include plans, goals, scripts, and themes, about voyeurs (for example, from "loitering in the dark"), male masturbation (for example, from "fingering something under his coat"), or sexual assaulters (for example, from "stalking the grounds of the RVI to see if a student nurse goes by"), and so on. These schemata will no doubt be starting points for readers generally, as they are for Fowler (see also section 6.1.1). However, on two occasions in my own reading of "Street Song," I did not experience similar world schemata activations to those of Fowler. Instead of the Chaucerian theme schema for "Monks" and "Friars," I experienced a more contemporary script/theme as regards members of the Catholic clergy who have been indicted for child molestation in recent years. *Raring to go* as associated with animals and hunting did not chime with my intuitions. This is not, of course, to say Fowler's schematal activations here are "wrong," but that questions might be raised about how stereotypical they are likely to be. Chaucer, for example, is usually only read these days as part of some university courses in English literature.

6.2.4 Using a Corpus to Find Evidence of Stereotypical Language Schemata

Let me return to how section 6.1 was rounded off: in what ways, then, might formulaic sequences as revealed through corpus analysis relate to schemata? Consider, firstly, the following from Cook (1994, 201):

> If we accept the existence of the three schemata types: world schemata, text schemata and language schemata (represented respectively by S(W), S(T), S(L)) we can assume that all of these are present in the mind of any reader. A reader's feeling that the text structure or linguistic choices of a

given discourse are normal or deviant derives from a comparison of its text structure (T) and its language (L) with the reader's pre-existing text schemata S(T) and language schemata S(L). The interaction of these interactions creates the illusion of a "world" in the discourse (W), which can then be compared with the world schemata of the reader, yielding a judgment as to the normality or deviance of that illusory world.

A large corpus provides evidence of typical formulaic sequences. It thus provides a form of evidence for typical language usage, that is, S(L). Typical language schemata, naturally enough, are associated with typical world schemata, that is, S(W). Indeed, for Moon (1998, 166) typical phrases trigger "agglomerates of cultural information." And, for Stubbs (2001, 211), common phrases such as:

"accosted by a stranger"; "lurking in the shadows"; "loitering on street corners"; "fighting one's way to the top"; "forced to undergo a serious operation" activate stored scenarios of the things which typically happen to people. We know how the world works, and given such a phrase, we can predict other components of the stories in which they occur. These ideas are also compatible with a theory of social cognition which sees linguistic repertoires (ways of talking) as sustaining certain views of social reality.

It should be stressed that saying typical world schemata are associated with typical formulaic sequences is not the same as saying that typical world schemata can only be activated by typical formulaic sequences. An abnormal form can also trigger a stereotypical world schema. "Combating one's route to the zenith" is intuitively less typical than "fighting one's way to the top" but could also activate stereotypical world schemata for career ambition, job hierarchies, and so forth. It must also be stressed that a large corpus only provides evidence for typical language use (S(L)), and prototypical language in text-types (S(T)), but not typical world schemata (S(W)). So a large corpus cannot be used to substantiate whether the world schemata activated in one person's head, in reading a poem, are stereotypical or not. (So I will not be able to use the Bank of English to substantiate whether the world schemata triggered by Fowler, for example, with regard to Chaucer, are likely to be stereotypical). A large corpus can, however, substantiate the "reader's feeling that . . . linguistic choices" of a literary work are "normal or deviant" (Cook 1994, 201) in some way from S(L). This is an important aspect of this chapter.

Having discussed the relationship between formulaic sequences and language schemata, let me now set out the theory and method for my corpus-informed analysis of "Street Song" that I use to show why it is likely to be stereotypically "dynamic and disturbing."

6.3 THEORY AND METHOD

6.3.1 Using a Corpus to Substantiate "Dynamic and Disturbing" Effects of a Literary Work

6.3.1.1 *Deviation versus Non-prototypicality*

In this chapter, departure from typical formulaic sequence is articulated through two notions: *deviation* and *non-prototypicality*. First, consider the title of an E. E. Cummings poem, "Love is more thicker than forget." Intuitively, this would seem to be a straightforward case of deviation from typical formulaic sequence. Nevertheless, investigation of a large corpus is useful for providing good empirical grounds for such deviation; that is, if there is little or no evidence for, say, this grammatical pattern in the corpus, then this provides empirical grounds for deviation from typical formulaic sequence. By contrast, other patterns in a literary work may be examples of non-prototypical formulaic sequences rather than instances of deviation from typical usage. For instance, evidence from a large corpus can give us grounds for deciding whether "*x* is waiting by something" or "*x* is waiting for something" is the less prototypical phraseology. (Compare "*x* is waiting of something," which is a deviant rather than non-prototypical form).

6.3.1.2 *Corpus Evidence for Potential Tensions in Reading*

Consider a situation where stereotypical world schemata (S(W)) that would be expected to be activated in reading a particular literary work are triggered through the following: deviation from typical formulaic sequence or non-prototypical formulaic sequence, which has been identified through comparison with a large corpus. In such a situation, S(W) would not correlate with (L). Moreover, because the identification of such deviation and non-prototypicality is corpus informed, there would be empirical grounds for supposing that a tension between S(W) and (L) in the reading of the literary work could occur. Let us assume there were many such tensions identified for the particular literary work, through the use of a large corpus. All the evidence could, then, empirically substantiate the evaluation that "dynamic and disturbing" effects in the reading of a literary work are likely to be stereotypical.

6.3.2 Equivalence and Deviation / Non-prototypicality

Given the influence of Roman Jakobson on stylistics, looking for equivalences (grammatical, semantic, and so forth) is a starting point for many stylistic analyses of literary texts,[3] as it is for Fowler (1996, 203) in his analysis of "Street Song":

> The Jakobsonian principle of equivalence should lead the experienced reader of poetry to link together the series of words and their meanings:

waiting, hiding, loitering, feeling, fingering, sidling, stalking, and *raring to go*. The poem is unified by this series.

A Jakobsonian focus on equivalences is a text-inherent one only. So the series that Fowler isolates and then judges to unify the poem does not take account of

- reader awareness (conscious or subconscious) of typical formulaic sequences (S(L)) in which the above *-ing* lexical verb forms appear;
- reader awareness (conscious or subconscious) of any non-prototypical / deviant collocations and phraseologies in the poem containing the *-ing* forms; and
- equivalences in the poem established from repeated non-prototypical / deviant collocations / phraseologies containing the *-ing* forms.

My focus here is on the *-ing* forms of the poem, since, like Fowler, I agree that they unify (most of) the text. In section 6.4, through investigation of the Bank of English corpus, I establish whether the *-ing* collocations and phraseologies in the poem are non-prototypical or deviant. On the basis of this evidence, in section 6.5, I explore possible tensions between the following:

1. activations of likely stereotypical world schemata (see section 6.2.3) *and* non-prototypicality / deviation in the *-ing* collocations / phraseologies of the poem; and
2. *-ing* equivalences that Fowler refers to *and* equivalences in the poem established from repetition of *-ing* collocations / phraseologies that are non-prototypical / deviant from typical usage.

Taken together, while the poem "on the page" is mostly unified by *-ing* forms, I explore to what extent it is likely to lead to a nonunified reading, which could account for its "dynamic and disturbing" effects.

To enable comparability between corpus results for the different *-ing* forms, one needs analytical consistency, as far as it is possible to achieve it. Semantic criteria are also needed to facilitate this, as well as to institute relevance for analytical focus. I move now to the three semantic criteria that guide my analysis.

6.3.3   Semantic Criteria for Corpus Analysis

6.3.3.1   *Place*

Place is a key topic in "Street Song," reflected in its title as well as the number of roads, and so forth, mentioned. The *-ing* forms, *waiting, hiding, loitering, sidling, stalking*, and *raring to go*, all relate to place in the poem and, apart from *waiting* and *stalking*, co-occur with locative-functional prepositions. My method of analysis here is to see how typically in the corpus the *-ing* forms collocate with locative-functional prepositions generally and those they co-occur with in the poem. I look immediately one place to the right of the node word (n+1) since this is the typical position for locative-functional prepositions, as indeed is the case in *hiding among, loitering in,* and *sidling along* in the poem. In the case of *stalking,* once again for consistency's sake I look to see whether or not it typically collocates with a place immediately after the node word, as it does in the poem ("stalking the grounds"). The locative "In Belle Grove Terrace or Fountain Row or Hunter's Road" (verse 4, lines 1–2) precedes *he's raring to go* (verse 4, line 2). Front-weighting, as with this long locative-functional prepositional phrase, is a marked phenomenon; it is much more common in literary texts than in other registers (Biber et al. 1999, 954). My investigation is concerned with whether *raring to go* co-occurs with a locative-functional preposition in "typical" usage. This is why I examine collocation after the node word. Once again, to facilitate comparability, I focus on n+1 collocates.

The realization of the present continuous is not consistent in the poem. Sometimes subject and auxiliary are present (*someone is waiting, someone is loitering, he's raring to go*); at other times subject and auxiliary verb are ellipted (*hiding among the nursery names, feeling the giggles rise in his throat, fingering something under his coat, stalking the grounds of the RVI*) or there is a modal verb (*he could be sidling along Forth Lane*). To enable comparability of collocational information at n+1, the corpus search form needs, as far as is possible, to be consistent. Since all the *-ing* forms are in the third-person singular, one candidate that recommends itself for investigation is the "*is+ -ing*" form. However, there is a problem here since there is not enough data in the Bank of English for *is loitering* (three instances). Much more data can be provided using lemma forms, of course, but then again such a focus would be moving away from one which is lexico-grammatically sensitive. In view of this, I decided the best solution is a search for *-ing* forms without the auxiliary. Where it would be appropriate to look at lemma forms so as to provide further substantiation, I do so.

6.3.3.2   *Intention to Act in a Place*

Another semantic criterion that guides analysis is 'intention to act in a place' (of a male sexual assaulter, voyeur, and so forth). Since I intuit, in part, that the dynamic and disturbing power of the poem comes from it being unclear whether (male) intention to act in a place is being expressed or not, I also examine the corpus data, where appropriate, to see to what extent intention is typically expressed around these *-ing* forms. Such a semantic focus may entail going well beyond investigating n+1 collocates, since much more cotext may be needed for this type of examination. For this focus, I use the cotextual facility of the Bank of English. (The Bank of English allows concordance lines to be expanded to five lines of cotext.) Since, as Jones and Sinclair (1974) argue, significant collocates are usually found within spans of only four words, *t*-score calculation (see section 6.3.4) for collocation, then, may not be appropriate for this semantic focus.

6.3.3.3   Action Around a Male Body

Rather than intention to act, or otherwise, in a place, the *-ing* forms of the second couplet of verse 2, *feeling* (in "feeling the giggles rise in his throat") and *fingering* ("fingering something under his coat") relate to actions around a male body. So I treat these two lines with a different semantic focus. I intuit *giggles* as being more associated with girls than with boys. Guided by this intuition, I look to see to what extent this is the case in the corpus. Since I had this intuition for *giggles*, and these two lines form a semantically related couplet, I also wondered whether in some way *fingering* in typical usage might be in tension with maleness, in this case with a stereotypical script (that is, a world schema) for male masturbation. So, this is something I also investigate.

As the reader can see, these three criteria are different, which in turn leads to differences in the way in which formulaic sequence evidence is investigated for each of them (see section 6.4).

6.3.4   Collocation and *T*-score

Comparing raw frequencies is useful, initially, in identifying which collocates are recurrent. However, it is difficult with raw frequencies to attach a precise level of attraction between a collocate and a node word. The statistical measure, *t*-score, provides this information.[4] More precisely, it measures the "certainty of collocation" (Hunston 2002, 73) because it takes into account the size of the corpus used. The Bank of English software automatically generates *t*-scores in collocate searches. A *t*-score of more than two is "normally taken to be significant" (Hunston 2002, 72) but a *t*-score in double figures is very significant (Hunston 2001, 16).

Unless otherwise stated, the whole of the Bank of English is used in the analysis. Where individual subcorpora of the Bank of English are used, this will be indicated and justified.

6.4   CORPUS ANALYSIS OF *-ING* FORMS IN "STREET SONG"

6.4.1   Place and Intention to Act

6.4.1.1   (Someone Is) Waiting (, I Don't Know Where) (Verse 1)

There are 49,852 instances of *waiting*. The first prepositions that occur at n+1, and which can be locative-functional, are *in* (1,834 instances; *t*-score 21.7) and then *at* (804 instances; 19.1 *t*-score). However, a locative-functional preposition is not the most common preposition. *For* and *to* (both to indicate purpose) are by far the most typical prepositions. *Waiting* collocates at n+1 with *for* 19,149 times and with *to* 7,748 times. The *t*-scores are well over 10 for both *for* (135.2) and *to* (73.8) and are thus extremely significant. The corpus evidence tells us that, habitually, *waiting* occurs in the phraseologies "is waiting for+something / someone" and "is waiting to do something," and much more so than in phraseologies with a locative-functional preposition. Indeed, corpus evidence (through expansion of cotext) overwhelmingly communicates that intention is indicated around *waiting* where there is a human subject.

From this corpus evidence, we can infer that in *someone is waiting, I don't know where*, there is *phraseological deviation* because nothing in the phraseology indicates intention being expressed. This is a form of deviation different to that which Jan Mukařovský (1932) highlighted, since deviation from phraseological norms is not immediately obvious, as compared with other forms of deviation such as grammatical deviation; for example, *someone are waiting*. But let us say I could have intuited that *someone is waiting, I don't know where* includes a phraseological deviation. With the statistical evidence gained through empirical exploration, I am in a stronger position: I am not just supposing that this is a phraseological deviation; I have shown that it is the case using data from the Bank of English corpus. Last, I have chosen "deviation" as a description here rather than "non-prototypicality" since expression of intention around *waiting* with a human subject is the overwhelming norm.

6.4.1.2   *Hiding among (The Nursery Names) (Verse 1)*
There are 9,461 instances of *hiding*. Fifty-eight instances of *hiding* have *among* as an n+1 collocate (*t*-score 5.0). For other prepositions that can be locative-functional, and which are n+1 collocates, the frequencies and *t*-scores are much higher: *in* (3,575 instances; *t*-score 36.8), *behind* (702 instances; *t*-score 25.8), *under* (283 instances; *t*-score 14.2). So *among* as an n+1 collocate of *hiding* is less common than other prepositions of place, and much less so in comparison with *in*. *Hiding among* in verse 1 is thus an example of non-prototypical collocation. And when people are hiding among others, on the evidence of the Bank of English, there is a minipattern: the intention to act on people is not indicated. *Hiding among* often means lying low, being dormant for a while; for example:

> Britain is likely in future to be involved in conflicts where there has been no declaration of war and where the job of British forces will be to locate and destroy an enemy **hiding among** a civilian population.

6.4.1.3   *(Someone Is) Loitering (in the Dark) (Verse 2)*
There are 361 instances of *loitering*. There are 72 instances of *in* as an n+1 collocate and with a *t*-score of 7.6. In fact, *in* has the highest *t*-score of all n+1 collocates. All instances of *in* relate to place so "loitering+in+the dark" in the poem is not deviant from a typical formulaic sequence (structurally or semantically), nor a non-prototypical formulaic sequence.

In section 6.1.2, I indicated that a second aim of the chapter is to test, where possible, whether Fowler's responses to the poem are likely to be stereotypical schematal activations or not. Recall that *loitering* activated in Fowler (1996) a text schema; that is, the crime of "loitering with intent." For Fowler (1996, 203), *loitering* involves intention to act, and "a person can only loiter with bad intent"; that is, Fowler's schemata also include language schemata for negative intention. There is evidence for this take on *loitering* in the Bank of English; for example:

> Mrs de Rosnay told the Old Bailey that she had seen a well-built man in a dark suit **loitering** near Miss Dando's house two hours before the killing.

There are also seventeen instances of the expression "loitering with intent" (*with* and *intent* have *t*-scores of 3.9) though all of these are ironic and not related to criminal activity. The following, for example, is from a football report:

> Instead, Gordon Marshall claimed the ball and launched his kicks at Hearts' left-back area, where Craig Dargo and Kris Boyd were **loitering with intent.**

But the corpus search also tells us that usage of *loitering* is more complicated. People may loiter with an intention to act, but an action that does not have (criminal) 'bad intent':

> When he arrived he had to make his way through a **loitering** group of journalists. They regarded him with brief interest, until they concluded he was neither a doctor not a policeman, and they ignored him.

Alternatively, people can loiter in the sense of just 'hanging about' with no clear and specific intention to act. Here is an example:

> Should you be **loitering** around Hyde Park Corner over the next three weeks, pop into Pizza on the Park for a comical crash course in the lost art of cabaret.

Indeed, around 40 percent of instances of *loitering* in the Bank of English occur without obvious intentions being indicated or being readily inferable. Thus, the corpus evidence usefully tells us that, stereotypically, *loitering* is sometimes associated with intention to act (sometimes negatively) and sometimes not associated with an intention to act.

In analyzing corpus evidence, one must be careful to distinguish quantitative frequency evidence from qualitative evidence about the salience of a phenomenon in a culture. The crime *loitering with intent* may be salient across a culture without it necessarily being talked or written about very much. Just because a phenomenon is not reflected by frequency of instances in a corpus does not mean it is not salient. The corpus evidence does not tell us that Fowler's generation of a language schema associated with bad intention for *loitering* is wrong. But it does tell us that *loitering* is not always associated with (bad) intention and thus, *pace* Fowler's (1996, 203) text schema, *loitering* is not then "uniaccentual" (see section 6.2.2). The corpus evidence tells us that *loitering* does carry a negative semantic prosody (Louw 1993), unsurprisingly, when used in relation to crime.[5]

6.4.1.4   *(He Could Be) Sidling along (Forth Lane) (Verse 3)*

There are 89 instances of *sidling* in the whole corpus. *Up* is the most common n+1 collocate featuring 42 times with a *t*-score of 6.4. By contrast, *along* only features 6 times with a *t*-score of 2.4. However, given there were only 89 instances of *sidling*, I went on to explore the lemma SIDLE (434 instances) to seek possible corroboration of this pattern. There are 211 instances (*t*-score, 14.5) of "SIDLE *up*+preposition+someone" but only 12 instances (*t*-score, 3.44) of "SIDLE *along* somewhere." The discrepancy between these respective *t*-scores is significant; secondly, only 5 percent of usage is for the lemma SIDLE+*along*. The corpus evidence shows that *sidling* / SIDLE collocate much more with *up* or *over* and with people (for example, *sidling up behind her*) than with a place. Thus, the corpus evidence reveals that *sidling along* exhibits non-prototypical collocation.

Let me shift focus to the second aim of the chapter as set out in section 6.1.2. For Fowler (1996, 203), verse 3 evokes the "vernacular, colloquial mode . . . as if some local people are talking about a voyeur," and so Fowler has a text schema activated here. To see whether this could be substantiated, I went on to look at the conversation corpora of the Bank of English (sixty-eight million words) only. *Sidling* occurs once and the lemma, SIDLE, seven times. On the evidence of the conversation corpora, it would not seem to be associated with colloquial usage, which is thus in tension with Fowler's text schema activation.

6.4.1.5   *(Or) Stalking (the Grounds of the RVI) (Verse 3)*

Analysis is a little different with this *-ing* form since there is no preposition at n+1. Also, consistent with the above line, where place features at n+2, I explore collocates at n+2 as well as n+1.

There are 1,788 instances of *stalking*. The top *t*-scores for stalking of place are *streets* (20 instances, *t*-score, 4.4) and *corridors* (13 instances, *t*-score 3.6). (These are n+2 collocates preceded by *the*.) These may be significant *t*-scores, but, in line with my semantic focus on place, it is important to semantically group the n+1 / n+2 collocates so as to see the extent to which *place* collocates with *stalking*. Taken together "stalking+place" only makes up around 10 percent of collocation in these positions. By contrast, around 80 percent of instances of *stalking* collocate, in these positions, with people as AFFECTED semantic roles; for example, "a psychopathic serial killer stalking a *woman*." Indeed, there are 63 instances of the n+1 collocate *her*, which has a *t*-score of 7.4. "Stalking+place," as we have in the poem, is thus another non-prototypical collocation.

6.4.1.6   (Or Hunter's Road He's) Raring to Go (–Unless) (Verse 4)

There are 520 instances of *raring* and 445 instances of *raring to go* with a *t*-score of 21.1. There seemed, then, to be evidence that *raring to go* is a formulaic sequence. Hence, I went on to investigate what its common collocates are at n+1, rather than just looking at *raring*. *Unless* immediately follows *raring to go* in verse 4 of the poem. However, there are no instances of *unless* as an n+1 collocate of *raring to go* in the corpus. Its most common n+1 collocate is <p> (78 instances; 8.3 *t*-score). This is mark-up in the corpus that indicates a new paragraph. The only n+1 preposition is *at* with 8 instances and a low *t*-score of 1.9; only one of these instances refers to a place (*at St James Park*). Other prepositions that can be locative-functional have nonsignificant *t*-scores; for example, *on* (6 instances, 1.2 *t*-score). The evidence suggests, then, that it is much more common for *raring to go* to finish a sentence rather than to co-occur with an n+1 locative-functional preposition. To sum up: (1) we can say that the collocation of *raring to go* with *unless* in verse 4 of the poem is deviant from a language schematic perspective; (2) the co-occurrence of *raring to go* with a locative-functional prepositional phrase in the poem ("In Belle Grove Terrace") is non-prototypical from a language schematic perspective; and, (3) since *raring to go* does not end a sentence in the poem, its use in "Street Song" is non-prototypical from a text schematic perspective.

Interestingly, *raring to go* commonly occurs in the sports report register, and particularly football news. The most common n+1 collocate of *raring to go*, is <p>, commonly followed by commentary by a sportsperson on their readiness for sport activity; for example:

> But despite his trials and tribulations the winger insists he's fit and raring to go.
> He said: "The pre-season training has been excellent so far. From my own point of view things have been going great and I feel fit and mentally ready as well."

Fowler experiences language schemata around 'hunting and animals' for line 2 of verse 4 (see section 6.2.2). On the basis of corpus evidence, we can at least go beyond Fowler's personal commentary in saying that many people are likely to have a text schema for sports reporting in relation to *raring to go*.

6.4.2   -ing Forms Relating to Male Body

6.4.2.1   Feeling the Giggles (Rise in His Throat) (Verse 2)

In section 6.4.1, I mainly explored n+1 collocates of *-ing* forms because of the focus on prepositions that are typically locative-functional in this position. In contrast, in section 6.4.2.1, I look for evidence as to whether *giggles* is typically associated with females or males. My focus is less positionally specific in relation to collocation, and so this is why I expand my collocate focus and use both an n–4 and an n+4 span. I choose up to four places, in line with Jones and Sinclair's (1974) judgment that significant collocates are usually found within spans of four.

There are 979 instances of *giggles* in the corpus. The most common collocates for *giggles* can be seen in figure 6.1. Notice the number of times females are referred to; for example, *Anna, Gerti, she, her, girls, girl,* and *girlish*. In contrast, males are only referred to three times through pronouns; there are no instances of the lemma, BOY, though there are two male names, *David* and *Gary*. While *she* at n–1 has a significant *t*-score of 9.2 and collocates ninety times, *he* at n–1 has a lower *t*-score of 4.7 and collocates only thirty-four times. Overall, the evidence seems to indicate that *giggles* is more likely to be language-schematically associated with girls (and perhaps females generally) rather than boys (perhaps males generally). This evidence thus contrasts with the information relating to the male gender in the line, "feeling the giggles rise in *his* throat."

a	fit	fit	**she**	NODE	and	**she**	**her**	i
into	a	fits	of	NODE	<p>	the	says	**her**
you	into	of	the	NODE	at	i	memory	**she**
i	**her**	got	and	NODE	when	**her**	audience	so
then	fits	me	into	NODE	as	<u>he</u>	**she**	hand
her	gave	into	<u>he</u>	NODE	but	s	me	my
Fun	both	get	few	NODE	from	lot	i	s
she	gary	getting	nervous	NODE	i	then	s	little
leary	**girl**	stifle	**her**	NODE	about	<u>his</u>	t	got
conversati	attack	collapsed	**girlish**	NODE	again	they	sadness	knows
sweet	**she**	collapse	uncontroll	NODE	over	**girls**	both	**girls**
had	still	few	with	NODE	it	ve	were	at
we	to	high	stifled	NODE	**she**	some	looks	t
like	my	wiggles	helpless	NODE	what	from	**girl**	but
says	burst	then	pitched	NODE	during	says	added	then
david	were	back	gerti	NODE	nervously	when	began	bistro
face	taste	<p>	between	NODE	then	drools	as	backstage
away	reduced	gerti	baby	NODE	or	cackles	doesn	toy
in	your	smirks	their	NODE	friendship	gurgles	you	jokes
were	bit	shrieks	more	NODE	anna	wiggles	down	Drives

Figure 6.1 Collocation grid for *giggles*, for collocates within n–4 and n+4, with the twenty highest *t*-scores in descending order. Word forms of the lemma *GIRL*, *her*, and *she* are shown in boldface. Instances of masculine pronouns are underlined.

6.4.2.2 *(And) Fingering (Something Under his Coat) (Verse 2)*

There are four hundred instances of *fingering* in the corpus. These are all verb forms. The stereotypical world schema likely to be activated from "fingering something under his coat" is male masturbation. The poem uses *something* as the object of *fingering*. I am interested in seeing what kinds of phenomena are fingered, that is, what would typically fill the *something* slot. So I look only to the right of the node word (see figure 6.2). For comparability with section 6.4.2.1, I use a span of n+4.

The kinds of thing that are fingered in the corpus are, for example, *beads, cashmere, diamond, goatee, and moustache*. The only things that are fingered that have a *t*-score higher than two are *beads* (five instances; *t*-score 2.3) and *gold* (five instances; *t*-score 2.2). So there is no collocate that has a pronounced relationship with *fingering*. Having said that, by viewing the cotextual information, we can see that many instances have something in common: many involve light touching. I will address the implications of this in section 6.5.1.

NODE	the	beads	of	his
NODE	his	gold	as	the
NODE	a	wound	and	her
NODE	her	little	beads	goatee
NODE	my	way	collar	paper
NODE	their	keys	gold	if
NODE	its	diamond	sprouted	of
NODE	through	wire	mustache	she
NODE	herself	tie	violin	cashmere
NODE	koba	small	buttons	keys
NODE	rolls	lacy	fence	bow
NODE	prayer	chords	cap	button
NODE	technique	folds	strike	reward
NODE	patterns	moustache	dark	actual
NODE	some	strand	trying	tie
NODE	them	dresses	on	ring
NODE	hand	sword	again	that
NODE	it	trigger	same	hair
NODE	one	stem	little	he
NODE	amorously	collar	man	didn

Figure 6.2 Collocation grid for *fingering* for collocates within n+4. Collocates for the twenty highest *t*-scores are shown in descending order.

6.4.3 (To Stop Some Girl from) Catching (Her Train) (Verse 3)

Catching in line 2 of verse 3, "some girl from catching her train," relates to the behavior of a *female* human being. This *-ing* form does not fit with my semantic foci (see section 6.3.3). In the interests of consistency, I thus ignore this *-ing* form (as indeed, interestingly, does Fowler).

I have highlighted departures from collocational and phraseological norms in a 450 million word corpus with regard to *-ing* forms in "Street Song." On the basis of the corpus evidence, in the next section I will indicate the various potential equivalences, or tensions between equivalences, that *-ing* forms contract into, which in turn can count as support for evaluation of the poem as one likely to be stereotypically "dynamic and disturbing."

6.5 USING CORPUS EVIDENCE IN LITERARY EVALUATION

6.5.1 Tensions between Phraseology and Stereotypical World Schemata

6.5.1.1 *Stereotypical Plan / Goal Schemata*
Stereotypically, people will activate plan and goal world schemata for (child) sex offenders in their reading of verse 1 (that is, schemata with specific intentions). So, the phraseological deviation in "someone is waiting, I don't know where" (verse 1, line 2), where intention is not indicated, is in tension with stereotypical world schemata. It could be argued, of course, that *someone is waiting* is elliptical where, for example, *to do something or other* or *for something* is implicit. But if this is the case, I would expect on the basis of corpus evidence as a follow-up *I don't know why* or *I don't know what for* rather than *I don't know where*. Indeed, the *where* in the poem would seem to have been already communicated in the first line of verse 1 with the locations of "Pink Lane, Strawberry Lane, Pudding Chare." A related tension emerges in verse 2. From the corpus evidence, *someone is loitering* in verse 2 may or may not be associated with intention. But, one would expect a reader to have stereotypical plan and goal schemata for a sex offender from verse 2; that is, activation of specific intentions.

6.5.1.2 *Stereotypical Script Schemata*
Fingering (verse 2, line 4) has the semantic prosody of 'light touching.' So, the corpus evidence is in tension with the stereotypical world schema of male masturbation, which includes the script that it is a vigorous activity.

6.5.2 Equivalences

6.5.2.1 *Non-prototypical Collocation*
We know from corpus evidence (sections 6.4.1.4 and 6.4.1.5) that (1) *sidling along (something)* is much less common than *sidling up (to someone)*; and,

(2) *stalking a place* is much less common than *stalking a person*. Thus, in verse 3, *sidling along Forth Lane* and *stalking the grounds of the RVI* are not only equivalent grammatically but equivalent because they are both instances of non-prototypical collocation in relating to places rather than human beings. A potentially "disturbing" tension is created, then, between actions in a place ("Forth Lane" and "the grounds of the RVI") and typical language schemata where *stalking* (especially in relation to voyeurism) and *sidling* associate with human beings. Lastly, it should be noted that *hiding among* (verse 1), as another instance of non-prototypical collocation, is then also equivalent to *sidling along* and *stalking the grounds of the RVI* in verse 3. This latter equivalence is not so visible on a text-focused stylistic analysis only.

6.5.2.2   Gender
In verse 2, *feeling* (line 3) and *fingering* (line 4) are equivalent morphologically. What a corpus-informed perspective illuminates is that *feeling the giggles rise in his throat* and *fingering something under his coat* are equivalent in another sense: because of stereotypical language schemata around gender that are *not* met. In turn, this equivalence also contributes to the "dynamic and disturbing" effects of the poem.

6.5.2.3   Phraseological Fragment
Raring to go has a high *t*-score for *and* (251 instances; *t*-score 9.6) at n–1. The evidence tells us that the formulaic sequence *raring to go* can regularly be longer before the node words, for example, *fit and raring to go, relaxed and raring to go, refreshed and raring to go*. This can be seen in figure 6.3. There is a relatively high *t*-score (7.43) for *fit* (56 instances). *Raring to go* has then a semantic preference of 'recovery' words.[6] However, we can go beyond semantic preference and identify a semantic prosody here also, that is, a common evaluative meaning that occurs with the expression *raring to go*. The semantic prosody here is something like 'despite the fact I was injured, following a period of rehabilitation I am now ready to return to playing sport.' The semantic preference and semantic prosody for *raring to go* commonly occur in the register of sports reporting, particular football reporting (see extract in section 6.4.1.6). So, as I pointed out earlier, *raring to go* is commonly bound up with a particular text schema.

On the basis of the Bank of English corpus, *raring to go* (verse 4, line 2) could be treated as a phraseological fragment. We also know that *someone is waiting* (verse 1, line 2) is a phraseological fragment since corpus evidence indicates that intention is normally expressed with, for example, an ensuing *for* or *to*. So we have equivalence between these lines in verses 1 and 4. This is a different form of equivalence from what we have observed so far: this might be called *phraseological fragment equivalence*. This equivalence is reinforced by the structure of the poem; each of the above lines referred to is a second one in the verses. Again, this is an equivalence that is not so visible on a text-focused stylistic analysis only.

others	and	i	and	NODE
he	indian	**fit**	is	NODE
and	now	he	be	NODE
<p>	he	will	m	NODE
i	is	ll	was	NODE
fit	i	it	are	NODE
</dt>	said	ready	firms	NODE
but	fully	they	s	NODE
friday	**fit**	should	were	NODE
now	m	back	am	NODE
sun	be	up	still	NODE
cup	<hl>	refreshed	re	NODE
feel	punters	relaxed	just	NODE
week	they	fresh	him	NODE
being	are	d	team	NODE
<hl>	feel	were	been	NODE
m	season	everybody	absolutely	NODE
back	but	everyone	now	NODE
raring	revved	strong	clearly	NODE
batteries	pumped	club	mendonca	NODE

Figure 6.3 Collocation grid for *raring to go* for collocates within n–4 (in line with Jones and Sinclair 1974). Collocates are for the twenty highest *t*-scores in descending order. Instances of *fit* are emboldened, as is "*and*: n–1."

6.5.3 Non-equivalences

6.5.3.1 *Phraseological*

There is quite a complicated relationship between *someone is waiting* (verse 1, line 2) and *someone is loitering* (verse 2, line 2). While they are grammatically and linearly equivalent in the poem, they are not phraseologically equivalent: *someone is waiting, I don't know where* is phraseologically deviant whereas *someone is loitering in the dark* is not.

There are infinitives in verse 3 expressing intentions to act: 'sidling . . . *to stop* some girl', 'stalking . . . *to see* if a student nurse.' There is a tension between the presence of these infinitive-of-purpose phraseologies in verse 3 and the lack of (infinitive of) purpose following *someone is waiting* in verse 1, which from the corpus evidence we know regularly follows *waiting* in English usage. So, on the basis of this phraseological evidence, *waiting* and *sidling / stalking* can be seen as non-equivalent in the poem.

The lines "Pink Lane, Strawberry Lane, Pudding Chare" (verse 1, line 1) and "Monk Street, Friars Street, Gallowgate" (verse 5, line 1) are semantically equivalent in the poem since they list road names and are linearly equivalent, too, being first lines of verses. Verse 5, line 1 is a subject of a verb and because of this *Monk Street, Friars Street, Gallowgate are better avoided when it's late* is grammatically prototypical. However, from the corpus evidence, we know that the absence of a locative-functional preposition, such as *in*, from verse 1, line 1 is non-prototypical in relation to *waiting*. Phraseologically, the lines are thus non-equivalent.

A last phraseological non-equivalence is between verse 2, lines 1 to 2, "In Leazes Terrace or Leazes Park / someone is loitering in the dark" and verse 4, lines 1 to 2, "In Belle Grove Terrace or Fountain Row/ or Hunter's Road he's raring to go–." These lines have linear and grammatical equivalence with the front-weighting of the locative-functional prepositional phrases in line 1 and the positions of the *-ing* forms in line 2. However, we know from corpus evidence that while *loitering* collocates typically with locative-functional prepositions such as *in*, this is not the case for *raring to go*.

6.5.3.2   *Intention to Act*

From corpus evidence, "HUMAN SUBJECT+(is)+waiting" (verse 1, line 2) is overwhelmingly associated with intention, but this is not expressed in verse 1 through, for example, use of the prepositions *to* or *for*. In verse 1, line 3, intention to act is not so apparent in *hiding among the nursery names*; the corpus evidence for *hiding among* provides some corroboration of this. However, in verse 1, line 4, "he wants to play peculiar games," intention to act is expressed. There is, then, non-equivalence in the first verse in the expressing of intention, which corpus evidence helps to reveal / substantiate. Furthermore, whereas from corpus evidence "HUMAN SUBJECT+(is)+waiting" is overwhelmingly associated with intention, corpus evidence also shows that "HUMAN SUBJECT+(is)+loitering" (verse 2, line 2) may or may not be associated with intention. Despite the fact that *someone is waiting* and *someone is loitering* are grammatically equivalent, with regard to expression of intention they are not equivalent.

6.5.4   Higher Resolution of Dynamic and Disturbing Effects

In verse 4, implicitly there are two kinds of male behavior associated with the preparation for sexual assault: one (type of) man who is *raring to go* and one who is a "quiet shape . . . on the cobbles." In section 6.5.2.3, I highlighted that *raring to go* has a semantic preference for 'recovery' words and a semantic prosody where someone expresses a positive evaluation that they have recovered from their injury and are now ready to engage in sport again. Commonly, this semantic preference and semantic prosody can be found in the sports report register. So this *raring to go* man can be given a "higher resolution" by the corpus evidence as one who is young and athletic.

Let me now move on to the "quiet shape . . . on the cobbles" man. In the Bank of English, there are only sixty-one instances of *on the cobbles*.

However, significantly, around two-thirds of these instances appear in book corpora (105 million words) that consist of historical fiction. Figure 6.4 shows concordance lines for these thirty-nine instances. In the book corpora, *on the cobbles* has, to a reasonable degree, a semantic preference: *cart, cloven, coach, hay, hoof, mule*, and so forth, belong to the same semantic field. Here is one example of *on the cobbles* with *horses* in "historical fiction":

> but her horse broke into a trot at the sight of the castle gate, and the moment was lost. As they entered the courtyard, the scrape of their horses' hooves echoing hollowly **on the cobbles**, Teidez burst from a side door, crying "Iselle! Iselle!". Cazaril's hand leapt to his sword hilt in shock–the boy's tunic and trousers were bespattered with blood–then fell away again

The activation in Fowler's (1996, 203) mind of 'medieval' (see section 6.2.2), and thus an historical association, is coincident with much of the collocation of *on the cobbles* (Fowler cites *cobbles*). So, the corpus evidence provides some substantiation of Fowler's language schema. Another point to make is that *on the cobbles* also has some semantic preference for expressions of sound. In other words, 'sound' could well be included in a stereotypical language schema for *on the cobbles*. This is interesting because the man *on the cobbles* referred to in verse 4 is a "*quiet* shape."

It is clear that, without the corpus evidence, there are two types of behavior being referred to in verse 4. However, the corpus evidence throws the two types of behavior into starker contrast since the types of men are given a higher resolution: young, sporty, athletic man in the first two lines versus a man who has some "historical" associations in the last two lines—two very different men. Use of corpus evidence, then, helps to substantiate the "dynamic" element of the poem that Fowler mentions, since it firms up the quick shift from one very different type of man to another. Lastly, corpus exploration provides more evidence for the "disturbing" tensions set up in reading the poem, that is, between the "*quiet* shape" man and sonorous associations of *on the cobbles*.

6.5.5 Textual Unity versus Disunity in Reading

Recall from section 6.3.2 that Fowler (1996, 203) argues that the poem is "unified" by the *-ing* series. On a Jakobsonian text-focused stylistic analysis only, there is "unity" in Fowler's sense: the *-ing* forms are morphologically and grammatically equivalent. On the basis of the corpus-informed analysis, however, there is likely to be disunity in reading the *-ing* verb forms of "Street Song." This is primarily due to

- tensions between stereotypical world schemata that are likely to be activated in reading and non-prototypical / deviant formulaic sequences in which the *-ing* forms occur in the poem; and

at the top was Anna Abraham.	On the cobbles	beside her were two baskets.frost
covered the town and	on the cobbles	of the Town Quay were scattered
the clatter of **hoof-beats**	on the cobbles	and, going to the doorway, saw a
his hair. He heard the boots	on the cobbles	behind him, put his head down.
the sound of their boots	on the cobbles,	their eyes glinting behind the
hooves, the trundle of **carts**	on the cobbles,	the shouts of **ostlers** and the
Sulieman's **hooves** clattering	on the cobbles.	Two **grooms** came running but
the burning building. Down	on the cobbles,	her face lit by the garish glow,
joined the rattling of feet	on the cobbles.	A woman's voice started up, sang
another. The sun gleamed	on the cobbles	as though they were metallic, the
hooves echoing hollowly	on the cobbles,	Teidez burst from a side door,
on him, the sound of **hoofs**	on the cobbles	almost louder than the rain. He
clang of **iron-shod hooves**	on the cobbles	of the forecourt covered Sebastian
of black feathers lay	on the cobbles	already, one still, one twitching.
Cloven feet clacking loudly	on the cobbles,	he **cantered** to the steps, then,
<p> Kids playing marbles	on the cobbles	ran to the pavement. Liza Atkin
clacking of their boot-nails	on the cobbles.	There were no birds, or animals.
horses trampled nervously	on the cobbles	by the yard's arched entrance. The
the mangled torso laid out	on the cobbles	of the courtyard, then looked up
of a **mule** and lay it out	on the cobbles.	The Zangre's castle warder.
White lines were painted	on the cobbles	right up to the end of Parliament
bound shook of **hay**, Rhodry	on the cobbles	while he cleaned his tack.
his heavy boots ringing	on the cobbles.	The boy waited until he had
to the yard, heels ringing	on the cobbles.	Her reading of the situation was
door bang, shoes scraping	on the cobbles	in indecision, and then the door
people abroad. Feet shifted	on the cobbles;	the largest of the sailors, the
was the scrape of a shoe	on the cobbles	behind them, and he swung round
<p> They found Trish sitting	on the cobbles	of the **stable yard**, staring at her
the gallows, were sleeping	on the cobbles	and were woken by the rain. They
but his club foot slipped	on the cobbles	and he fell full length. 'I
as he jerked spasmodically	on the cobbles.	'Well done,' Lavisser said
suicide, wasted, spattered	on the cobbles	far below. Bag jerking in his
legs of the chair splintered	on the cobbles	as the rope's cut end flicked
to see her sprawled	on the cobbles	beneath, but she was quite simply
a small gallery breaking up	on the cobbles.	Two Armenian artists, Krikor and
both already waiting	on the cobbles.	Devil and Honoria had already
coach still glistened wetly	on the cobbles,	though the buckets were gone.
hooves or carriage wheels	on the cobbles	and the shouting and cursing of
at the sound of their **wheels**	on the cobbles.	She recognized Phyllida and came

Figure 6.4 Concordance lines for all thirty-nine instances of *on the cobbles* from the book corpora of the Bank of English. Highlighted in bold are things that belong to the semantic field of equine animals; expressions that indicate sound are underlined.

- the existence of different, and thus nonunified, patterns of equivalence and non-equivalence for the *-ing* forms in the poem in relation to non-prototypical / deviant formulaic sequences.

Since regular collocations and phraseologies are bound up with stereotypical language schemata, the tensions and nonunified patterns identified provide some corroboration of how the poem is likely to be stereotypically "dynamic and disturbing" for readers in the first instance.

6.6 CONCLUSION

While the patterns of corpus-informed equivalence or non-equivalence I have highlighted are not so readily detectable with the text-focused approach of Jakobsonian stylistics, this is not to say I think that stylistics should abandon a Jakobsonian approach. Rather, I would argue that analysis of a large corpus should complement a Jakobsonian text-focused approach if the analyst is seeking the following: corroboration for their evaluation of a literary work's capacity to establish itself, in the first instance, in readers' minds generally. With this evaluative focus, then, I have not been conjecturing the kinds of interpretations that might be made of "Street Song." Clearly, it is impossible to forecast what individual interpretations different readers in different contexts will make in their sustained reflections on this poem.

It must be borne in mind that individual readers, like Fowler, will approach a literary text with a mix of stereotypical schemata and not so stereotypical schemata such as "Chaucer" in Fowler's reading of verse 5, line 1, of "Street Song," "Monk Street, Friars Street, Gallowgate." This does not affect the method of this chapter, since I have provided an explanation of the poem *only* where readers have stereotypical activations of (world, language, and text) schemata in their reading of it.

With my focus on evaluating the capacity of a poem to establish itself in the minds of readers in the first instance, I have in essence been discussing a particular aspect of literary creativity. In literary studies in the 1970s and 1980s, investigations of the nature of creativity largely lay dormant while oppositional critique (deconstructionist, feminist, neo-Marxist, postcolonial) became ascendant. This was understandable in times of social change when it became readily apparent that what was regarded as canonically creative was to some extent a reflection of mainstream sociopolitical forces as well as literary merit. However, since oppositional critique has now become fairly established, this is allowing a revisiting of issues of creativity (for example, Attridge 2004, Carter 2004, Cook 2000, Goodman and O'Halloran 2006, Jones 2012, Maybin and Swann 2006, Pope 2005, Swann et al. 2011). On the basis of this chapter, I would argue that corpus investigation is valuable for

- showing "jarring" between stereotypical world schemata activated and the "surface" form of a literary work; and
- investigating the relationships between equivalences of forms in a literary work and the formulaic sequences S(L) in which those forms habitually occur.

Both can give insight into how the creativity in a literary text works to establish the text in readers' minds in the first instance by creating "dynamic and disturbing" effects. I would also argue that the above method is valuable for other reasons:

- to help reduce individual reader-relative, speculative analysis of schemata through using a corpus to investigate the kinds of stereotypical language and text schemata likely to be activated more generally by a literary work; and
- pedagogically: using the corpus as a tool, students could examine literary critics' evaluations of creativity in a literary text to see if these evaluations can be verified or falsified. This can also benefit students (especially students of a second language or foreign literature) in testing their own evaluations of literary texts and thus contribute to their learning autonomy.

Literary reading is of course a highly complex phenomenon. "Literary schemata" will also affect our evaluation of whether something succeeds or not in its creation of effects. In their reception of a text, readers are expected by writers to take account of the form of a poem (or novel or play) and its associated expectations, which are often established over time. So what also needs to be measured is something generic as well as what exists in the language as a whole. This is not, however, something that can easily be done by corpus means. For a comprehensive exploration of literary evaluation, mixed-method interdisciplinary research is needed—something of an ideal that would only really be possible as part of a well-resourced research project. While large corpus exploration in relation to a poem, like any method, ultimately only offers partial insights, it is both convenient and powerful for indicating the following: the degree to which what is activated in a literary critic's reading is likely to be shared by readers generally—if not universally—as well as being useful in substantiating (or not) evaluation of the cognitive effects of a literary work.

NOTES

1. However, Fowler (1996, 203) moves towards a schema-theoretical account when he states that, "the last stanza . . . would allow us to construct a *situation* [my emphasis] of, say, someone addressing a local support or self-defence group." "Situation" seems to me to be akin to a script schema.
2. I only analyze here what Fowler presents in his analysis. Naturally, other schemata will have been activated in his reading but for which there is no trace

in what he details. For example, (a) "loitering with (bad) intent" will also involve scripts (for example, a lone man in a park looking shifty).

3. One of the most famous quotations in stylistics is the following by Roman Jakobson: "The poetic function projects the principle of equivalence from the axis of selection into the axis of combination. Equivalence is promoted to the constitutive device of the sequence" (Jakobson [1960] 1996, 17).

4. *T*-score depends on a number of calculations. The first is the number of instances of the co-occurring word in the specified span. This value is known as "the Observed." The second calculation is based on the null hypothesis: the co-occurring word has no effect at all on its lexical environment. In other words, its relative frequency of co-occurrence with the node word in the specified span is the same as its relative frequency in the entire corpus being investigated. This value is known as "the Expected." The final calculation that *t*-score depends on is the "standard deviation." This calculation involves the probability of co-occurrence of the node and the collocate and the number of words in the specified span in all concordance lines. *T*-score is calculated by subtracting "the Expected" from "the Observed" and dividing this number by the standard deviation value.

5. The concept of "semantic prosody" has had wide currency in corpus-based linguistics (for example, Sinclair 1991, Louw 1993, Hunston 1995, Stubbs 1996, Channell 2000; Sinclair 2004). Here is a definition from Sinclair (2003, 178):

   A corpus enables us to see words grouping together to make special meanings that relate not so much to their dictionary meanings as to the reasons why they were chosen together. This kind of meaning is called a semantic prosody; it has been recognised in part as connotation, pragmatic meaning and attitudinal meaning.

   Sinclair (2004, 30–35) gives the example of the seemingly "neutral" phrase, *the naked eye*. Corpus investigation reveals a common phraseology, "visibility + preposition + the + naked + eye," which in turn reveals a negative semantic prosody, such as in "too faint to be seen with the naked eye" or "it is not really visible to the naked eye."

6. The concept of "semantic preference" is another common one in corpus-based linguistics. It refers to a set of different, frequently occurring collocates that are from the same semantic field. Here is more information on semantic preference from Sinclair (2003, 178):

   Sometimes in the structure of a phrase there is a clear preference for words of a particular meaning. The word class is not important, and any word with the appropriate meaning will do (though there are often collocational patterns within semantic preference). While the majority of the choices will show the preference clearly, there may be a small number of marginal cases where the preferred meaning has to be interpreted in a rather elastic fashion, and some which appear to be exceptions. For this reason, we do not use a word like "restriction" instead of "preference."

7 Performance Stylistics
Deleuze and Guattari, Poetry, and (Corpus) Linguistics

Kieran O'Halloran

7.1 INTRODUCTION

7.1.1 Orientation

A common approach to reading a poem is initially to ask "what is this poem about?" or "what is the poet trying to say?" and to come to a general interpretation about the poem that could be shared by others. Another conventional move is to offer a more personal interpretation of the poem and thus answer the question "what does this poem mean to me?"

Taking as stimulus some key ideas of the philosopher, Gilles Deleuze, and his collaborator the psychoanalyst, Félix Guattari, as well as web search engine literacy, I demonstrate an alternative interpretative engagement—one that *performs* a poem. It is a literacy practice where the poem is seen as an invitation to the reader to be creative via a web-based, interpretative journey that is individual, edifying, and refreshing. This alternative approach puts a poem to work, allowing its obliqueness and suggestiveness to trigger, randomly, knowledge and resources on the World Wide Web that are new for the reader; in turn, these can be used as fresh perspectives on the poem in order to perform it in individual ways, to "fill in" creatively personas and scenarios in the poem.[1]

Interpretation with this approach is not concerned with asking "what is this poem about?" "what is the poet trying to say?" nor "what does this poem mean to me?" Instead, the reader asks a very different question: "How can I connect up a poem with different things outside of it in order to help dramatize it in a singular way?" With this literacy practice, the reader does not seek to form a singular interpretation *of* the poem itself exactly. This is because the reader's interpretative performance is *across* a series of connections between the poem and a number of things outside of it. This web-based engagement with a poem involves stylistic analysis in order to lead to an interpretative performance of it—I refer to this approach as *performance stylistics*.

7.1.2 Stylistic and Corpus Analysis in Performance Stylistics

There are two elements necessary to performance stylistics. They are employed in the following order: (1) use of the World Wide Web; (2) stylistic analysis. The web-based element of performance stylistics is centrifugal, taking the reader outside of the poem, travelling from website to website. This centrifugal movement is balanced by a centripetal one that takes the reader into the patterns of the poem. Stylistic analysis meets this centripetal need effectively. Stylistic analysis has traditionally been used to provide linguistic evidence for interpretation of a literary work. However, influenced by ideas in the work of Deleuze and Guattari, I also use stylistic analysis in a nontraditional way—to *mobilize* interpretation of a poem. There is a third element in performance stylistics: corpus analysis. This also helps the reader to mobilize interpretation but, unlike stylistic analysis, it is an optional element. Corpus analysis in performance stylistics takes place between the web-based stage and the stylistic analysis.

The poem I use to demonstrate performance stylistics is Robert Frost's "Putting in the Seed," written in 1916. I have numbered each line below; numbers in square brackets in this chapter refer to lines from the poem.

Putting in the Seed[2]

1. You come to fetch me from my work tonight
2. When supper's on the table, and we'll see
3. If I can leave off burying the white
4. Soft petals fallen from the apple tree
5. (Soft petals, yes, but not so barren quite,
6. Mingled with these, smooth bean and wrinkled pea;)
7. And go along with you ere you lose sight
8. Of what you came for and become like me,
9. Slave to a springtime passion for the earth.
10. How Love burns through the Putting in the Seed
11. On through the watching for that early birth
12. When, just as the soil tarnishes with weed,
13. The sturdy seedling with arched body comes
14. Shouldering its way and shedding the earth crumbs.

In section 7.2, I lay out some key interrelated ideas of Deleuze and Guattari and indicate how they inspire performance stylistics. In section 7.3, I outline how stylistic analysis and corpus analysis are used in this chapter and how their use is also influenced by the ideas of Deleuze and Guattari. The performance stylistic reading of "Putting in the Seed" takes place in sections 7.4–7.8. As the reader will see, I am not advocating a "method" for mechanically generating an interpretation of a poem. Instead, I am proposing a process that guides and facilitates experimentation out of which an individual interpretative performance can develop.

7.2   HOW CONCEPTS IN DELEUZE AND GUATTARI'S WORK INSPIRE PERFORMANCE STYLISTICS

Over more than forty years, Gilles Deleuze (1925–1995) wrote voluminously on philosophy, literature, cinema, and painting. Among his central works are *Nietzsche and Philosophy* (1983) and *Difference and Repetition* (2004). Félix Guattari (1930–1992) collaborated with Deleuze on a number of books. Probably, their most influential collaboration is *A Thousand Plateaus* (1987). While the work of Deleuze and Guattari has had influence in a range of disciplines in the social sciences and humanities, their work has yet to be taken up in a sustained manner in applied linguistics generally or more specifically in stylistics.

7.2.1   Rhizome

A key notion for performance stylistics is Deleuze and Guattari's (1987) botanical metaphor—the *rhizome*. An actual rhizome is a horizontal, underground stem that can sprout roots or shoots from any part of its surface. Plants that have rhizomes include ginger, bamboo, orchids, Bermuda grass, and poison oak. Because roots or shoots can sprout from any part of their stems, rhizomes do not have a top or bottom. This property makes them distinct from most seeds, bulbs, and trees. Rhizomes also grow via subterranean networks that connect, helping to spread the plant over a large area.

Deleuze and Guattari view the rhizome as a productive image of creative thought—unpredictable, growing in various directions from multiple inputs and outputs:

> The rhizome operates by variation, expansion, conquest, capture, offshoots . . . the rhizome pertains to a map that must be produced, constructed, a map that is always detachable, connectible, reversible, modifiable, and has multiple entryways and exits and its own lines of flight. (Deleuze and Guattari 1987, 23)

The World Wide Web is a super resource for exploring knowledge rhizomatically. In relation to a poem, we can allow whatever ideas the poem triggers to move us in a variety of directions, from hyperlink to hyperlink, website to website. The rhizomatic movement helps to accrue knowledge in unpredictable manners. In turn, this can offer fresh perspectives on the poem, allowing the reader to "fill in" the poem's personae and scenarios in surprising ways.[3]

7.2.2   Connecting and Experimenting

Reading for Deleuze is something that sends us *outside* of the text to experimenting with making new *connections*. Deleuze (1995, 7–9) refers to this mode of reading as "reading with love":

> There are, you see, two ways of reading a book: you either see it as a box with something inside and start looking for what it signifies, . . . And you annotate and interpret and question, and write a book about the book, and so on and on. Or there's the other way: you see the book as a little non-signifying machine, and the only question is "Does it work, and how does it work?" How does it work for you? If it doesn't work, if nothing comes through, you try another book. This second way of reading's intensive, . . . is quite different from the first, because it relates a book directly to what's Outside. A book is a little cog in much more complicated external machinery. . . . This intensive way of reading, in contact with what's outside the book, as a flow meeting other flows, one machine among others, as a series of experiments for each reader in the midst of events that have nothing to do with books, as tearing the book into pieces, getting it to interact with other things, absolutely anything . . . is reading with love. That's exactly how you read the book.

An "intensive" way of reading, for Deleuze, is one that connects out to new potentials, to new ways of seeing and doing. And when he uses the term *machine*, as he does above, Deleuze refers to anything that is made of connections without an organizing center (Deleuze and Guattari 2004). So, if a book is read "machinically"—a term that Deleuze and Guattari employ—the reading produces a set of unpredictable connections with a series of outsides.[4]

In this chapter, my performance stylistic reading of "Putting in the Seed" will connect with the following from different websites: contemporary information on a personality disorder, information on germination, a recent scientific research press release, an existing interpretation of "Putting in the Seed," and recent sexual health advice. In the interests of rigor, I ensure that each textual resource cited carries an academic reference that I have subsequently checked. Finding productive connections with knowledge from different websites, for purposes of performance stylistics, is necessarily an experimental process.

7.2.3   Becoming

Deleuze and Guattari are less interested in states of being and more in what we can *become* (Deleuze and Guattari 1987). Relating a poem to our life experience is to relate a poem to what we are and what we already know—our being.[5] This may mean that a reader's default intuitions about a poem may not be particularly surprising. An approach that uses the poem to trigger a set of rhizomatic web searches forces the reader out of their "being comfort zone" into new *becomings*, into learning new things through a set of unpredictable connections. This becoming enhances the possibility of novel perspective on a poem.

7.2.4   Non-representationalism

Deleuze highlights the limitations of a representational perspective on language, an outlook that sees a key purpose of language to describe or to represent reality. It is not so much that this key purpose is inherently misguided—it is after all how we use language much of the time. However, if we want to look at things creatively, it is limiting because representation of reality by language does not easily mobilize thinking in new directions:

> Representation has only a single centre . . . and in consequence a false depth. It mediates everything, but mobilises and moves nothing. (Deleuze 2004, 67)

In a nutshell, our habitual describing of reality through language is limiting for Deleuze because this representation does not easily lead to becoming and transformation.

A reading of "Putting in the Seed" that echoes Deleuzean non-representationalism would not be "about" someone's passion for planting seeds or "about," say, the act of impregnation. Since these readings "capture the reality" of the poem, "representing" what it is "about," they involve no becoming. With these readings, the poem has not been used to produce new learning and mobilize thinking.

7.2.5   The Untimely and Context

For Deleuze, to engage with literature, or indeed any art form, does not entail looking at how it originally responded to a particular context, but to understand its capacity to take us beyond that context. One possible approach to interpreting "Putting in the Seed" would be to situate the reading in 1916 and assume that the poem's persona is Robert Frost, especially as he was a farmer at the time. Such an historicist reading, perhaps interesting in its own terms, would nevertheless miss the potential of "Putting in the Seed" to be put to work to produce a reading that goes beyond this historical context. In other words, it would miss the potential for what Deleuze calls *untimely* effects (Deleuze 2004, xix).[6] In this chapter, I connect "Putting in the Seed" to contemporary knowledge (see section 7.2.1), as well as to a corpus of contemporary English, and thus take an untimely perspective on the poem.

7.2.6   Flow

A recurring image in the work of Deleuze and Guattari is "flow." For them, flow is seemingly everywhere, not only air, blood, electricity, magma, sun, but conversations, culture, ideas. In discussing literature, Deleuze and Guattari specify a link between flow and style:

> Style . . . is the moment when language is no longer defined by what it says, even less by what makes it a signifying thing, but by what causes it to move, to flow, and to explode—desire. For literature is . . . a process and not a goal, a production and not an expression. (Deleuze and Guattari 2004, 145)

Deleuze and Guattari's images of flow and the rhizome, together with their emphasis on connection, stimulate, for me, a perspective where different elements of an interpretation flow into one another—that is, a procedure where interpretation is *phased*. Phasing interpretation of a poem allows different but related elements of interpretation to connect in unpredictable and thus rhizomatic ways that, in turn, can augment a singular perspective on the poem. In performance stylistics, interpretation of a poem is a process of continual becoming.

7.2.7   Multiplicity

This is one of the first principles in Deleuze and Guattari (1987). A multiplicity is a whole greater than its parts. Packs, swarms, shoals, mobs, or crowds are multiplicities where the qualities of the whole are different from and greater than the qualities of the particular. How does this idea of multiplicity inspire performance stylistics? The phasing of different forms of knowledge garnered from the web, as a result of what the poem triggers, will facilitate the growth of an interpretative multiplicity. Developing an interpretative multiplicity helps to avoid an unrealistic reading of a poem that does not evoke the plural dimensions of life.

I have outlined some key ideas in the work of Deleuze and Guattari and how they inspire an approach to the interpretation of poetry. Key aspects of this literacy practice are its connective, experimental, rhizomatic, and phased nature. I have so far only highlighted the first stage of performance stylistics—the centrifugal element that propels the reader beyond the poem to the web. To reiterate from the introduction, performance stylistics requires two elements in the following order: (1) use of the web, and (2) stylistic analysis; corpus analysis is an optional element that occurs between (1) and (2). This chapter makes use of all three elements.

In section 7.3, I indicate how the other necessary element—stylistic analysis—is used centripetally in performance stylistics to take the reader back into the poem. This centripetal movement not only uses linguistic evidence to support the web-based element of a performance stylistic reading but to mobilize it too. Moreover, in section 7.3, I indicate how corpus analysis—the optional element—can be used to mobilize interpretation also.

7.3   STYLISTIC ANALYSIS AND CORPUS ANALYSIS: SUPPORTING AND MOBILIZING INTERPRETATION

7.3.1   Stylistic Analysis

7.3.1.1   *Stylistic Analysis Independent of Already Emerged Rhizomatic Interpretation*

In traditional stylistics, when an analyst makes an interpretation of a literary work, analysis and interpretation are usually synchronous. It is my contention that this synchronous approach in stylistics can hinder singular interpretation. This is because the stylistic analysis may just reinforce, albeit systematically, default intuitions the interpreter has about the poem. The result may be a rigorous analysis, but the interpretation may not be particularly singular if the initial default intuitions are unsurprising.

In the interests of rigor, in performance stylistics it is important to connect the emerging rhizomatic interpretation, where possible, to the patterns of the poem. Stylistic analysis can, in principle, provide empirical support for, as well as specifying, interpretation. However, crucially, this stylistic analysis will be specifying rhizomatic interpretation that has already emerged *independently* of it; that is, previously in the web-based and corpus analysis components. As a result, this stylistic analysis stands a better chance of also *mobilizing* interpretation than when analysis and interpretation are synchronous.

7.3.1.2   *Stylistic Analysis Spread Over Different Phases*

On this Deleuze and Guattari–inspired approach to reading poetry, stylistic analysis takes place in different phases of interpretation. This reduces the potentially inhibiting effect on interpretation of too much linguistic description in one place—and thus potentially of too much representationalism—which in turn might hinder mobilization of thinking. This is not to deny that a stylistic analysis should be comprehensive. But, for "Putting in the Seed," I shall achieve reasonably comprehensive description of the poem *over* different phases.

7.3.2   Corpus Analysis

7.3.2.1   *Supporting Interpretation with Corpus Evidence*

In the last few years, corpus analysis has begun to be used to help support interpretation (and evaluation) of poetry and other literary genres (see, for instance, Adolphs and Carter 2002, Biber 2012, Culpeper 2009,

Fischer-Starcke 2010, Hoey 2007, Hoover 2002, Louw 1993, McIntyre and Walker 2010, Mahlberg 2013, O'Halloran 2007, Romaine 2010, Stubbs 2005, Toolan 2006). In this chapter, one of my uses of a corpus will be in this established sense, that is, to provide empirical support for interpretation. However, I will use a corpus in a less established sense too—to mobilize interpretation.

7.3.2.2   Mobilizing Interpretation: Collocation

A poem, like any text, is composed to a significant degree of different language patterns. One type of language patterning that corpus analysis reveals to be especially common is *collocation*—a statistically significant local association between lexical words (usually pairs of lexical words). So, for example, *heavy* is a collocate of *rain* in the collocations *heavy rain* and *the rain will be heavy today*. Investigation of a corpus is useful, since it can substantiate with quantitative evidence intuitions we have about unusual collocation in a poem that, in turn, might be used to support a burgeoning interpretation.

That said, in using a large corpus to discern common collocates for a particular word, one can often find collocations that would have been difficult to predict. When a corpus search leads to unpredictable results, this discovery process could be construed as rhizomatic. In the spirit of Deleuzean and Guattarian "flow," I will show that, if in using a corpus we find out unpredictable collocates of words or phrases in a poem, this can help evolve previously generated interpretation of the poem in the web-based stage, rather than just support it. Importantly, it would be a mobilizing of interpretation that is grounded in general patterns of language use. In other words, there would be an empirical basis for the evolution of the interpretation. Moreover, since collocation analysis means necessarily going outside the language of the poem, it can be construed as *non-representational*. On the basis of Deleuze's position as set out in section 7.2.4, a non-representational approach should aid production of a singular interpretation.

7.3.2.3   Mobilizing Interpretation: Phraseology

Language patterns can consist of both lexical words and grammatical words, for example, *the first time I saw*. Corpus investigation may reveal such patterns to be regular. Such regular patterns of lexical words and grammatical words, which may or may not correspond to complete grammatical units, are known as *phraseologies* (Hunston 2002, 9–12; Hunston 2010). In my performance stylistic reading of Frost's poem, I also conduct a corpus analysis of phraseologies within it. In order to institute analytical consistency, when I examine phraseologies from Frost's poem in a corpus, (as far as possible) each phraseology has only one lexical word in it, but it will have one or more grammatical words.

Similar to section 7.3.2.2, one reason for conducting a corpus analysis of phraseologies could be to substantiate intuitions about their unusuality that, in turn, might be used to support an evolving interpretation. At other times, phraseologies might be examined for a different reason, one also indicated in section 7.3.2.2: to discover collocates that otherwise are difficult to predict and thus can help mobilize interpretation—again where mobilizing of interpretation is grounded in general patterns of language use, providing an empirical basis for the development of the interpretation.

7.3.2.4   *Corpus Exploration and Experimentation*

In performance stylistics, the collocates of words or phraseologies in a poem that an analyst runs with will be ones they regard as productive for progressing interpretation—either by supporting an evolving interpretation or by pushing it in an unusual direction. Not every collocation investigation will yield useful, interesting, surprising, and so forth, results that could be used to move interpretation along. Corpus analysis in performance stylistics is, thus, used in a less comprehensive manner than stylistic analysis. In other words, corpus analysis is used to progress interpretation where this is possible.

7.3.2.5   *The "Machinic" Corpus*

A corpus rigged up to search software can be construed as a "Deleuze and Guattari machine," since it has no center; we can start with any word / phraseology and explore its collocates or, in more "machinic" terms, explore which words *connect* tightly with the search word / phraseology. It is not only the unpredictability but the *particularity* of the collocational connections that help excite interpretation, as I shall show. Ultimately, it is the "machinic" nature of a corpus that affords its rhizomatic potential for progressing an interpretative performance of a poem.

In the corpus-based analysis, I draw on the 1.5 billion-word corpus, UKWaC,[7] using Sketch Engine software.[8] For ascertaining the statistical significance of collocation, I use t-score values. A t-score of more than two is "normally taken to be significant" (Hunston 2002, 72), but a t-score in double figures is very significant (Hunston 2001, 16). Unless stated otherwise, I use a word span of $n \pm 4$ (where n is the node word, that is, the word being investigated), the standard word span for looking at collocations (Jones and Sinclair, 1974). Using a consistent word span helps institute rigor and comparability for different investigations of collocation.

7.3.3   Connecting to an Existing Interpretation

The reader will have noticed that performance stylistics involves two different types of movement: (1) evolving interpretative engagement *within* each phase; (2) evolving interpretative engagement *across* different phases. In this chapter, the bulk of interpretation of "Putting in the Seed" is done in three phases A to C (sections 7.4–7.6), each phase employing different knowledge from World Wide Web searches.

Phases D to E (sections 7.7–7.8) involve a different form of web connection from Phases A to C. They connect the burgeoning reading of "Putting in the Seed" in Phases A to C to an existing interpretation of this poem randomly found on the web. One reason for this engagement is to augment rhizomatic movement by taking a different connective turn; that is, instead of connecting to a web resource indirectly related to the poem, I alter course by using one *directly* related to it. Another reason is to show how an existing interpretation can be regenerated (rather than plagiarized) for my own continuing performance stylistic reading of "Putting in the Seed." Corpus-based critique of the existing interpretation in Phase D (section 7.7) will become the basis for furthering the growth of my own interpretative performance in Phase E (section 7.8). This part of the procedure is, thus, "critical-creative." I take my cue here from the important work of Rob Pope (2003; 2005) who argues that any critical engagement is creative, and any creative engagement is critical. (Pope is a scholar inspired, in part, by the work of Deleuze.)

In what follows, I put "Putting in the Seed" to work along the lines of the tripartite phasal procedure presented and inspired by Deleuze and Guattari's concepts of rhizome, machinic connections, becoming, non-representationalism, the untimely, flow, and multiplicity. A performance stylistic reading of a poem is best seen as the following: an interpretation that moves *across* the poem's connections with a series of outsides rather than as an interpretation *of* the poem itself; the latter description evokes neither the movement of the interpretative multiplicity nor how it is dependent to a large extent on the particular *emergent* sequence of phases.

7.4 PHASE A: OBSESSIVE COMPULSIVE PERSONALITY DISORDER (OCPD)

7.4.1 Orientation

For me, the first four lines of the poem suggest the poem's persona has a certain obsession with burying apple blossom. This is because they have to be fetched inside; they question whether they would be able to stop burying apple blossom instead of going into the house for supper when presumably they would be hungry. This behavior does not strike me as particularly normal. Moreover, the persona mentions "my work" [1] and that they are a "slave to a springtime passion for the earth" [9]. This suggests that they are regularly in the garden, and, in turn, that this seemingly obsessive behavior may not be a unique event. Indeed, later in the poem, we learn that the poem's persona is "watching for that early birth" [11] of a seedling—another apparently obsessive action that could well occur on different occasions. With a hunch that the behavior of the persona could be construed as a disorder, I explored the web on search terms such as *obsession* and *disorder*.

Consider the following criteria for judging a particular disorder: Obsessive Compulsive Personality Disorder (OCPD). These criteria are used by the American Psychiatric Association (APA 2000):[9]

Obsessive-Compulsive Personality Disorder (OCPD)

1. is preoccupied with details, rules, lists, order, organization, or schedules to the extent that the major point of the activity is lost;
2. shows perfectionism that interferes with task completion;
3. is excessively devoted to work and productivity to the exclusion of leisure activities and friendships (not accounted for by obvious economic necessity);
4. is over conscientious, scrupulous, and inflexible about matters of morality, ethics, or values (not accounted for by cultural or religious identification);
5. is unable to discard worn-out or worthless objects even when they have no sentimental value;
6. is reluctant to delegate tasks or to work with others unless they submit to exactly his or her way of doing things;
7. adopts a miserly spending style toward both self and others; money is viewed as something to be hoarded for future catastrophes;
8. shows rigidity and stubbornness.[10]

For an OCPD diagnosis, the person must fulfill at least four of the eight criteria (APA 2000).

Consider also this fragment of information from the same website:

OCPD *and men*

Obsessive-Compulsive Personality Disorder is . . . almost twice as prevalent in males as females (McGlashan et al. 2005).[11]

Let me hypothesize that the persona has OCPD. How might a corpus linguistic perspective on the poem help support this idea in relation to the APA criteria?

7.4.2   Corpus-Based Analysis

7.4.2.1   *On through the Watching for that Early Birth [11]*

Intuitively, *the watching for* [11] is an unusual phraseology, and, indeed, it does not occur in UKWaC. When I examined collocates for *the watching*, I found that the most common collocates were *crowd, audience, spectators, millions*, such as in *the watching crowd. The watching* is used normally as a modifier of a large group of people; it is also a description of a watching separate from the describer of the event. In stark contrast, in the poem *the watching* relates to a single person, and it is their *own* description of what they are doing. Its unusuality points, on my reading, to a sense of detachment on the part of the persona and thus a marked concentrative focus on the task. This goes hand in hand with the marked conscientiousness of OCPD sufferers (APA criteria 3 and 4). From corpus investigation, then, there is some initial support for the OCPD interpretation.

7.4.2.2   *When, Just as the Soil Tarnishes with Weed [12]*

Tarnish [12] is in the present tense and in conjunction with the preposition *with*. I compared the phraseologies *tarnishes with* and *tarnished with* in UKWaC; there are only 2 instances of the former and 50 instances of the latter (a ratio of 1/25). In comparison, there are 207 instances of *tarnishes* and 3,441 instances of *tarnished* (a ratio of 1/16).

This relative quantitative perspective lends support to the OCPD interpretation; would one normally notice the soil just as it tarnishes with weed? One would more likely notice the *result*—that something *had* tarnished. The persona might be said to have a marked form of empirical obsession that dovetails with the keen focus on schedule of the OCPD sufferer (APA criterion 1)—in this case the schedule from planting seeds to seedling growth.

Let us see how stylistic analysis might further support this interpretation.

7.4.3   Stylistic Analysis

7.4.3.1   *Morphology*

The persona's task, as indicated by the poem's title, would seem to be planting seeds. However, we never actually encounter the persona planting any seeds. Instead, the only contact with organic nature referred to is the burying of soft petals [4, 5]. In light of the title, is the explicit burying of apple blossom in contrast to the implicit planting of seed not a little odd? We know from APA criteria 1–2 that the perfectionism of OCPD sufferers interferes with completion of a task. Could this explicit / implicit contrast not reflect a form of task interference—the burying of apple blossom impedes the task of planting seeds (though seed planting is not, on my interpretation, the primary reason the persona is in the garden—see section 7.6)? This OCPD task inference interpretation is reflected to some extent by the following: *soft petals* [4, 5] is morphologically plural and mentioned twice whereas plural morphology is absent for *bean* [6], *pea* [6], *Seed* [title, 10] and *seedling* [13]. Indeed, one could construe lines [13] and [14] as focusing on just *one* seedling.

7.4.3.2   *Orthography*

"Putting in the Seed" is a particular form of lyric poem—a sonnet. A sonnet consists of fourteen lines and can have different rhyme schemes. The sonnet rhyme scheme that Frost uses is close to the Petrarchan form of the sonnet.[12] This form consists of an octet (eight lines) and a sestet (six lines).

The delineation of the octet and sestet is indicated through a different rhyme scheme in each. A Petrarchan sonnet usually takes different perspectives in the octet and sestet (Thornborrow and Wareing 1998, 41); a more general, perhaps even universal, perspective is suggested in the sestet. Frost uses the sestet, seemingly, to adopt a universal position; this seems to be in relation to the capitalized *Love* [10].

There are two full stops in the poem. One of these is after line fourteen where the poem and thus the sestet ends. While we might expect the other full stop to come at the end of the octet, in fact it comes at the end of line 9. In viewing the sonnet as a window on the persona's mental life, the lack of "success" in constructing the sonnet connects with the OCPD interpretation. It reflects that the persona's mind is detached and on other things; that is, when they should be putting in seed, the burying of apple blossom interferes with this task (APA criteria 1–2).

Using stylistic analysis, as well as corpus analysis, I have taken my first steps towards an interpretative performance of Frost's poem that the persona has OCPD. Taking my cue from the evidence in section 7.4.1 that men are more likely to have OCPD than women, let me assume the persona in the poem is a man; let me also assume that the male persona is in a relationship with the person who comes to fetch him.

In Phase B, we move to a different topic in the poem: germination. That Phase B is different in knowledge content from Phase A is valuable from a rhizomatic perspective since attempts to connect Phase A to Phase B are less likely to be predictable. Using corpus analysis and then stylistic analysis in Phases B and C, we shall see not only the emerging interpretative performance supported by linguistic evidence, but mobilized too.

7.5   PHASE B: GERMINATION

7.5.1   Orientation

Germination refers to the development from seed into seedling. Researching germination in *Wikipedia*, I found the following:

> Seed germination depends on both internal and external conditions. The most important external factors include temperature, water, oxygen and sometimes light or darkness. (Raven, Evert, and Eichhorn 2005).[13]

Using corpus analysis, let me see if I can connect with this information on germination so as to progress my interpretative performance of the poem.

7.5.2   Corpus-Based Analysis

We can assume that light, oxygen, the right soil temperature, and water are extant in the scenario of the poem—otherwise the seedling in the poem would not have germinated. The first three factors can be reasonably treated as being fairly constant but the last is dependent on rain falling and / or watering by a gardener. To provide some empirical perspective on the latter, I explored the extent to which *rain* or *water* collocates with *seed*. There are 60,757 instances of *seed* in UKWaC. To try to restrict my search to horticultural meanings of *seed*, using the Sketch Engine filtering function I filtered these concordance lines on the search term, *garden*, for a word span of $n \pm$ 100. I chose this span since a very narrow one such as $n \pm 4$ would make it unlikely I would find concordance lines where *rain* or *water* and *seed* and *garden* all featured. This filtering reduced the number of concordance lines to 5,567. In a subsequent collocate search for *seed* at $n \pm 4$, *rain* did not feature but *water* did (47 instances; t-score 6.6),[14] such as in this example where *water* is used as a verb:

> Lightly rake the seed in and roll to ensure the seed comes into contact with the moisture in the soil; gently water the seed bed.

This sentence reflects how *water* is discussed habitually in relation to germination in a garden—watering by a gardener rather than via rain. In turn, this evolves perspective on the poem. If the persona is really obsessed with the germination of the seeds, on an untimely reading of "Putting in the Seed," why is there no evidence in the poem that he is watering, since this would seem to be so habitual after planting seeds? The corpus-based evidence helps progress my interpretative performance that the poem's persona is not primarily concerned with germination, as I shall contend (see section 7.6). But, for now, since watering is not signaled in the poem, the water for germination must come from rain.

Is there anything in the patterns of the poem that connects with this interpretation and can further specify and progress it?

7.5.3 Stylistic Analysis

The poem is packed with voiceless sibilants or hissing sounds[15]—as well as voiceless plosives. Indeed, the title itself "Putting in the Seed" contains two voiceless plosives /p/ and /t/ as well as a voiceless sibilant /s/. Figure 7.1 shows, in Frost's poem, the voiceless plosives /p/ and /t/ in bold and voiceless sibilants underlined.

The most dominant plosive is /t/, which occurs twenty-five times. Other voiceless sounds receive emphasis by fronting words. For example, /s/ begins fourteen words and occurs seventeen times; /p/ begins six words and occurs nine times. In contrast, the voiced equivalents of these sounds are, in total, fewer and less foregrounded. The consonant sound /z/ occurs ten times, but at or near the end of words; while /b/ does begin eight words and occurs nine times, /d/ occurs fifteen times, but never begins a word, just as in *seed* in the title "Putting in the Seed" and its repeat [10]. Given the overall different

Putting in the Seed

You come to fe<u>tch</u> me from my work to-night

When <u>s</u>upper's on the table, and we'll <u>s</u>ee

If I can leave off burying the white

<u>S</u>oft petals fallen from the apple tree

(<u>S</u>oft petals, ye<u>s</u>, but not <u>s</u>o barren quite,

Mingled with these, <u>s</u>mooth bean and wrinkled pea;)

And go along with you ere you lose <u>s</u>ight

Of what you came for and become like me,

<u>S</u>lave to a <u>s</u>pringtime pa<u>ss</u>ion for the earth.

How Love burns through the **P**utting in the <u>S</u>eed

On through the wa<u>tch</u>ing for that early birth

When, ju<u>s</u>t as the <u>s</u>oil tarni<u>sh</u>es with weed,

The <u>s</u>turdy <u>s</u>eedling with ar<u>ch</u>ed/t/ body comes

<u>Sh</u>ouldering it<u>s</u> way and <u>sh</u>edding the earth crumbs.

Figure 7.1   Voiceless plosives /p/ and /t/ (*bold*) and sibilants /s/, /ʃ/, /tʃ/ (*underlined*) in "Putting in the Seed"

proportions of these voiceless and voiced plosives / sibilants and their different emphases, I would argue we have an onomatopoeic effect of *light* rainfall.[16]

How can we connect this with the OCPD interpretation in Phase A? We saw in section 7.4.2 how unusual *the watching for* [11] and *tarnishes with* [12] are. Given also the present-tense verbs in the sestet—*burns* [10], *comes* [13]—as well as use of the continuous aspect—*shouldering, shedding* [14]—and the time taken for the *schedule* (APA criterion 1) of germination, the persona must be obsessively observing the earth over a lengthy amount of time. Since the water necessary for germination is very likely to come from rain, how could the persona not get wet at some point with such empirical obsession and detachment? Moreover, the onomatopoeia of *light* rainfall dovetails with an interpretation that the OCPD sufferer who is a "Slave to a springtime passion for the earth" [9]—which can be seen as chiming with APA criterion 3—barely notices the rain. When his partner comes to fetch him [1], they could be fetching him out of the rain.

7.6   PHASE C: GARDENING AND DEPRESSION

7.6.1   OCPD and Depression

From the same website that supplied the APA criteria for diagnosing OCPD, I also found out that there is a relationship between depression and OCPD:

> A side effect of OCPD is frequent anxiety or depression, but not usually to the point of a serious disorder. (Williams 2009)

> People with OCPD usually have problems with social relationships, which can lead to clinical depression. They tend to focus on organization, perfection, or improvement over fun or social activities. (Williams 2009)[17]

Phase C begins with the hunch that perhaps gardening—for that is how I see what the persona of the poem is doing—is recommended for sufferers of depression.

7.6.2   Mycobacterium vaccae

Employing the search terms *gardening* and *depression*, I discovered on the web that gardening is, indeed, encouraged for the depressed since it can lift their mood. Recent research offers an explanation for this. Consider the following press release for research that was conducted at the University of Bristol, UK:

Getting dirty may lift your mood

Press release issued 2 April 2007
    "Friendly" bacteria activated a group of neurons that produce the brain chemical serotonin.
    Treatment of mice with a "friendly" bacteria, normally found in the soil, altered their behavior in a way similar to that produced by antidepressant drugs, reports research published in the latest issue of Neuroscience.[18]
    These findings, identified by researchers at the University of Bristol and colleagues at University College London, aid the understanding of why an imbalance in the immune system leaves some individuals vulnerable to mood disorders like depression.
    Dr Chris Lowry, lead author on the paper from Bristol University, said: "These studies help us understand how the body communicates with the brain and why a healthy immune system is important for maintaining mental health. They also leave us wondering if we shouldn't all be spending more time playing in the dirt."
    Interest in the project arose after human cancer patients being treated with the bacteria Mycobacterium vaccae unexpectedly reported increases in

their quality of life. Lowry and his colleagues reasoned that this effect could be caused by activation of neurons in the brain that contained serotonin.

When the team looked closely at the brains of mice, they found that treatment with M. vaccae activated a group of neurons that produce the brain chemical serotonin. The lack of serotonin in the brain is thought to cause depression in people, thus M. vaccae's effects on the behavior of mice may be due to increasing the release of serotonin in parts of the brain that regulate mood.[19]

Playing around in soil, on the above research, leads to contact with *mycobacterium vaccae*. The research suggests that this can increase serotonin in the brain and thus lead to a lifted mood for those experiencing depression. One might conjecture that this is what is happening to the OCPD / depression suffering persona in "Putting in the Seed," via his frequent contact with soil (without him necessarily knowing why). Since mycobacterium vaccae live in soil, this allows a reading of *passion for the earth* [9] where *the earth* is not functioning as a metonym—that is, it is not standing in for "nature"—but is literally soil. In other words, the primary reason the persona is in the garden is because contact with the soil cheers him. The "*Love*" that "*burns* (through the Putting in the Seed")] [10] can be construed (at least in part) as the love for contact with soil and its beneficial effects. Indeed, as previously noted (section 7.4.3.1), we never encounter the persona explicitly planting seeds. So, "Putting in the Seed" seems hardly a title we should trust as being indicative of the primary reason the persona is in the garden.

Let us see how we can mobilize this interpretation via corpus analysis.

7.6.3   Corpus-Based Analysis

There are 10,056 instances of the phraseology *passion for* [9] in UKWaC; I found that its top lexical verb collocate is *share* (357; t-score 18.8). Figure 7.2 shows twenty randomly generated concordance lines for *share* + *passion for*. *Share a passion for*, naturally, presupposes the existence of an *established* passion that links two or more people. While *share* is the highest collocate of *passion for*, this does not mean that *passion for* necessarily has to be used with *share*. It is, of course, quite possible for one person to say they have a passion for doing something on their own.

That said, in the poem we do have *two* people seemingly in a relationship and who, presumably, share the same house and garden. There is no evidence to the contrary that they have not *both* been in the garden before. Moreover, we know that the persona supposes that his partner is capable of having a springtime passion for the earth through use of "become like me" [8]. Given all this, that *share* is the highest lexical verb collocate of *passion for* mobilizes the following line of thinking: why would the persona's partner

Our goal is to help people **share** a **passion for** plants, to encourage excellence in horticulture in private and public spaces, to help create healthy, sustainable communities and support long-term environmental improvements.

Hanif Joseph Alam, Jonathan Cornell, David Edwards, Yee Yen Goh, Junie Koay and Jane Peng represent a range of the university's departments–History, Medicine, Psychology and Slavonic & East European Studies–and hail from Hong Kong and Malaysia as well as the UK, but they all **share** one thing: a **passion for** cycling.

You, like us, **share** a **passion for** education.

They want to **share** an enthusiasm and **passion for** this wonderfully communicative art form without the trappings and social cachet of red carpet, chandeliers and champagne.

A record lover's paradise and you get the feeling that Track Records is run by people who **share** your **passion for** music.

My real highlight is working with people that want to believe and **share** the **passion for** Dunn-Line—they are what counts and they are what make me proud.

Imagine spending a vacation learning how to swim, developing new bike and run skills and meeting people from all over the world who **share** your **passion for** triathlon and fun.

We are looking for 5 core team members to develop their own departments who can **share** the vision and the **passion for** St Luke's future.

If you would like to **share** your **passion for** science and engineering with young people, visit: www.scenta.co.uk or www.setnet.co.uk The Construction Ambassadors Scheme allows you to promote your industry in schools and offers presentation training.

Perus rich cultural tapestry presents the visitor with an array of cities, rich in colonial architecture and alive with friendly people who **share** a typically Latin American **passion for** life.

Whatever your reason for moving to a new home, we're here to **share** the **passion for** your dream home and we want to make the whole process an easy and enjoyable one.

the nice thing about it is David and I **share** a **passion for** old movies, so we can talk in shorthand

I **share** a **passion for** renewable energy with my hon.

Figure 7.2 Twenty randomly generated concordance lines for *share + passion for* (bold)

Both **share** a **passion for** reform, yet only one has been honoured—Miss Florence Nightingale.

Drafting and reviewing the business plan Persuading third parties—particularly investors—to **share** your **passion for**, and belief in, your business is no mean feat!

Check out www.flook.co.uk for lots of great information about this band & their history; and their relentless energy seems to extend to their desire to **share** their great **passion for** their music with others–they run music workshops and tour extensively!

"Kewal and Nimmi are childhood sweethearts who **share** a **passion for** theatre.

"Membership of the association is available to all who **share** our **passion for** sailing and the sea.

He is married with two children both of whom **share** his **passion for** all things related to Robin Hood.

It was obvious to us all that our colleagues in Ulster and Eire **share** the NCCAs **passion for** our industry, but that they can sometimes feel left out as distance from the Uk's mainstream events can leave them at a disadvantage.

Figure 7.2   (*Continued*)

not already *share* this passion with the persona, regardless of whether they are in a garden or not? It seems odd that the persona's partner would *suddenly* become like their partner, a slave to a springtime passion for the earth, just by stepping into the garden from the house. Might we then say that the persona is deluding himself here, something to do with the detachment from reality that his OCPD induces? Due to his OCPD and depression, is it not *only* he who is a *slave* [9] to a springtime passion for the earth, largely because of the serotonin buzz he gets from contact with the soil? Indeed, there is no evidence that the persona's partner has OCPD or depression: they do not need their serotonin level raised through prolonged contact with soil; moreover, they do not want to get wet.

Another way of reading the lack of *share*, or similar meanings, around *passion for* [9] is in relation to the knowledge that OCPD sufferers have a reluctance to trust a work assignment or task to someone else for fear that their standards will not be met (APA criterion 6). Recognizing that his partner has the capacity for a springtime passion for the earth, the persona does not, in fact, want to share his *work* [1] with his partner. This is why he is weighing up whether to go inside with his partner (not because he is getting wet, as he does not register this). Indeed, OCPD sufferers are likely to prefer asocial activities (see section 7.6.1).

Let us see how we can support and further mobilize this combined web and corpus-based performing of the poem via stylistic analysis.

7.6.4 Stylistic Analysis

7.6.4.1 *Just as*

Consider the ambiguity with *just as* in lines 12–14:

> When, just as the soil tarnishes with weed,
> The sturdy seedling with arched body comes
> Shouldering its way and shedding the earth crumbs.

On the one hand, we can isolate a temporal meaning associated with *just as*: at the same time as the soil tarnishes with weed, the seedling emerges. On the other hand, a comparative meaning is also possible: *in the same way* as the soil tarnishes with weed, so the earth is tarnished by the seedling emerging. The seedling when it arrives, just like weed (and just like apple blossom), in a sense "adulterates" the soil for the persona. By this I mean, it is physical contact with soil that is the primary reason for the persona gardening—since it lifts their mood. Naturally, once plants grow, not only does ready access to soil eventually reduce but the horticultural need for physical contact with soil reduces also.

7.6.4.2 *Pronouns*

There are pronouns in the octet: *you* [1], *we* [2], *I* [3], *you* x2 [7], *you* [8], and *me* [8]. There are no pronouns in the sestet. As a result, the sestet offers a more impersonal perspective. So, instead of *our love* or *love between us*, and so forth, we find the non-pro-nominalized *Love* in "How Love burns through the Putting in the Seed" [10].

This gap, this absence of *our* around *Love* (or any other grammatical and / or lexical indicator of shared love) supports the corpus-based interpretation I made around *passion for* [9] that the persona's *hyper*enthusiasm for soil contact (in light rain) is (1) not shared by their partner; (2) the persona prefers to garden on their own.

7.6.5 The Interpretative Multiplicity So Far

On my interpretative multiplicity so far, the persona of the poem has OCPD (the persona fulfills at least four of the American Psychiatric Association criteria necessary for diagnosis). He has depression but achieves a serotonin high through regular contact with soil (that is, with mycobacterium vaccae); his primary reason for being in the garden is contact with soil; he is so obsessed and detached he does not notice the light rain; his partner does not share his passion for soil contact since they do not have OCPD nor depression and do not want to get wet.

It is time to disturb the nature of the phasal movement so far. This is in the interests of inducing further unpredictability into my performance stylistic reading; that is, in keeping things rhizomatic. Firstly, in Phase D, from the vantage of Phases A to C, I critically engage with an existing interpretation of "Putting in the Seed" that I randomly found on the web; this critical engagement is facilitated by corpus analysis. In Phase E, I use the results of this corpus-based critical engagement to evolve further my performance stylistic reading of "Putting in the Seed." In other words, sections 7.7 and 7.8 involve a "critical-creative" process.

7.7   PHASE D: CRITICALLY CONNECTING TO A WEB-BASED INTERPRETATION

7.7.1   Orientation

I reproduce different excerpts from the interpretation of "Putting in the Seed" that I found on the web.[20] Here is the first excerpt:

> [Lines 1–2] would seem to reflect the typical lives of American country dwellers in the early twentieth century: the man working outside while his partner tends the house and prepares the dinner.

From the perspective of Deleuze and Guattari, the author evinces a representational attitude through the use of "reflects"; the critic is not looking at the power of the poem to open up an untimely connection to the past, present, or future.

7.7.2   "Nature"

Beauty of Nature

> [In lines 3–9] the speaker suggests he will find it difficult to tear himself away from the natural world long enough to have his meal, and says they must go quickly into the house before they are both seduced by the beauty of the natural world around them.

The interpretation seems, to me, hyperbolic. Would anyone act in this way if they possessed mental equilibrium (compare Phases A to C)? Intuitively, part of the reason it is hyperbolic is because the categories "nature" in the heading and "natural world" above are too general. Can we really say that the persona is expressing a love of something so general as nature if they are burying apple blossom—the only explicitly flagged contact with organic nature in the poem? (In contrast, my reading related the poem to the much less general "a love for getting dirty in garden soil"). Having said this, my judgment here that use of *nature* is too general is ungrounded in evidence. On the reasonable assumption that the persona is in the couple's garden, it would be interesting to see to what extent *nature* is a common collocate of *garden*.

In UKWaC, for $n \pm 4$, *nature* occurs 362 times (t-score 19.0) as a collocate of *garden*. *Nature* and *garden* are, indeed, part of the same discourse. However, *nature* is not the most common collocate by a long stretch. The most common lexical collocates of *garden* are *house* (4,574; t-score 67.3), *rear* (3,879; t-score 62.1), and *front* (3,497; t-score 58.6). *Garden*, then, is much more commonly talked and written about, in UKWaC, in relation to the home rather than *nature*. This corpus information problematizes, or at least puts into perspective, a rather automatic projection of the general category of *nature* on to the poem. And, as I show in section 7.8, this corpus information helps mobilize interpretation.[21]

In the excerpt that immediately follows on from the previous one, the author moves focus to "physical love."

7.7.3 "Love and Sex"

Love and Sex

However, a closer examination of the lexical choices leaves the reader in no doubt that a strong sense of physical love runs through this poem as well.

The title of the poem can have two meanings: reflecting the job that the speaker is doing, but also suggesting the physical act of impregnation.

The title of the poem "Putting in the Seed" suggests impregnation to the interpreter.[22] In line with corpus linguistic principles, I have been taking a phraseological perspective on the poem, and so let me do this for the title. What are the most common lexical collocates of the phraseology *putting in the*? In UKWaC, at $n + 4$, they are *effort* (forty-eight; t-score 6.9), *work* (twenty-nine; t-score 5.3), and *time* (twenty-eight; t-score 5.2). Thus, *putting in the* has a semantic preference for *effort / time*.[23] Once again, by connecting to corpus evidence, the "projectional" nature of the interpretation via a general category—*sex* in the heading above—is illuminated. This is not to say something sexual is not suggested by *seed* (or elsewhere in the poem). However, a phraseological approach to the language of the poem means that, though *seed* could suggest semen, we need to appreciate how its meaning in the poem could be mediated by the semantic preference for *putting in the*.

7.7.4   Summary

The interpretation of "Putting in the Seed" that I found randomly on the web is unsatisfying on Deleuzean / Guattarian criteria since it does not open up the poem to its interpretative potential. Instead, it remains at a representational level in commenting on what the poem "reflects" or "what it is about"; it does not even seek to connect the two different interpretations it offers. Moreover, because "nature" and "sex" are rather general categories, their use does not easily mobilize interpretation beyond default, and thus unsurprising, commentary on the poem.

In section 7.8, I show how the corpus evidence in this section that I used to criticize this interpretation can be used to evolve my own. In such a way, Phase E below *regenerates* (rather than plagiarizes) the web-based interpretation.

7.8   PHASE E: OCPD, DEPRESSION, AND REDUCED SEX DRIVE

7.8.1   Reduced Sex Drive

In section 7.8, it is the rather general "sexual" reading in the web data excerpted in section 7.7 that I regenerate. I do so by travelling outside the poem to see whether I can connect "Putting in the Seed" to a more specific sexual perspective and, simultaneously, to my performance stylistic reading from Phases A to C.

The reader will know from section 7.6.1 that depression is a symptom of OCPD. On further web-based research, I found out that depression is associated with reduced sex drive:

> one commonly overlooked symptom of depression . . . is reduced sex drive, or in more extreme cases, hypoactive sexual desire disorder (HSDD).[24]

We have a basis for supposing that the persona's OCPD not only leads to depression, but this depression leads to diminishment of libido. Let me now see if this interpretation can be specified / mobilized via the results of the corpus analysis in section 7.7.

7.8.2   Corpus-Based Analysis

While sex would seem to be suggested by *seed* and elsewhere in the poem, collocations of the phraseology *putting in the* [*effort* (forty-eight; t-score 6.9), *work* (twenty-nine; t-score 5.3), and *time* (twenty-eight; t-score 5.2)] lead to an interpretation of joylessness in the persona's attitude to his sexual relationship (as well as chiming with the marked conscientiousness of the OCPD sufferer—APA criteria 3 and 4). Consider also collocates for *shouldering its* [14]: out of the eight instances of this phraseology in UKWaC, *responsibility/ies* occurs five times. Using only *shouldering* as a node word, the highest lexical collocates are *responsibility* (forty-six; t-score 6.8) and *burden* (thirty-four; t-score 5.8). Moreover, the image of the laden *arched body* [13] can connect with the idea of burden. All this information allows me to develop my performance stylistic reading: not only does the OCPD persona of the poem find their sex life a joyless effort and burden, "putting in the seed" can be seen as a rather listless way of describing coitus. In other words, the corpus evidence chimes with an interpretation of reduced sex drive.

Recall the corpus evidence in section 7.7.2 that the most common lexical collocates of *garden* are *house*, *rear*, and *front*. The collocation evidence for *garden* in UKWaC indicates that gardens are talked about most commonly in relation to a house: put another way, it is usual to consider a garden in relation to the home. This corpus evidence mobilizes my interpretative performance as follows. While the persona wants to stay in the garden to get his serotonin high, there could be another reason for this: inside the house is associated with his absent sex life, a by-product of the depression associated with OCPD. Staying outside the house for the marked amount of time that must elapse to allow "the watching for that early birth" [11] of a seedling, or to be able to notice the soil just "tarnishing with weed" [12], might also be construed as an avoidance of his partner and the *burden* of their sex life.

How might a stylistic analysis connect with this enriched interpretative performance?

7.8.3   Stylistic Analysis

7.8.3.1   *Long Vowel to Short Vowel Movement*
Allow me to discuss an internal deviation in the poem that supports and mobilizes an interpretation that there are sexual problems in the relationship. This relates to vowel length in the end-rhyme scheme. The vowels in the end rhymes in lines 1–12 are all "double-vowels" (/aɪ/) or long vowels (/iː/ and /ɜː/). However, in lines 13–14, the rhyme involves the short vowel /ʌ/. One of these short vowels occurs in the orgasmic *comes*, the last word in line 13. An obvious way of symbolizing a delirious orgasm would have been to move from short vowels to long vowels in the end rhymes. Instead, the vowel length scheme in the end rhymes moves from long to short. All this phonological information connects with the evolving interpretation: attempts at sexual union are somewhat unsuccessful due to the persona's reduced sex drive.

7.8.3.2   *Lexis*
We previously saw that *soft petals* [4, 5] is repeated twice. The repetition of *soft* connects with, and further specifies, the reduced sex drive interpretation in suggesting erectile dysfunction—as, indeed, does the entire phraseology *soft petals fallen* [4] in concert with the movement from long vowels to short in the end rhymes. (Indeed, might the burying of the *soft petals fallen* be construed as a symbolic attempt to forget this physical limit?)

For this reading, however, there is an apparent inconsistency in the poem. *Sturdy* in *the sturdy seedling* [13], as the opposite of soft, may at first glance signal erective proficiency:

> The sturdy seedling with arched body comes
> Shouldering its way and shedding the earth crumbs.

That said, common collocates around *shouldering* [14] do rather suggest that achieving *sturdiness* is an effort or a burden—the apparent contradiction is resolved. Lastly, problems in the relationship are also suggested by the evidence in section 7.6.4.2; for example, the lack of the pronoun *our*, or similar meaning, around *Love* [10].

In sum, in section 7.8, I have shown how a corpus-based analysis regenerates the general, and thus rather dead-end, representational "sex" and "nature" based interpretations that I found randomly on the web.[25] In turn, this has not only facilitated connection with the flowing interpretative performance of Phases A, B, and C, but mobilized it further. Indeed, Phase E has reinforced how an interpretation that works with such general representational categories as "sex" and "nature" is debilitating on seeing specific, connective possibilities for the poem.

7.9   CONCLUSION

7.9.1   Review

This chapter has demonstrated a performance stylistic reading. This is an approach, inspired by ideas from Deleuze and Guattari, that connects out to web-based resources for the purposes of generating a singular interpretative performance of a poem. Interpretation with this literacy practice is not concerned with asking "what is this poem about?" "what is the poet trying to say?"[26] nor "what does this poem mean to me?" Nor does a performance stylistic reading of a poem mean interpretation *of* the poem itself. This is because the reading is *across* a series of connections between the poem and a number of outsides, a reading that uses these connections to perform the poem by filling in its personas and scenarios in specific and surprising ways. And, because the emphasis is on the individuality of the interpretative travelling and filling-in, performance stylistics does not seek to do the following: form a universal perspective on the human condition from the particulars of the poem—as is often the case in traditional literacy practices around poetry.

In phasing analysis / interpretation rhizomatically, my evolving interpretation in effect became a multiplicity of elements (OCPD, germination, gardening and depression, depression and reduced sex drive, and relationship difficulties in a couple because one partner has a personality disorder), which is greater than the sum of its parts. Looking at interpretation in terms of a multiplicity helps to circumvent an unrealistic reading of a poem that does not evoke the plural dimensions to life. Moreover, it helps to avoid closing down creative options in interpretation. Given the ever-expanding World Wide Web, there is potentially no end point for interpretation using the procedure of this chapter. Moreover, phasing analysis / interpretation has the advantage of staggering linguistic description; too much stylistic analysis early on, I would argue, can stunt the prospect of generating a singular interpretative performance because of the difficulties of shaking off default associations with linguistic representations.[27]

To reiterate from the introduction, stylistic analysis is a *necessary* centripetal force in performance stylistics rather than a choice. One cannot do this kind of poetry interpretation without linguistic analysis of a poem's structural elements, since this centripetal analysis is needed to connect up the web-based centrifugal phases via description of the patterns of the poem. This not only connects interpretative elements from the centrifugal phases into the poem's language patterns, but this act of connection crucially mobilizes interpretation also. Since the analyst needs to be guided by the idiosyncratic patterns of the poem in the forging of these connections, there is a certain unpredictability to the interpretation that helps the progressing of a singular performance. In contrast, the use of corpus analysis is not a necessary component of performance stylistics. Corpus analysis can be used in a less comprehensive manner than the stylistic analysis, used at different points to mobilize interpretation where this works. Furthermore, since the initial web-based connections made with the poem are based, as far as is possible, in fact / current research, this means that, when interpretation is progressed through use of (corpus) stylistic analysis, it is grounded in fact / current research rather than mere speculation.

7.9.2 "What Is This Poem About?"

Since novels, plays, and films commonly have explicit plots and characters, asking the question, "what is this novel / play / film about?" is often apposite. In contrast, much poetry (particularly many lyric poems of the last hundred years or so) does not contain explicit characters and plot; it is common for poetry to feature a much greater degree of obliqueness and suggestiveness than in many novels, plays, and films. Since making sense of many poems is dependent, to a large degree, on how the reader fills in the "gaps," asking "what is this poem about?" does not always seem to me to be so apposite a question, or at least a completely apposite question. Indeed, this question could limit the interpretative potential of the poem. Asking "what is 'Putting in the Seed' about?" is, I think, unlikely to lead to a response that the persona of the poem has OCPD and regularly gardens because of the side-effect condition of depression, and so forth. This is because the very posing of this question—a "representational" one in Deleuze's terms—restricts the possibilities of a reader opening out the poem to a new set of connections that could then help perform the poem in this way. Naturally, there are limitations to the validity of making connections between a poem and things outside of it; for a connection to be valid, there needs to be an empirical basis in the poem for forming a semantic link with something outside. For example, I began my performance stylistic reading of "Putting in the Seed" from the suggestion that the poem's persona has a certain obsession with burying apple blossom, given they have to be fetched in for supper and question if they will be capable of leaving their work.

7.9.3   Divergence in Interpretative Performances

Due to the vastness of the web, interpretative travels initiated by a poem are likely to diverge markedly for different interpreters; indeed, the obliqueness and suggestiveness of much poetry make it likely that the web searches triggered from reading a poem will vary. And, because of this divergence, and also because a performance stylistic reading is phased, how stylistic analyses and corpus analyses will be used to support / mobilize the web-based element of the reading is likely to vary for different interpreters. By its very nature, there cannot be one definitive, performance stylistic reading of a poem. But, can all poetry be put to work in this way? Lyric poetry that has openness in its textuality is more likely to be productive for performance stylistic ends, for allowing movement through and around the poem, than other forms.[28]

No doubt there are other possible sequences and hookups between Deleuze and Guattari and (corpus) stylistics. The image of the rhizome is anything but inflexible.[29] Finally, I hope I have shown how a performance stylistic reading of a poem is a pleasurable, creative challenge for the reader: putting a poem to work in order to produce, in their own unique way, a series of dynamic connections with a variety of outsides, pulling these into the unpredictably mobilizing machine of the corpus and then into the specific patterns of the poem, evolving a rhizomatic riff, an untimely and singularly performative journey.

NOTES

1. "The best craftsmanship always leaves holes and gaps in the works of the poem, so that something that is *not* in the poem can creep, crawl, flash, or thunder in." Dylan Thomas (quoted in Leech 1969, 227).
2. Frost (1995, 120).
3. This process could work, of course, with a paper-based encyclopedia, moving rhizomatically from one entry to another. However, the web is so much better for this process, since, given its size, it affords greater potential for movement variation, not only from website to website, but from one different text type to another.
4. A "Deleuze and Guattari machine" is not the same as a mechanism, since the latter is organized for a particular purpose (for example, a clock is organized for telling the time). See Deleuze and Guattari (2004).
5. This is not to say that Deleuze and Guattari set up a dichotomy of being and becoming; for Deleuze and Guattari, *being* is part and parcel of *becoming*. Rob Pope indicates this via his neographism, "human be(com)ing" (Pope 2005, 113).

6. This does not necessarily mean that an untimely interpretation needs to relate an old work of literature to the present day or to the future. An untimely perspective on "Putting in the Seed" could, potentially, link it back to 1916. But, it would show, in some way, how the poem renews existing appreciation of that context.

7. The UK Web as Corpus (UKWaC) was built in 2007. It consists of around 1.5 billion words from World Wide Web sites with a UK internet domain name. It contains a wide variety of topics and genres. Since the aim was to build a corpus of British English, only UK internet domains were included (see Ferraresi et al. 2008).

8. http://www.sketchengine.co.uk/

9. http://www.brainphysics.com/oc-personality.php [Accessed June 2012]

10. http://www.brainphysics.com/oc-personality.php [Accessed June 2012]

11. http://www.brainphysics.com/oc-personality.php [Accessed June 2012]. OCPD is not to be confused with "Obsessive Compulsive Disorder" (OCD). OCD is an anxiety disorder (APA 2000) not a personality disorder. Someone with OCD is focused on particular obsessions, such as repeated hand-washing, which distress the sufferer. In contrast, someone with OCPD is not distressed by their abnormality. See http://www.brainphysics.com/oc-personality.php [Accessed June 2012].

12. There are two well-known forms of sonnet, each with different rhyme schemes The Shakespearean sonnet is end rhymed *a-b-a-b, c-d-c-d, d-e-d-e, g-g,* where these letters refer to a particular vowel (+consonant[s]) at the end of a line. The other well-known form of sonnet is the Petrarchan or Italian sonnet. The rhyme scheme of the Petrarchan octet is usually *a-b-a-b-a-b-a-b* For the sestet, there are different possibilities, for example: *c-d-e-c-d-e, c-d-c-c-d-c,* and *c-d-c-d-c-d.* Frost uses the following rhyme scheme: *a-b-a-b-a-b-a-b, c-d-c-d-e-e.*

13. http://en.wikipedia.org/wiki/Germination [Accessed June 2012]

14. Henceforth, the first number in curved brackets refers to the frequency of a collocate and the second number the t-score for the collocation).

15. I include the voiceless affricate /tʃ/.

16. To check this, the reader may want to listen to http://www.youtube.com/watch?v = 1pSyYhRYeIM&feature = related [Accessed June 2012].

17. http://www.brainphysics.com/oc-personality.php [Accessed June 2012].

18. See Lowry et al. (2007).

19. http://www.bristol.ac.uk/news/2007/5384.html [Accessed June 2012]

20. See http://www.suite101.com/content/robert-frosts-putting-in-the-seed-a33831 [Accessed June 2012]

21. The next chunk of text from the website is not part of the interpretation but an advert with a hyperlink (underlined) that appears within it:

How To Study A Poem
    Whether you are reading a poem for pleasure, or simply trying to pass an exam, these helpful hints should allow you to get to grips with what the poet is trying to say.

With "what the poet is trying to say," we have more un-Deleuzean, representational discourse. Such pedagogy would push us in the direction of a timely rather than an untimely interpretation.

22. "Not so barren quite" [5] rather protrudes in an interpretation around 'impregnation' in suggesting only a little fertility.

23. "Semantic preference is the restriction of regular co-occurrence to items that share a semantic feature, for example that they are all about, say, sport or suffering" (Sinclair 2004, 142).

24. http://www.everydayhealth.com/sexual-health/depression-and-hypoac
tive-sexual-desire-disorder.aspx_[Accessed June 2012] This website does not
carry a reference for an academic source. However, it is validated by Pat F
Bass III, MD, MPH, an associate professor of medicine and pediatrics at
Louisiana State University Health Services Center-Shreveport.

25. As an alternative, one could use comments from a web discussion forum to engage
with critically-creatively. Here, for example, is a comment from a randomly discovered forum discussing "Putting in the Seed" that offers a sexual interpretation:

   Frost is a deep poet "Putting in the seed" has definatley got a sexual agenda,
   the title alone conveys this "if i leave off burrying the white soft petals"
   seems to be Frost describing love making outside and the sheer weight buries
   the soft white petals This may be related to Frost's mistress Definatley a light
   hearted poem which uses love making as a metaphor to convey his love for
   nature Good luck in your exams everyone XXX. http://www.americanpoems.
   com/poets/robertfrost/12084/comments/2 [Accessed June 2012].

26. In not taking the writer's intentions into account, performance stylistics
accords with Barthes's "Death of the Author" thesis (Barthes 1967).

27. The interpretative performance I have generated is, naturally, one of many
possibilities. I was raised as a Christian: for me, *fallen, the apple tree, garden,*
and *passion* resonate biblically: the fall, tree of knowledge, Garden of Eden /
Garden of Gethsemane, the Passion, respectively. On this train of thought,
might *shouldering* connect with Christ's shouldering of a wooden cross as
part of the Passion? Then again, these are ideas related to my "being" and
not "becoming"—I need to go beyond what I know already.
This website http://www.bbc.co.uk/news/uk-10905070 [Accessed June 2012]
tells me that *love* and *seed* have the same etymological root in Arabic and that
this is mentioned in the Koran. Especially as these words occur in the same line
(10) in "Putting in the Seed," possibilities for a bifaith rhizome in and around the
poem thus present themselves, one that could become both critical and creative.

28. As a coda, one might argue that what we regard as a literary or valuable
poem on Deleuzean / Guattarian criteria is one that has the potential to do
the following: set off the greatest number of readers to generate unique rhizomes of creative, connective possibilities.

29. And the procedure I have demonstrated is protean too. A performance stylistics reading of a poem that consists of three phases is manageable for a
short undergraduate project (in my case, Phases A to C come to around
3,700 words). If the project is longer in scope, then the critical-creative
Phases D to E could also be accommodated (the substantive parts being
around 1,700 words in my case). A short assignment could just involve a
corpus-based, critical engagement with an existing web-based interpretation
along the lines of Phase D.

Glossary

This glossary focuses on key terms that may not be familiar to some readers, defining them as they are used in this book. See the index for terms that are not covered here but may be defined in the text.

aboutness. Relating to the text's content, what it is about. The term has similarities with Halliday's (1994) *ideational function*.

abstract noun. A noun that refers to an abstract or nonphysical concept, rather than to a material object. See also *intangible noun*.

annotation. Corpus annotation involves associating chunks of language with a category chosen from a set, which could be predefined or derived from preliminary analyses of the data. It is achieved through adding appropriate codes or tags to relevant chunks. Linguistic categories typically relate to grammatical parts of speech or syntactic functions, prosodic forms, or, more recently, semantic fields. But annotation need not be confined to linguistic categories; it could, for example, contain social or contextual categories like sex, social status, genre, or event type. See also *tagging*.

associate. A keyword that has a statistical association with another keyword. See also *keyword*.

authorship attribution. The process of attributing a text to an author; the use of computational methods to do so.

cleft sentence. A complex sentence that emphasizes one part of a simple proposition by expressing it as a clause. For example, in contrast to the simple proposition *John likes coffee*, the cleft sentence *It is John who likes coffee* emphasizes *John* while the cleft sentence *It is coffee that John likes* emphasizes *coffee*.

closed class word. A grammatical word (function word). So called because grammatical words comprise a set inventory to which new members cannot easily be added. Compare *open class word*.

cluster analysis. An exploratory data-analysis method in which a set of observations (texts) is grouped or clustered into categories on the basis of the frequencies of a set of variables (words).

collocation. A statistically significant local association between words (usually pairs of lexical words). For example, *heavy* is a collocate of *rain* in the collocations *heavy rain* and *the rain will be heavy today*.

computational stylistics. The use of computational methods to investigate or characterize (literary) style. The related term *stylometry* more strongly emphasizes the measurement of style than investigation or characterization of it.

concordance. An index to a place in a text where particular words and phrases occur. Concordance lines show the cotexts for the node word in a corpus of texts.

concrete noun. A noun that refers to a material object or any thing that can be apprehended through the senses.

consonant. A basic speech sound in which the breath is at least partly obstructed and which can be combined with a vowel to form a syllable; a letter representing a consonant sound.

content analysis. Content analysis involves the analysis, usually involving statistics, of the semantic content or referential meanings of texts. Today, perhaps its most widespread application is the kind of content analysis performed by search engines, such as Google, to retrieve web pages with a particular content.

cotext (co-text). The words that appear before and after any given word of interest; the linguistic context in which a word appears.

culling. The process of automatically removing from a word frequency list words that are very frequent in it only because of very high local frequency in one or a small number of texts. Its goal is to exclude from analysis words that are very closely related to local context, such as proper names.

Delta. A measure of textual difference based on the frequencies of the most frequent words and specially designed for authorship attribution problems involving multiple candidate authors; introduced by John F. Burrows (2002a, 2002b, 2003).

DeltaLz. A modification of Delta that limits the word list for each authorship attribution test to those words that show large differences in frequency (Hoover 2004b).

dendrogram. A tree diagram produced by cluster analysis, in which texts are classified into groups based on the similarities and differences among the frequencies of the words of the texts. Similarity is indicated by how quickly a pair or a group of texts joins together into a single cluster.

discourse marker. A discourse marker, such as *ah*, *oh*, and *well*, is considered by some linguists not to be part of the grammar or the lexicon. It tends to be peripheral to the syntax, instead playing a role in the organization of dialogue. It has little semantic content, but rather pragmatic import, often expressing speaker attitudes.

Distinctiveness Ratio (DR). A measure of textual difference, defined as the rate of occurrence of a word in one text divided by its rate of occurrence in another text; invented by Ellegård (Kenny 1982, 69–70).

epistolary novel. A novel in which the text consists entirely or predominantly of fictional letters (and occasionally other documents) written or received by characters in the novel.

expletive. A word that acts as a grammatical filler or place-holder without contributing to the meaning of a sentence; for example, *it* in *It is raining*, or *there*, in *Is there any cake left?*

formulaic sequence. For Sinclair (1991), much language use follows the *idiom principle*: the hearer or reader understands language in chunks, rather than as individual words in a grammatical sequence. These chunks vary in size from the short (for example, the marker of politeness, *after you*), to the long (for example, *a bird in the hand is worth two in the bush*.) These chunks may be fixed, such as the above examples, or semifixed, such as *Peter thinks the world of you*, where *Peter* and *you* could be replaced by many other possibilities and *think* could take different forms, such as *thinks* or *thought*. Wray refers to such chunks as *formulaic sequences*: "*formulaic* carries with it some associations of 'unity' and of 'custom' and 'habit,' while *sequence* indicates that there is more than one discernible unit, of whatever kind" (Wray 2002, 9). On this broad definition, formulaic sequences can include both collocation and phraseology.

function word. See *grammatical word*.

grammatical word. A word that expresses a grammatical relationship and classification; for example, a determiner (*a, one, the, three*), a conjunction (*and, if, when*), a preposition (*at, in, on*), a pronoun (*he, she, him, its*), or an auxiliary verb (*be, do, have*). See also *noise word*; compare *lexical word*.

hapax legomenon (plural ***hapax legomena***). A word that occurs exactly once in a text or corpus.

head. The required element in any phrase; for example, a noun phrase has a noun (or pronoun) as the head. Thus *rules* is the head in the noun phrase *the standard rules of behavior*).

ideational function. One of Halliday's (for example, 1978, 1994) three semantic or functional components of language (also called *metafunctions* in systemic theory). The ideational function concerns meanings relating to experience, including processes, participants, and circumstances. It is the referential aspect of language.

idiolect. A character's idiolect is the total set of linguistic choices made by the author for that character, and it is thrown into relief by relationships of contrast or similarity with the idiolects of other characters. In other words, an idiolect is a foregrounded style, which may deviate from or be parallel to the idiolectal styles of other characters.

intangible noun. A noun that refers to any thing that cannot be thought of as a substance or as matter, and cannot be apprehended by the senses. See also *abstract noun*.

interpersonal function. One of Halliday's (for example, 1978, 1994) three semantic or functional components of language (also called *metafunctions* in systemic theory). The interpersonal function concerns the attitudes and emotions expressed among participants in language.

keyword. A word that occurs with a frequency that is statistically unusual relative to some norm. The term *keyword* in corpus linguistics is not to be confused with lexical items that are *key* because they are of particular social, cultural, or political significance.

keyword, positive and negative. A positive keyword is one that is unusually frequent in a text; a negative keyword is one that is unusually infrequent.

key keyword. A keyword that is key in a number of different texts; that is, a word that is generally key across a corpus.

lemma. The lemma of a word consists of all its grammatical forms. Lemmas are indicated conventionally by capitals. The noun lemma COLLAPSE includes the noun singular form *collapse*, the noun possessive form *collapse's*, and the noun plural form *collapses*. The verb lemma COLLAPSE includes the verb forms *collapse, collapses, collapsed*, and *collapsing*. A broad conception of the lemma COLLAPSE would include its noun and verb forms.

lemmatize. The process of analyzing the words of a text on the basis of lemmas rather than word forms; for example, in a lemmatized text, all forms of the word *collapse* would be counted together.

lexical word. A word that contributes to the main information content of a spoken or written text, and belongs to one of four grammatical classes: noun (*Peter, Moscow, dictionary, air*); lexical verb (*walk, think, pray*); adjective (*hot, thirsty, angry, ugliest*); or adverb (*slowly, recently, often*). Compare *grammatical word*; *noise word*.

lexis. The vocabulary, diction, or wording of a text, especially as opposed to its syntax or grammar.

log-likelihood test. A statistical measure of how likely data is, given the parameters of a model. It is used as a test of statistical significance—to quantify how unlikely it is that similar frequencies are due to chance. Compare t-*score*; z-*score*.

modal verb. A verb that has specific function to express modality; for example, *may* and *can't*, respectively, in *he may be out*, and *you can't smoke here*.

modality. The expression of a writer's or speaker's judgment about the likelihood of what he or she is saying (How sure am I about it?) or about levels of obligation (Do I have to do it?).

morphology. The study of the structure of word forms; the structure itself.

multidimensional analysis. Multidimensional analysis, or factor analysis, involves statistical operations on the frequency counts of linguistic features, mostly grammatical, and identifies statistical relationships of co-occurrence between those features. Features that co-occur or group together constitute bipolar *factors* or *dimensions*, which can be labeled according to the kinds of features that constitute them.

multiple narration. The use of two or more distinct narrators in a fictional text.

narrative voice. The idiolect of a single narrator in a text with *multiple narration*.

nearest neighbor. In cluster analysis, a text that is more similar to a given text or group of texts than to any other text or group of texts.

node word. In a concordance, the word or phrase that is searched for.

noise word. A word, typically a grammatical or function word, that has so little meaning or significance that its presence in a word list can be considered 'noise' for some purposes. Such words are sometimes eliminated from consideration in studies of authorship or style. See also *grammatical word*; *closed class word*; compare *lexical word*.

noun phrase. A phrase with a noun or a pronoun as head; for example, *we, holidays, all the right answers, the man in the moon*.

open class word. A lexical word, so called because new lexical words can easily be added to the vocabularies of languages. Compare *closed class word*.

orthography. The study of spelling and punctuation; the spelling and punctuation itself.

PCA. See *principle components analysis*.

phrasal verb. A phrase that consists of a verb plus a preposition or adverb, or both, in which the meaning is (typically) not predictable from the meaning of the parts; for example, *to drive up the price*, or *to go out with someone*. Compare *to drive up the driveway*, and *to go out with an umbrella*, in which *up*, *out*, and *with* are normal prepositions and adverbs.

phrase. A structural unit of one or more words, consisting of a head plus (optional) modifiers.

phraseology. Language patterns can consist of both lexical words and grammatical words; for example, *the first time I saw*. Corpus investigation may reveal such patterns to be regular. Such regular patterns of lexical words and grammatical words, which may or may not correspond to complete grammatical units, are known as *phraseologies*.

plosive. A consonant produced by stopping the airflow using the lips, teeth, or palate, followed by a sudden release of air. The basic plosives in English are /t/, /k/, /p/ (voiceless) and /d/, /g/, and /b/ (voiced).

prepositional phrase. A phrase consisting of a preposition together with its associated noun phrase (*in the box, with his hands up, after the party*).

principle components analysis. An exploratory method of data analysis that attempts to explain the maximum amount of variation in the frequencies of variables by combining variables that occur in similar ways into new, unrelated variables called *principle components*. For example, the variables of height, weight, arm span, inseam, shoe size, and ring size seem likely to be highly related to (correlated with) each other. Principle components analysis would likely combine all of them into a single variable that might be called *size*. In an authorship attribution context, the variables are typically word frequencies and the first, or most significant, component is typically authorship.

reference corpus. A body of electronic textual data—a corpus—that provides a point of comparison for the data to be analyzed. Keywords, indeed keyness, relies on such a comparison.

semantic preference. A set of different, frequently occurring collocates that are from the same semantic field; for example, words that are about sports.

semantic prosody. Sinclair (2004, 30–35) discovered an interesting phraseological pattern around the seemingly neutral collocation *naked eye*. His corpus investigation revealed a common phraseology, *negativity + visibility + preposition + the + naked + eye* such as in *too faint to be seen with the naked eye* or *it is not really visible to the naked eye*. What is interesting here is that, while the collocation *naked eye* would seem to be neutral, in the sense of being devoid of connotational meaning, the regular phraseology in which it appears is not neutral. It carries the evaluative meanings of constraint or limitation. This type of evaluative meaning is spread over the phraseology and thus absorbs seemingly neutral meanings like *naked eye*. This corpus-illuminated type of evaluative meaning is referred to as *semantic prosody*. It is different from connotational meaning, since the latter is regarded as conventionally associated with a word; for example, *devil* has conventionally associated negative meaning.

sibilant. A speech sound that carries a hissing effect; for example, /s/, /sh/ (or in phonemic representation /ʃ/).

SGML (standard generalized markup language). A markup language is a metalanguage, a series of instructions about, for example, how the text is to be structured and presented. The most common example of a markup language is HTML, which is consistent with SGML and underlies all web pages. A tag in this context contains a command for the computer about what to do with the text, and the markup system is a standardized way of (or syntax for) organizing the tags. For example, using angle brackets to form tags, placing them so that they touch the text to which they pertain, and having a beginning (a "switch on") and an end (a "switch off") tag is derived from SGML. See also *annotation*; *tagging*; *TEI*.

sociopragmatic. The branch of pragmatics that is particularly concerned with how meanings are shaped by, and in turn shape, social contexts.

span. The number of words chosen on either side of the node word to determine the scope of a concordance investigation of a corpus. Four places to the left of a node word and four places to the right of it is the standard span for searching for collocation in corpus linguistics (Jones and Sinclair 1974). This standard span is referred to, in short, as an n ± 4 span (where *n* = node word).

speech marker. A phrase that identifies part of a text as a character's speech; for example, *he said*, or *she quietly responded*. As in the last example, a speech marker sometimes also characterizes the speech in some way.

standard deviation. A measure of how widely dispersed a set of values is. The standard deviation is calculated from the mean (average) frequency and the difference of all the values from the mean. When all of the values are close to the mean, the standard deviation is small, but when the values fluctuate a great deal, the standard deviation is large. Large differences in frequency are thus more significant if the standard deviation is small.

standard generalized markup language. See *SGML.*

style marker. Style markers are words (or other textual features) that are associated with particular contexts. They have frequencies of occurrence that differ significantly from words that are restricted, at least to some degree, to other contexts. They are closely related to statistically defined *keywords.*

style variation. Any significant change in style over a given corpus, which may be as small as a few hundred words or as large as an entire authorial oeuvre.

style variation method. An alternate method of creating a word frequency list for a corpus; rather than listing words in descending order of total frequency in the corpus, they are listed in descending order of each word's highest frequency in any text in the corpus (Hoover 2003c).

stylometry. Statistically based approaches to textual style; the measurement of style. The related term *computational stylistics* more strongly emphasizes investigation and characterization of style than measurement of it.

syntax. The ways words, phrases, and clauses are combined to form sentences.

tagging. Codes appended to chunks of text that allow a computer to assign those chunks to particular categories (or the process of appending such chunks). Tags appended to words are often linked by an underscore; for example, ball_NN. Tags appended to larger portions of text often involve pairs of brackets; for example, <s>This is a sentence<\s>. See also *annotation*; *SGML*; *TEI.*

TEI (Text-Encoding Initiative). A consortium that collectively develops and maintains a standard for representing digital texts. It produces guidelines that specify encoding methods for machine-readable texts, mainly in the humanities, social sciences, and linguistics. See also *annotation*; *SGML*; *tagging.*

textual function. One of Halliday's (for example, 1978, 1994) three semantic or functional components of language (also called *metafunctions* in systemic theory). The textual function concerns the thematic, informational, and cohesive structure of language.

t-score. A statistical measure of the likelihood that two or more words occur together by chance.

token. An individual instance of a type or class; an individual instance of a unique word or spelling. The previous sentence contains fifteen tokens (words). See also *type.*

type. A class or category; a unique spelling. Six types are represented by the seven tokens of the previous sentence.

voiced / voiceless sound. When the vibration of the vocal chords is necessary for a speech sound, it is said to be voiced. The consonant sound /b/ is voiced, but the consonant sound /p/ is not voiced—it is voiceless. The production of English vowels requires the vibration of the vocal chords; thus, all English vowels are also voiced.

vowel. A speech sound that is produced by vibration of the vocal cords but without audible air friction, and which is a unit of the sound system of a language that forms the nucleus of a syllable; a letter representing a vowel sound, such as *a, e, i, o, u*. Compare *consonant*.

word family. A group of morphologically related words, typically including all forms of a lemma, but sometimes also including words that would not normally be considered part of the lemma. For example, *sharply-cut* might be considered part of a word family formed around *sharp*, but would not normally be considered part of the lemma SHARP. See also *lemma; lemmatize*.

z-score (standard score). The number of standard deviations above or below the mean (average) at which a given raw score falls, calculated by subtracting the mean score from the raw score and dividing by the standard deviation for the word. See also *standard deviation*.

References

Adcock, Fleur. 2000. *Poems 1960–2000*. Tarset, Northumberland: Bloodaxe Books Ltd.

Adolphs, Svenja, and Ronald Carter. 2002. "Corpus Stylistics: Point of View and Semantic Prosodies in *To the Lighthouse*." *Poetica* 58: 7–20.

Ali, Afida Mohamad. 2007. "Semantic Fields of Problem in Business English: Malaysian and British Journalistic Business Texts." *Corpora* 2 (2): 211–39.

American Psychiatric Association (APA). 2000. *Diagnostic and Statistical Manual of Mental Disorders*. 4th ed. Washington, DC.

Archer, Dawn, ed. 2009. *What's in a Word-List? Investigating Word Frequency and Keyword Extraction*. Aldershot: Ashgate.

Archer, Dawn, and Derek Bousfield. 2010. " 'See better, Lear'? See Lear Better! A Corpus-Based Pragma-stylistic Investigation of Shakespeare's *King Lear*." In *Language and Style: Essays in Honour of Mick Short*, edited by Dan McIntyre and Beatrix Busse, 183–203. New York: Palgrave.

Archer, Dawn, and Jonathan Culpeper. 2003. "Sociopragmatic Annotation: New Directions and Possibilities in Historical Corpus Linguistics." In *Corpus Linguistics by the Lune: A Festschrift for Geoffrey Leech*, edited by Andrew Wilson, Paul Rayson, and Anthony M. McEnery, 37–58. Frankfurt/Main: Peter Lang.

Archer, Dawn, Jonathan Culpeper, and Paul Rayson. 2009. "Love–'a familiar of a devil'? An Exploration of Key Domains in Shakespeare's Comedies and Tragedies." In *What's in a Word-list? Investigating Word Frequency and Keyword Extraction*, edited by Dawn Archer, 137–57. Aldershot: Ashgate.

Archer, Dawn, Tony McEnery, Paul Rayson, and Andrew Hardie. 2003. "Developing an Automated Semantic Analysis System for Early Modern English." In *Proceedings of the Corpus Linguistics 2003 Conference*, edited by Dawn Archer, Paul Rayson, Andrew Wilson, and Tony McEnery, 22–31. *UCREL Technical Paper Number 16*. UCREL: University of Lancaster.

Archer, Dawn, and Paul Rayson. 2004. "Using an Historical Semantic Tagger as a Diagnostic Tool for Variation in Spelling." Paper presented at the Thirteenth International Conference on English Historical Linguistics, University of Vienna, Austria, August 2004.

Archer, Dawn, Paul Rayson, Scott Piao, and Tony McEnery. 2004. "Comparing the UCREL Semantic Annotation Scheme with Lexicographical Taxonomies." In Vol. 3 of *Proceedings of the 11th EURALEX (European Association for Lexicography) International Congress (EURALEX 2004), Lorient, France, 6–10 July 2004*, edited by Geoffrey Williams and Sandra Vessier, 817–27. Lorient: Université de Bretagne Sud.

Argamon, Shlomo. 2008. "Interpreting Burrows's Delta: Geometric and Probabilistic Foundations." *Literary and Linguistic Computing* 23 (2): 131–47.

Attridge, Derek. 2004. *The Singularity of Literature*. London: Routledge.

Baker, Dorothy Z. 1996. " 'Detested Be the Epithet!': Definition, Maxim, and the Language of Social Dicta in Hannah Webster Foster's *The Coquette.*" *Essays in Literature* 23 (1): 58–68.

Baker, Paul. 2004. "Querying Keywords: Questions of Difference, Frequency and Sense in Keywords Analysis." *Journal of English Linguistics* 32 (4): 346–59.

Baker, Paul. 2011. "Times May Change, But We Will Always Have Money: Diachronic Variation in Recent British English." *Journal of English Linguistics* 39 (1): 65–88.

Barcelona Sánchez, Antonio. 1995. "Metaphorical Models of Romantic Love in *Romeo and Juliet.*" *Journal of Pragmatics* 24 (6): 667–88.

Baron, Alistair, and Paul Rayson. 2008. "VARD 2: A Tool for Dealing with Spelling Variation in Historical Corpora." In *Proceedings of the Postgraduate Conference in Corpus Linguistics.* Birmingham: Aston University.

Barthes, Roland. (1967) 1977. "The Death of the Author." In *Image, Music, Text,* translated by Stephen Heath, 142–48. London: Fontana.

Barthes, Roland. (1970) 1975. *S-Z.* Translated by Richard Miller. London: Cape.

Beach, Joseph Warren, ed. 1963. *The American.* New York: Holt.

Bennett, Anna Maria. 1789. *Agnes De-Courci: A Domestic Tale.*

Biber, Douglas. 1988. *Variation Across Speech and Writing.* Cambridge: Cambridge University Press.

Biber, Douglas. 2012. "Corpus Linguistics and the Study of Literature: Back to the Future?" *Scientific Study of Literature* 1 (1): 15–23.

Biber, Douglas, Susan Conrad, and Randi Reppen. 1998. *Corpus Linguistics: Investigating Language Structure and Use.* Cambridge: Cambridge University Press.

Biber, Douglas, Stig Johansson, Geoffrey Leech, Susan Conrad, and Edward Finegan. 1999. *Longman Grammar of Spoken and Written English.* Harlow: Pearson Education.

Blake, Norman F. 1983. *Shakespeare's Language: An Introduction.* London: MacMillan.

Bondi, Marina, and Mike R. Scott, eds. 2010. *Keyness in Texts.* Amsterdam: John Benjamins.

Bontatibus, Donna. "Foster's *The Coquette.*" *Explicator* 58 (4): 188–90.

Brinton, Laurel, and Elizabeth C. Traugott. 2005. *Lexicalization and Language Change.* Cambridge: Cambridge University Press.

Brook, George L. 1976. *The Language of Shakespeare,* London: Andre Deutsch.

Brown, Gillian. 1997. "Consent, Coquetry, and Consequences." *American Literary History* 9 (4): 625–52.

Brown, Penelope, and Stephen C. Levinson. 1987. *Politeness: Some Universals in Language Usage.* Cambridge: Cambridge University Press.

Brown, Roger, and Albert Gilman. 1960. "The Pronouns of Power and Solidarity." In *Style in Language,* edited by Thomas A. Sebeok, 253–76. Cambridge, MA: MIT Press.

Burney, Fanny. 1778. *Evelina.* http://www.gutenberg.org/dirs/etext04/eveli10.txt.

Burrows, John F. 1987. *Computation into Criticism.* Oxford: Clarendon Press.

Burrows, John F. 1992a. "Computers and the Study of Literature." In *Computers and Written Texts,* edited by Christopher S. Butler. Oxford: Blackwell.

Burrows, John F. 1992b. "Not Unless You Ask Nicely: The Interpretive Nexus Between Analysis and Information." *Literary and Linguistic Computing* 7 (2): 91–109.

Burrows, John F. 2002a. " 'Delta': A Measure of Stylistic Difference and a Guide to Likely Authorship." *Literary and Linguistic Computing* 17 (3): 267–87.

Burrows, John F. 2002b. "The Englishing of Juvenal: Computational Stylistics and Translated Texts." *Style* 36 (4): 677–99.

Burrows, John F. 2003. "Questions of Authorship: Attribution and Beyond." *Computers and the Humanities* 37 (1): 5–32.

Burrows, John F. 2005. "Who Wrote *Shamela*? Verifying the Authorship of a Parodic Text." *Literary and Linguistic Computing* 20 (4): 437–50.

Burrows, John F. 2006. "All the Way Through: Testing for Authorship in Different Frequency Strata." *Literary and Linguistic Computing* 22 (1): 27–47.

Burrows, John F. 2012. "A Second Opinion on 'Shakespeare and Authorship Studies in the Twenty-First Century.'" *Shakespeare Quarterly* 63 (3): 355–392.

Carter, Ronald. 2004. *Language and Creativity: The Art of Common Talk*. London: Routledge.

Carter, Ronald, and Peter Stockwell, eds. 2008. *The Language and Literature Reader*. London: Routledge.

Channell, Joanna. 2000. "Corpus-Based Analysis of Evaluative Lexis." In *Evaluation in Text: Authorial Stance and the Construction of Discourse*, edited by Susan Hunston and Geoffrey Thompson, 38–55. Oxford: Oxford University Press.

Chatman, Seymour B. 1972. *The Later Style of Henry James*. Oxford: Blackwell.

Clement, Ross, and David Sharp. 2003. "Ngram and Bayesian Classification of Documents." *Literary and Linguistic Computing* 18 (4): 423–47.

Collins, Wilkie. 1868. *The Moonstone*. http://www.gutenberg.org/dirs/etext94/mston10.txt.

Cook, Guy. 1994. *Discourse and Literature: The Interplay of Form and Mind*. Oxford: Oxford University Press.

Cook, Guy. 2000. *Language Play, Language Learning*. Oxford: Oxford University Press.

Cooper, Susannah Maria. 1813. *Caroline Herbert*. London: Becket and Porter. http://www.chawton.org/novels/wife/index.html.

Costas, Gabrielatos, and Paul Baker. 2008. "Fleeing, Sneaking, Flooding: A Corpus Analysis of Discursive Constructions of Refugees and Asylum Seekers in the UK Press 1996–2005." *Journal of English Linguistics* 36 (1): 5–38.

Craig, Hugh. 2011. "Shakespeare's Vocabulary: Myth and Reality." *Shakespeare's Quarterly* 62 (1): 53–74.

Craig, Hugh, and Arthur F. Kinney, eds. 2010. *Shakespeare, Computers, and the Mystery of Authorship*. Cambridge: Cambridge University Press.

Craig, William J. 1914. *The Oxford Shakespeare*. Oxford: Oxford University Press.

Culpeper, Jonathan. 2001. *Language and Characterisation: People in Plays and other Texts*. Harlow: Pearson Education.

Culpeper, Jonathan. 2002. "Computers, Language and Characterisation: An Analysis of Six Characters in *Romeo and Juliet*." In Vol. 15 of *Conversation in Life and in Literature: Papers from the ASLA Symposium*, edited by Ulla Melander-Marttala, Carin Ostman, and Merja Kytö, 11–30. Uppsala: Association Suedoise de Linguistique Appliquee (ASLA). (Also available at http://www.lexically.net/wordsmith/corpus_linguistics_links/papers_using_wordsmith.htm).

Culpeper, Jonathan. 2009. "Keyness: Words, Parts-of-Speech, and Semantic Categories in the Character-Talk of Shakespeare's *Romeo and Juliet*." *International Journal of Corpus Linguistics* 14 (1): 29–59.

D'Andrade, Roy G. 1965. "Trait Psychology and Componential Analysis." *American Anthropologist* 67 (5): 215–28.

Deignan, Alice. 2005. *Metaphor and Corpus Linguistics*. Amsterdam: John Benjamins.

Deignan, Alice, and Elena Semino. 2010. "Corpus Techniques for Metaphor Analysis." In *Metaphor Analysis: Research Practice in Applied Linguistics, Social Sciences and the Humanities*, edited by Lynne Cameron and Robert Maslen, 161–79. London: Equinox.

Deleuze, Gilles. (1962) 1983. *Nietzsche and Philosophy*. Translated by Hugh Tomlinson. London: Athlone.

Deleuze, Gilles. (1968) 2004. *Difference and Repetition*. Translated by Paul Patton. London: Continuum.

Deleuze, Gilles. 1995. *Negotiations 1972–1990*. Translated by Martin Joughin. New York: Columbia University Press.

Deleuze, Gilles, and Félix Guattari. (1972) 2004. *Anti-Oedipus*. London: Continuum.

Deleuze, Gilles, and Félix Guattari. (1980) 1987. *A Thousand Plateaus*. Translated by Brian Massumi. London: Athlone.

Demmen, Jane E. J. 2013. "A Corpus Stylistic Investigation of the Language Style of Shakespeare's Plays in the Context of Other Contemporaneous Plays." PhD diss., Lancaster University.

Dovring, Karin. 1954. "Quantitative Semantics in 18th Century Sweden." *Public Opinion Quarterly* 18 (4): 389–94.

Eder, Maciej. 2013. "Mind Your Corpus: Systematic Errors in Authorship Attribution." *Literary and Linguistic Computing*. Published electronically, July 23, 2013.

Eder, Maciej, and Jan Rybicki. 2013. "Do Birds of a Feather Really Flock Together, or How to Choose Training Samples for Authorship Attribution." *Literary and Linguistic Computing* 28 (2): 229–36.

Edgeworth, Maria. 1798. *Letters for Literary Ladies*. 2nd ed. http://digital.library.upenn.edu/women/edgeworth/ladies/ladies.html.

Elliott, Ward E. Y. and Robert J. Valenza. 2011. "Shakespeare's Vocabulary: Did it Dwarf All Others?" In *Stylistics and Shakespeare's Language*, edited by Mireille Ravassat and Jonathan Culpeper, 34–57. London: Continuum.

Enkvist, Nils Erik. 1964. "On Defining Style." In *Linguistics and Style*, edited by Nils Erik Enkvist, John Spencer, and Michael J. Gregory, 1–56. Oxford: Oxford University Press.

Enkvist, Nils Erik. 1973. *Linguistic Stylistics*. Berlin: Mouton.

Evans, Gareth. 1995. "Rakes, Coquettes and Republican Patriarchs: Class, Gender and Nation in Early American Sentimental Fiction." *Canadian Review of American Studies* 25 (3): 41–62.

Faulkner, William. (1930) 2000. *As I Lay Dying: The Corrected Text*. New York: Modern Library.

Ferraresi, Adriano, Eros Zanchetta, Marco Baroni, and Silvia Bernardini. 2008. "Introducing and Evaluating ukWaC." In *Proceedings of the 4th Web as Corpus Workshop*, edited by Stefan Evert, Adam Kilgarriff, and Serge Sharoff, 47–54. Marrakech: LREC.

Finseth, Ian. 2001. "'A Melancholy Tale': Rhetoric, Fiction, and Passion in *The Coquette*." *Studies in the Novel* 33 (2): 125–59.

Fischer-Starcke, Bettina. 2010. *Corpus Linguistics in Literary Analysis: Jane Austen and Her Contemporaries*. London: Continuum.

Foster, Hannah Webster. 1797. *The Coquette*. http://digital.library.upenn.edu/women/foster/coquette/coquette.html.

Fowler, Roger. 1986. *Linguistic Criticism*. Oxford: Oxford University Press.

Fowler, Roger. 1996. *Linguistic Criticism*. 2nd ed. Oxford: Oxford University Press.

Frost, Robert. (1916) 1995. "Putting in the Seed." In *Robert Frost: Collected Poems, Prose and Plays*, edited by Richard Poirier and Mark Richardson, 120. New York: The Library of America.

Garside, Roger. 1987. "The CLAWS Word-Tagging System." In *The Computational Analysis of English: A Corpus-Based Approach*, edited by Roger Garside, Geoffrey Sampson, and Geoffrey N. Leech. London: Longman.

Gettmann, Royal A. 1945. "Henry James's Revision of *The American*." *American Literature* 16 (4): 279–95.

Gibbon, Dafydd, Inge Mertins, and Roger Moore, eds. 2000. *Handbook of Multimodal and Spoken Dialogue Systems: Resources, Terminology and Product Evaluation*. New York: Kluwer Academic Publishers.

Gilbert, Anthony J. 1979. *Literary Language from Chaucer to Johnson*. London: MacMillan.

Goodenough, Ward H. 1956. "Componential Analysis and the Study of Meaning." *Language* 32 (1): 195–216.

Goodman, Sharon, and Kieran A. O'Halloran, eds. 2006. *The Art of English: Literary Creativity.* Basingstoke: Palgrave.

Guiraud, Pierre. (1954) 1970. *Les Caractères Statistiques du Vocabulaire,* 64–67. Paris: Presses Universitaires de France. Reprinted in *La Stylistique Lectures,* edited by Pierre Guiraud and Pierre Kuentz, 222–4. Paris: Klincksieck.

Halliday, Michael A.K. 1973. *Explorations in the Functions of Language.* London: Edward Arnold.

Halliday, Michael A.K. 1978. *Language as Social Semiotic: The Social Interpretation of Language and Meaning.* London: Edward Arnold.

Halliday, Michael A.K. 1994. *An Introduction to Functional Grammar.* 2nd edition. London: Edward Arnold.

Harris, Sharon M. 1995. "Hannah Webster Foster's *The Coquette*: Critiquing Franklin's America." In *Redefining the Political Novel: American Women Writers, 1797–1901,* edited by Sharon M. Harris. Knoxville: University of Tennessee Press.

Ho, Yufang. 2011. *Corpus Stylistics in Principles and Practice: A Stylistic Exploration of John Fowles' "The Magus."* London: Continuum.

Hochmann, Baruch. 1985. *Character in Literature.* Ithaca: Cornell University Press.

Hoey, Michael. 2005. *Lexical Priming: A New Theory of Words and Language.* London and New York: Routledge.

Hoey, Michael. 2007. "Lexical Priming and Literary Creativity." In *Text, Discourse and Corpora: Theory and Analysis,* edited by Michael Hoey, Michaela Mahlberg, Michael Stubbs, and Wolfgang Teubert, 7–29. London: Continuum.

Holmes, David I. 1994. "Authorship Attribution." *Computers and the Humanities* 28 (2): 87–106.

Hoover, David L. 1999. *Language and Style in The Inheritors.* Lanham, Maryland: University Press of America.

Hoover, David L. 2002. "Frequent Word Sequences and Statistical Stylistics." *Literary and Linguistic Computing* 17 (2): 157–80.

Hoover, David L. 2003a. "Another Perspective on Vocabulary Richness." *Computers and the Humanities* 37 (2): 151–78.

Hoover, David L. 2003b. "Frequent Collocations and Authorial Style." *Literary and Linguistic Computing* 18 (3): 261–86.

Hoover, David L. 2003c. "Multivariate Analysis and the Study of Style Variation." *Literary and Linguistic Computing* 18 (4): 341–60.

Hoover, David L. 2004a. "Testing Burrows's Delta." *Literary and Linguistic Computing* 19 (4): 453–75.

Hoover, David L. 2004b. "Delta Prime?" *Literary and Linguistic Computing* 19 (4): 477–95.

Hoover, David L. 2004c. "Altered Texts, Altered Worlds, Altered Styles." *Language and Literature* 13 (2): 99–118.

Hoover, David L. 2007. "Corpus Stylistics, Stylometry, and the Styles of Henry James" *Style* 41 (2): 174–203.

Hoover, David L. 2009. "Word Frequency, Statistical Stylistics, and Authorship Attribution." In *What's in a Word-List? Investigating Word Frequency and Keyword Extraction,* edited by Dawn Archer, 35–51. Aldershot: Ashgate.

Hoover, David L. 2010a. "Some Approaches to Corpus Stylistics." In *Stylistics: Past, Present, and Future,* edited by Yu Dongmin, 40–63. Shanghai: Shanghai Foreign Language Education Press.

Hoover, David L. 2010b. "Authorial Style." In *Language and Style: Essays in Honour of Mick Short,* edited by Dan McIntyre and Beatrix Busse, 250–71. New York: Palgrave Macmillan.

Hori, Masahiro. 2004. *Investigating Dickens' Style: A Collocational Analysis*. New York: Palgrave Macmillan.

Hunston, Susan. 1995. "A Corpus Study of Some English Verbs of Attribution." *Functions of Language* 2 (2):133–58.

Hunston, Susan. 2001. "Colligation, Lexis, Pattern, and Text." In *Patterns of Text: In Honour of Michael Hoey*, edited by Mike R. Scott and Geoff Thompson, 13–33. Amsterdam: John Benjamins.

Hunston, Susan. 2002. *Corpora in Applied Linguistics*. Cambridge: Cambridge University Press.

Hunston, Susan. 2010. *Corpus Approaches to Evaluation: Phraseology and Evaluative Language*. Abingdon: Routledge.

Hunston, Susan, and Gill Francis. 2000. *Pattern Grammar: A Corpus-Driven Approach to the Lexical Grammar of English*. Amsterdam: John Benjamins.

Jakobson, Roman. (1960) 1996. "Closing Statement: Linguistics and Poetics." In *The Stylistics Reader: From Roman Jakobson to the Present*, edited by Jean Jacques Weber, 10–35. London: Routledge.

James, Henry. 1871. *Watch and Ward*. http://www2.newpaltz.edu/hathawar/watchandward.html.

James, Henry. 1875. *Roderick Hudson*. http://www.gutenberg.org/dirs/etext94/rhuds10.txt.

James, Henry. 1877. *The American*. http://eserver.org/fiction/the-american.txt.

James, Henry. 1878. *Daisy Miller*. http://www2.newpaltz.edu/hathawar/daisy0.html.

James, Henry. 1878. *The Europeans*. http://www2.newpaltz.edu/hathawar/european.html.

James, Henry. 1880. *Confidence*. http://www.gutenberg.org/dirs/etext94/confi10.txt.

James, Henry. 1881. *The Portrait of a Lady*. http://www.bartleby.com/311/.

James, Henry. 1886. *The Bostonians*. http://www2.newpaltz.edu/hathawar/bostonians1.html; http://www2.newpaltz.edu/hathawar/bostonians2.html.

James, Henry. 1886. *The Princess Casamassima*. http://www.henryjames.org.uk/pcasa/home.htm.

James, Henry. 1890. *The Tragic Muse*. http://www.henryjames.org.uk/tmuse/home.htm.

James, Henry. 1896. *The Other House*. http://books.google.com/books.

James, Henry. 1897. *The Spoils of Poynton*. http://www.henryjames.org.uk/spoynt/home.htm.

James, Henry. 1899. *The Awkward Age*. http://www.henryjames.org.uk/aage/home.htm.

James, Henry. 1901. *The Sacred Fount*. http://www2.newpaltz.edu/hathawar/sacredfount.html.

James, Henry. 1907. *The American*. Electronic edition created and provided by John F. Burrows.

James, Henry. 1907–09. *The New York Edition of the Novels and Tales of Henry James*, 24 vols. New York: Scribner.

James, Henry. 1908. *The Reverberator*. http://www2.newpaltz.edu/hathaway/reverberator.html.

James, Henry. 1908. *What Maisie Knew*. http://www2.newpaltz.edu/hathaway/maisie1.html; http://www2.newpaltz.edu/hathawar/maisie2.html.

James, Henry. 1909. *The Ambassadors*. http://www.gutenberg.org/dirs/etext96/ambas10.txt.

James, Henry. 1909. *Daisy Miller*. http://www2.newpaltz.edu/hathawar/daisynye.html.

James, Henry. 1909. *The Golden Bowl*. http://www2.newpaltz.edu/hathawar/goldenbowl1.html; http://www2.newpaltz.edu/hathawar/goldenbowl2.html.

James, Henry. 1909. *The Portrait of a Lady*. http://www2.newpaltz.edu/hathawar/portrait1.html; http://www2.newpaltz.edu/hathawar/portrait2.html.

James, Henry. 1909. *The Wings of the Dove*. http://www2.newpaltz.edu/hathaway/wings1.html; http://www2.newpaltz.edu/hathawar/wings2.html.

James, Henry. 1911. *The Outcry*. http://www.henryjames.org.uk/outcryn/home.htm.

James, Henry. 1917. *The Sense of the Past*. http://books.google.com/books.

James, Henry. 1917. *The Ivory Tower.* http://www.henryjames.org.uk/itower/home.htm.

Jeffries, Lesley, and Dan McIntyre. 2010. *Stylistics.* Cambridge: Cambridge University Press.

Jockers, Matthew L., Daniela M. Witten, and Craig S. Criddle. 2008. "Reassessing Authorship of the Book of Mormon Using Delta and Nearest Shrunken Centroid Classification." *Literary and Linguistic Computing* 23 (4): 465–91.

Johnson, Sally, Jonathan Culpeper, and Stephanie Suhr. 2003. "From 'Politically Correct Councillors' to 'Blairite Nonsense': Discourses of Political Correctness in Three British Newspapers." *Discourse and Society* 14 (1): 28–47.

Jones, Martha, Paul Rayson, and Geoffrey N. Leech. 2004. "Key Category Analysis of a Spoken Corpus for EAP." Paper presented at The 2nd Inter-Varietal Applied Corpus Studies (IVACS) International Conference on "Analyzing Discourse in Context," the Graduate School of Education, Queen's University, Belfast, Northern Ireland, June 2004.

Jones, Rodney, ed. 2012. *Discourse and Creativity.* Harlow: Pearson.

Jones, Susan, and John Sinclair. 1974. "English Lexical Collocations." *Cahiers de Lexicologie* 24 (1): 15–61.

Kenny, Anthony. 1982. *The Computation of Style.* Oxford: Pergamon Press.

Koller, Veronika, Andrew Hardie, Paul Rayson, and Elena Semino. 2008. "Using a Semantic Annotation Tool for the Analysis of Metaphor in Discourse." *Metaphorik.de.* http://www.metaphorik.de/15/koller.pdf.

Krause, Sydney J. 1958. "James's Revisions of the Style of *The Portrait of a Lady*." *American Literature* 30 (1): 67–88.

Krook-Gilead, Dorothea. 1962. *The Ordeal of Consciousness in Henry James.* Cambridge: Cambridge University Press.

Lee, Vernon. 1968. *The Handling of Words.* Lincoln: University of Nebraska Press.

Leech, Geoffrey N. 1969. *A Linguistic Guide to English Poetry.* Harlow: Longman.

Leech, Geoffrey N. 1981. *Semantics.* Middlesex: Penguin Books.

Leech, Geoffrey N. 1997. "Introducing Corpus Annotation." In *Corpus Annotation: Linguistic Information from Computer Text Corpora*, edited by Roger Garside, Geoffrey N. Leech, and Tony McEnery, 1–18. Harlow: Longman.

Leech, Geoffrey N. 2008. *Language in Literature: Style and Foregrounding.* Harlow: Pearson Education.

Leech, Geoffrey N., Roger Garside, and Michael Bryant. 1994. "CLAWS 4: The Tagging of the British National Corpus." In *Proceedings of the 15th International Conference on Computational Linguistics (COLING 94)* Kyoto, Japan, 622–28. Also available at http://www.comp.lancs.ac.uk/computing/research/ucrel/papers/coling.html.

Leech, Geoffrey N., Paul Rayson, and Andrew Wilson. 2001. *Word Frequencies in Written and Spoken English Based on the British National Corpus.* London: Longman.

Leech, Geoffrey N., and Mick Short. 2007. *Style in Fiction: A Linguistic Introduction to English Fictional Prose.* 2nd ed. Harlow: Pearson Education.

Lodge, David. 1966. *Language of Fiction.* London: Routledge and Kegan Paul.

Louw, Bill. 1993. "Irony in the Text or Insincerity in the Writer? The Diagnostic Potential of Semantic Prosodies." In *Text and Technology: In Honour of John M. Sinclair*, edited by Mona Baker, Gill Francis and Elena Tognini-Bonelli, 157–76. Amsterdam: John Benjamins.

Louw, Bill. 1997. "The Role of Corpora in Critical Literary Appreciation." In *Teaching and Language Corpora*, edited by Anne Wichmann, Steven Fligelstone, Tony McEnery, and Gerry Knowles, 240–51. London: Longman.

Love, Harold. 2002. *Attributing Authorship: An Introduction.* Cambridge: Cambridge University Press.

Lowry, C., J. Hollis, A. de Vries, B. Pan, L. Brunet, J. Hunt, J. Paton, E. van Kampen, D. Knight, A. Evans, G. Rook, and S. Lightman. 2007. "Identification of an

Immune-responsive Mesolimbocortical Serotonergic System: Potential Role in Regulation of Emotional Behavior." *Neuroscience* 146 (2–5): 756–72.

Mahlberg, Michaela. 2007. "Clusters, Key Clusters and Local Textual Functions in Dickens." *Corpora* 2 (1): 1–31.

Mahlberg, Michaela. 2013. *Corpus Stylistics and Dickens's Fiction*. New York: Routledge.

Mahlberg, Michaela, and Dan McIntyre. 2011. "A Case for Corpus Stylistics: Ian Fleming's *Casino Royale*." *English Text Construction* 4 (2): 204–27.

Maybin, Janet, and Joan Swann, eds. 2006. *The Art of English: Everyday Creativity*. Basingstoke: Palgrave Macmillan.

McArthur, Tom. 1981. *Longman Lexicon of Contemporary English*. London: Longman.

McEnery, Tony, and Andrew Wilson. 2001. *Corpus Linguistics: An Introduction*. 2nd ed. Edinburgh: Edinburgh University Press.

McGlashan, T., C. Grilo, C. Sanislow, E. Ralevski, L. Morey, J. Gunderson, A. Skodol, M. Shea, M. Zanarini, D. Bender, R. Stout, S. Yen, and M. Pagano. 2005. "Two-Year Prevalence and Stability of Individual DSM-IV Criteria for Schizotypal, Borderline, Avoidant, and Obsessive-Compulsive Personality Disorders: Toward a Hybrid Model of Axis II Disorders." *American Journal of Psychiatry* 162 (5): 883–89.

McIntosh, Angus. 1963. "'As You Like It': A Grammatical Clue to Character." *A Review of English Literature* 4 (2): 68–81.

McIntyre, Dan. 2004. "Point of View in Drama: A Socio-pragmatic Analysis of Dennis Potter's *Brimstone and Treacle*." *Language and Literature* 13 (2): 139–60.

McIntyre, Dan. 2010. "Dialogue and Characterization in Quentin Tarantino's *Reservoir Dogs*: A Corpus Stylistic Analysis." In *Language and Style: Essays in Honour of Mick Short*, edited by Dan McIntyre and Beatrix Busse, 162–83. New York: Palgrave Macmillan.

McIntyre, Dan, and Dawn Archer. 2010. "A Corpus-Based Approach to Mind Style." *Journal of Literary Semantics* 39 (2): 167–82.

McIntyre, Dan, and Brian Walker. 2010. "How Can Corpora Be Used to Explore the Language of Poetry and Drama?" In *The Routledge Handbook of Corpus Linguistics*, edited by Anne O'Keeffe and Michael McCarthy, 516–30. Abingdon: Routledge.

McWhirter, David, ed. 1995. *Henry James's New York Edition: The Construction of Authorship*. Stanford: Stanford University Press.

Minitab Statistical Software. 1999. State College, Pennsylvania: Minitab.

Moon, Rosamund. 1998. *Fixed Expressions and Idioms in English*. Oxford: Clarendon Press.

Mower, C. Leiren. 2002. "Bodies in Labor: Sole Proprietorship and the Labor of Conduct in *The Coquette*." *American Literature* 74 (2): 315–44.

Mukařovský, Jan. 1970. "Standard Language and Poetic Language." Edited and translated by Paul L. Garvin. In *Linguistics and Literary Style*, edited by Donald C. Freeman, 40–56. New York: Holt, Rinehart, and Winston.

Mulholland, Joan. (1967) 1987. "'Thou' and 'You' in Shakespeare: A Study in the Second Person Pronoun." In *A Reader in the Language of Shakespearean Drama*, edited by Vivian Salmon and Edwina Burness, 153–61. Amsterdam: John Benjamins.

NLP. 2001. Language Technology Group / Infogistics Ltd. http://www.infogistics.com/textanalysis.html.

O'Halloran, Kieran A. 2007. "The Subconscious in James Joyce's 'Eveline': A Corpus Stylistic Analysis That Chews on the 'Fish Hook.'" *Language and Literature* 16 (3): 227–44.

Ohmann, Richard. (1964) 1970. "Generative Grammars and the Concept of Literary Style." *Word* 20 (1964): 424–39. Reprinted in *Linguistics and Literary Style*, edited by Donald C. Freeman, 258–39. New York: Holt, Rinehart, and Winston.

Page, Norman. 1988. *Speech in the English Novel.* 2nd ed. Houndmills, Hampshire: MacMillan.

Petter, Henri. 1971. *The Early American Novel.* Columbus: Ohio State University Press.

Pfister, Manfred. 1988. *The Theory and Analysis of Drama.* Cambridge: Cambridge University Press.

Phillips, Martin. 1989. *Lexical Structure of Text.* Discourse Analysis Monographs, 12. Birmingham: English Language Research, University of Birmingham.

Piao, Scott S. L., Paul Rayson, Dawn Archer, and Tony McEnery. 2004. "Evaluating Lexical Resources for a Semantic Tagger." In Vol. 2 of *Proceedings of 4th International Conference on Language Resources and Evaluation (LREC 2004), May 2004, Lisbon, Portugal,* 499–502.

Poirier, Richard. 1960. *The Comic Sense of Henry James: A Study of the Early Novels.* New York: Oxford University Press.

Pope, Rob. 2003. "Re-writing Texts, Re-constructing the Subject: Work as Play on the Critical-Creative Interface." In *Teaching Literature: A Companion,* edited by Tanya Agathocleous and Ann C. Dean. London: Palgrave Macmillan, 105–24.

Pope, Rob. 2005. *Creativity: Theory, History, Practice.* London: Routledge.

Project Gutenberg. http://www.gutenberg.org/.

QTAG. 2003. Oliver Mason. http://www.english.bham.ac.uk/staff/omason/software/qtag.html.

Raven, Peter H., Ray F. Evert, and Susan E. Eichhorn. 2005. *Biology of Plants.* 7th ed. New York: W. H. Freeman.

Rayson, Paul. 2003. "Matrix: A Statistical Method and Software Tool for Linguistic Analysis Through Corpus Comparison." PhD diss., Lancaster University.

Rayson, Paul. 2004. "Keywords Are Not Enough." Invited talk for JAECS (Japan Association for English Corpus Studies) at Chuo University, Tokyo, Japan. http://www.comp.lancs.ac.uk/computing/users/paul/public.html.

Rayson, Paul. 2005. WMatrix: A Web-Based Corpus Processing Environment. Computing Department, Lancaster University. http://www.comp.lancs.ac.uk/ucrel/wmatrix/.

Rayson, Paul. 2008. "From Key Words to Key Semantic Domains." *International Journal of Corpus Linguistics.* 13 (4): 519–49.

Rayson, Paul, Dawn Archer, Scott S. L. Piao, and Tony McEnery. 2004. "The UCREL Semantic Analysis System." In *Proceedings of the Workshop on Beyond Named Entity Recognition Semantic Labelling for NLP Tasks in Association with 4th International Conference on Language Resources and Evaluation (LREC 2004), 25th May 2004, Lisbon, Portugal,* 7–12. Paris: European Language Resources Association.

Rayson, Paul, Dawn Archer, and Nicholas Smith. 2005. "Vard Versus Word: A Comparison of the UCREL Variant Detector and Modern Spell Checkers on English Historical Corpora." *Proceedings from the Corpus Linguistics Conference Series On-line E-journal* 1 (1).

Romaine, Suzanne. 2010. "19th Century Key Words, Key Semantic Domains and Affect: 'In the Rich Vocabulary of Love "Most Dearest" be a True Superlative.'" *Studia Neophilologica* 82 (1): 12–48.

Rondal, J. A., M. Elbouz, M. Ylieff, and L. Docquier. 2003. "Françoise, a Fifteen Year Follow-up." *Down Syndrome Research and Practice* 8 (3): 89–99.

Rybicki, Jan, and Maciej Eder. 2011. "Deeper Delta Across Genres and Languages: Do We Really Need the Most Frequent Words?" *Literary and Linguistic Computing* 26 (3): 315–21.

Rybicki, Jan, and Magda Heydel. 2013. "The Stylistics and Stylometry of Collaborative Translation: Woolf's *Night and Day* in Polish." *Literary and Linguistic Computing.* Published electronically, May 27, 2013.

Salmon, Vivian, and Edwina Burness, eds. 1987. *A Reader in the Language of Shakespearean Drama.* Amsterdam: John Benjamins.

Schank, Roger C., and Robert P. Abelson. 1977. *Scripts, Plans, Goals and Understanding.* Hillsdale, NJ: Lawrence Erlbaum.

Scherer, Klaus Rainer. 1979. "Personality Markers in Speech." In *Social Markers in Speech*, edited by Klaus Rainer Scherer and Howard Giles, 147–209. Cambridge: Cambridge University Press.

Schmitt, Norbert, and Ronald Carter. 2004. "Formulaic Sequences in Action: An Introduction." In *Formulaic Sequences: Acquisition, Processing and Use*, edited by Norbert Schmitt, 1–22. Amsterdam: John Benjamins.

Schmitt, Norbert, Sarah Grandage, and Svenja Adolphs. 2004. "Are Corpus-Derived Recurrent Clusters Psycholinguistically Valid?" In *Formulaic Sequences: Acquisition, Processing and Use*, edited by Norbert Schmitt, 127–51. Amsterdam: John Benjamins.

Scott, Mike R. 1997. "PC Analysis of Key Words—And Key Key Words." *System* 25 (2): 233–45.

Scott, Mike R. 1999. *WordSmith Tools.* Oxford: Oxford University Press. See also http://www.liv.ac.uk/~ms2928/.

Scott, Mike R. 2000. "Focusing on the Text and Its Key Words." In *Rethinking Language Pedagogy from a Corpus Perspective*, vol. 2, edited by Lou Burnard and Tony McEnery, 103–22. Frankfurt: Peter Lang.

Scott, Mike R. 2008. *WordSmith Tools Help Manual.* Version 5.0. Liverpool: Lexical Analysis Software.

Scott, Mike R. 2013. *WordSmith Tools Manual.* Version 6.0. Liverpool: Lexical Analysis Software Ltd. http://www.lexically.net/downloads/version6/wordsmith6.pdf.

Scott, Mike R., and Chris Tribble. 2006. *Key Words and Corpus Analysis in Language Education.* Amsterdam: John Benjamins.

Semino, Elena. 1997. *Language and World Creation in Poems and Other Texts.* London: Longman.

Semino, Elena, and Mick Short. 2004. *Corpus Stylistics: Speech, Writing and Thought Presentation in a Corpus of English Writing.* New York: Routledge.

Semino, Elena, and Kate Swindlehurst. (1996). "Metaphor and Mind Style in Ken Kesey's *One Flew Over the Cuckoo's Nest*," *Style* 30 (1): 143–166.

Short, Raymond W. 1946. "The Sentence Structure of Henry James." *American Literature* 18 (2): 71–88.

Simpson, Paul. 2004. *Stylistics: A Resource Book for Students.* London: Routledge.

Sinclair, John. 1991. *Corpus, Concordance, Collocation.* Oxford: Oxford University Press.

Sinclair, John. 2003. *Reading Concordances.* Harlow: Longman.

Sinclair, John. 2004. *Trust the Text: Language, Corpus and Discourse.* Edited with Ronald Carter. London: Routledge.

Smith-Rosenberg, Carroll. 2003. "Domesticating Virtue: Coquettes and Revolutionaries in Young America." In *American Literary Studies: A Methodological Reader*, edited by Michael A. Elliott and Claudia Stokes. New York: New York University Press.

Smollett, Tobias. 1771. *The Expedition of Humphry Clinker.* http://www.gutenberg.org/dirs/etext00/txohc10.txt.

Starcke, Bettina. 2006. "The Phraseology of Jane Austen's *Persuasion*: Phraseological Units as Carriers of Meaning." *ICAME Journal* 30: 87–104.

Stefanowitsch, Anatol. 2006. "Corpus-Based Approaches to Metaphor and Metonymy." In *Corpus-Based Approaches to Metaphor and Metonymy.* Trends in Linguistics 171, edited by Anatol Stefanowitsch and Stefan Thomas Gries, 1–16. Berlin: Mouton de Gruyter.

Stubbs, Michael. 1996. *Text and Corpus Analysis: Computer-Assisted Studies of Language and Culture.* Oxford: Blackwell.

Stubbs, Michael. 2001. *Words and Phrases: Corpus Studies of Lexical Semantics.* Oxford: Blackwell.

Stubbs, Michael. 2004. Review of *Stylistics*, by Peter Verdonk. *Applied Linguistics* 25 (1): 126–29.

Stubbs, Michael. 2005. "Conrad in the Computer: Examples of Quantitative Stylistic Methods." *Language and Literature* 14 (1): 5–24.

Swann, Joan, Rob Pope, and Ronald Carter, eds. 2011. *Creativity in Language and Literature: the State of the Art.* Basingstoke, Hants: Palgrave Macmillan.

Taavitsainen, Irma. 1999. "Personality and Styles of Affect in *The Canterbury Tales.*" In *Chaucer in Perspective: Middle English Essays in Honour of Norman Blake*, edited by Geoffrey Lester, 218–34. Sheffield: Sheffield Academic Press.

Thomas, Jenny, and Andrew Wilson. 1996. "Methodologies for Studying a Corpus of Doctor-Patient Interaction." In *Using Corpora for Language Research: Studies in Honour of Geoffrey Leech*, edited by Jenny Thomas and Michael H. Short, 92–109. London: Longman.

Thornborrow, Joanna, and Shân Wareing. 1998. *Patterns in Language: An Introduction to Language and Style.* London: Routledge.

Toolan, Michael J. 1985. "Syntactical Styles as a Means of Characterisation in Narrative." *Style* 19 (1): 78–93.

Toolan, Michael J. 1988. *Narrative: A Critical Linguistic Introduction.* London and New York: Routledge.

Toolan, Michael J. 2006. "Top Keyword Abridgements of Short Stories: A Corpus Linguistic Resource?" *Journal of Literary Semantics* 35 (2): 181–94.

Tribble, Chris. 2000. "Genres, Keywords, Teaching: Towards a Pedagogic Account of the Language of Project Proposals." In *Rethinking Language Pedagogy from a Corpus Perspective*, edited by Lou Burnard and Tony McEnery, 75–90. Frankfurt: Peter Lang.

Underwood, Geoffrey, Norbert Schmitt, and Adam Galpin. 2004. "The Eyes Have It: An Eye- Movement Study into the Processing of Formulaic Sequences." In *Formulaic Sequences: Acquisition, Processing and Use*, edited by Norbert Schmitt, 153–72. Amsterdam: John Benjamins.

van Dalen-Oskam, Karina. 2012. "The Secret Life of Scribes. Exploring Fifteen Manuscripts of Jacob van Maerlant's Scolastica (1271)." *Literary and Linguistic Computing* 27 (4): 355–72.

van Dalen-Oskam, Karina, and Joris van Zundert. "Delta for Middle Dutch–Author and Copyist Distinction in *Walewein.*" *Literary and Linguistic Computing* 22 (3): 345–62.

Van Doren, Carl. 1921. *The American Novel.* New York: Macmillan. http://www.bartleby.com/187/11.html.

Verdonk, Peter. 2002. *Stylistics.* Oxford: Oxford University Press.

Wales, Katie. 2011. *A Dictionary of Stylistics.* 3rd ed. London: Longman.

Watt, Ian. (1960). 1964. "The First Paragraph of *The Ambassadors.*" In *Essays in Criticism* 10 (3): 250–74. Reprinted in *The Ambassadors: An Authoritative Text, the Author on the Novel, Criticism*, edited by Stanford P. Rosenbaum, 442–55. New York: Norton.

Wenska, Walter P., Jr. 1977. "*The Coquette* and the American Dream of Freedom." *Early American Literature* 12 (3): 243–55.

White, Devon. 1995. "Contemporary Criticism of Five Early American Sentimental Novels, 1970–1994: An Annotated Bibliography." *Bulletin of Bibliography* 52 (4): 293–305.

Widdowson, Henry G. 1992. *Practical Stylistics: An Approach to Poetry.* Oxford: Oxford University Press.

Williams, Carrington. B. 1970. *Style and Vocabulary: Numerical Studies.* London: Griffin.

Williams, Monnica. 2009. "Obsessive-Compulsive Personality Disorder: When Everything Has to Be 'Just Right.'" *OCD Resource Center of Florida*, http://www.ocdhope.com/oc-personality-disorder.php.

Williams, Raymond. 1983. *Keywords: A Vocabulary of Culture and Society*. London: Fontana.

Wilson, Andrew, and Paul Rayson. 1993. "The Automatic Content Analysis of Spoken Discourse." In *Corpus-Based Computational Linguistics*, edited by Clive Souter and Eric S. Atwell. Amsterdam: Rodopi.

Wray, Alison. 2002. *Formulaic Language and the Lexicon*. Cambridge: Cambridge University Press.

Wynne, Martin. 2006. "Stylistics: Corpus Approaches." In *Encyclopedia of Language and Linguistics,* edited by Keith Brown, 223–25. 2nd ed. Oxford: Elsevier.

Xiao, Zhonghua, and Tony McEnery. 2005. "Two Approaches to Genre Analysis: Three Genres in Modern American English." *Journal of English Linguistics* 33 (1): 62–82.

Index

For Product Safety Concerns and Information please contact our EU
representative GPSR@taylorandfrancis.com
Taylor & Francis Verlag GmbH, Kaufingerstraße 24, 80331 München, Germany